The Sacred Poets of the Nineteenth Century
Edward Hayes Plumptre to Selwyn Image

Alfred H. Miles

This work has been selected by scholars as being culturally important, and is part of the knowledge base of civilization as we know it. This work was reproduced from the original artifact, and remains as true to the original work as possible. Therefore, you will see the original copyright references, library stamps (as most of these works have been housed in our most important libraries around the world), and other notations in the work.

This work is in the public domain in the United States of America, and possibly other nations. Within the United States, you may freely copy and distribute this work, as no entity (individual or corporate) has a copyright on the body of the work.

As a reproduction of a historical artifact, this work may contain missing or blurred pages, poor pictures, errant marks, etc. Scholars believe, and we concur, that this work is important enough to be preserved, reproduced, and made generally available to the public. We appreciate your support of the preservation process, and thank you for being an important part of keeping this knowledge alive and relevant.

The Sacred Poets of the Nineteenth Century.

Edward Hayes Plumptre to Selwyn Image.

Edited by
ALFRED H. MILES

LONDON
GEORGE ROUTLEDGE & SONS, LTD.
NEW YORK: E. P. DUTTON & CO.
1907.

In the prefatory note of the first edition this work (1891) the Editor invited criticism with a view to the improvement of future editions. Several critics responded to this appeal, and their valuable suggestions have been considered in preparing this re-issue. In some cases the text has been revised and the selection varied; in others, additions have been made to complete the representation. The biographical and bibliographical matter has been brought up to date.—A.H.M.

PREFATORY.

THIS and the preceding volume of " The Poets and the Poetry of the Nineteenth Century " are devoted to the sacred, moral, and religious verse of the period.

Some of the acknowledgments made in the former volume cover, to some extent, the contents of this one; but, even at the risk of repetition, the Editor desires to express his high sense of the favour shown to him in this connection by poets and publishers alike.

His special thanks are due to Dr. Alexander, Dr. Bickersteth, Dr. Walter C. Smith, and Mr. Selwyn Image, for kind permission to include selections from their works, and to their publishers for gracious acquiescence. Beyond these there are many who since the publication of the first edition of this work have passed the bourn — many whose sympathetic interest is gratefully remembered and whose correspondence is treasured. These include the late Francis Turner Palgrave, Aubrey de Vere, Coventry Patmore, George Macdonald, E. H. Plumptre, W. Walsham How, H. S. Sutton, John Ellerton, Richard Wilton, Christina Rossetti, Alexander Grosart and S. J. Stone.

At the end of this volume the reader will find a list of the twelve volumes which comprise the series, in chronological order, the order of the arrangement of the work, also a general index of authors, and a list of the authors included in each separate volume. A reference to these will enable him to find the exact position of the work of any poet he may desire to consult.

The Editor feels that the not inconsiderable time, thought, and expense devoted to the perfecting of this edition has greatly added to its value, and hopes that the study and enjoyment of the poetry of the period may be thereby facilitated and enhanced.

A. H. M.

INDEX.

	PAGE
E. H. PLUMPTRE (1821—1891) . *W. G. Horder*	1
LAZARUS AND OTHER POEMS—	
Three Cups of Cold Water	5
MASTER AND SCHOLAR—	
Gilboa	13
THINGS NEW AND OLD—	
Chalfont St. Giles	17
HYMNS—	
I. "Rejoice, ye pure in heart"	20
II. "Thine arm, O Lord"	21
JAMES DRUMMOND BURNS (1823—1864) *Grosart*	23
POEMS—	
I. The Vesper Hour	27
II. The Child Samuel	28
III. Humility	29
IV. The Footsteps of the Flock . . .	30
V. The Bird and the Bee . . .	32
SONNETS—	
I. Presentiment	33
II. Reason and Faith	33
III. My First Birthday in a Foreign Land .	34
IV. Memory of a Dear Friend . . .	34
V. Imagination	35
VI. By the Sea-Side	35
VII. Evening Picture	36
VIII. Great Britain	36
CECIL FRANCES ALEXANDER (1823—1895) *Miles*	37
HYMNS FOR CHILDREN—	
I. "Every morning the red sun" . .	39
II. "There is a green hill far away" . .	40
HYMNS AND SACRED POEMS—	
I. Earth and Heaven	41
II. Touched with a Feeling of Our Infirmities .	42
III. The Burial of Moses	43
IV. Ruth	46

		PAGE
W. W. HOW (1823—1897) . . . *Alfred H. Miles*		49

POEMS—
    I. Stars and Graves 51
    II. Converse 52
    III. "Pasce Verbo, Pasce Vita" . . . 53
    IV. A Starlit Night by the Sea-Shore . . 54

HYMNS—
    I. Jesus at the Door 55
    II. "O God, enshrined" 56
    III. Offertory 50
    The New Jerusalem 57

WILLIAM ALEXANDER (1824) . *Alfred H. Miles* 59

POEMS—
    I. A Sea Gleam 61
    II. Very Far Away 62
    III. Christ on the Shore 63
    IV. A Fine Day in Holy Week . . . 64
    V. The Birthday Crown 65

SONNETS—
  St. John at Patmos—
    I. "What be his dreams" 67
    II. "Not fancies of the soft Ionian clime" . 67
    III. "But ere heaven's cressets burn" . . 68

WILLIAM JOSIAH IRONS (1812—1883) *A. H. Miles* 69
  ("*The God of heav'n*," by Joseph Irons) . 69

PSALMS AND HYMNS FOR THE CHURCH—
    I. "Evening has come" 73
    II. "Hail, holy rest!" 74
    III. "Lo, signs in sun, and moon, and stars" . 75
    IV. "Clouds around the mountains" . . 75
    V. "Mother mine, why hast thou borne me" . 77
    VI. "Is not this our King and Prophet?" . 78
    VII. "O silent Night" 79
    VIII. "'He loved His own unto the end'" . 79
    IX. "Pause now, and think, O Christian soul" . 80
    X. "O All-surpassing Splendour" . . 82

INDEX.

	PAGE
AUBREY DE VERE (1814—1902) . *Alfred H Miles*	83
(All but unutterable Name)	83
(The lights o'er yonder snowy range) . .	84
POEMS—	
I. Spring	85
II. Spring Thoughts	86
III. Sense, Faith, and Glory. . . .	87
IV. Martha and Mary	88
COVENTRY PATMORE (1823—1896) *Alfred H Miles*	89
THE TOYS	91
F. T. PALGRAVE (1824—1897) . . *A. H. Miles*	93
AMENOPHIS AND OTHER POEMS—	
I. At Ephesus	95
II. An Incident at Mendrisio . . .	98
III. On the Love of Children . . .	100
IV. Hymn to Our Saviour	102
V. Christus Consolator	103
VI. The Garden of God	104
VII. A Hymn of Repentance. . . .	105
VIII. Death and the Fear of it . .	106
IX. I am the Resurrection and the Life .	108
WALTER CHALMERS SMITH (1824) *W G Horder*	109
HYMNS—	
I. "Earth was waiting"	115
II. "Lord, I would choose" . . .	116
OLRIG GRANGE (*Selected Lines*)—	
I. "But my Faith is not gone" . .	117
II. "My sun sinks without clouds or fears" .	118
RABAN, OR, LIFE SPLINTERS—	
Work and Spirit	119
NORTH COUNTRY FOLK—	
A Cry from the Merse	121
THOUGHTS AND FANCIES—	
I. "One thing I of the Lord desire" .	123
II. "Be still"	124
III. "O'er land and sea"	124
A HERETIC AND OTHER POEMS—	
I. Creeds	126
II. The Vision of God	128

INDEX.

	PAGE
GEORGE MACDONALD (1824—1905) *Alfred H. Miles*	129
(Lie, little cow, and chew thy cud) . .	130
(God gives His child upon his slate a sum) .	130

ORGAN SONGS—
    I. "I know what beauty is" 131
    II. Longing 132
    III. "I would I were a child" . . . 133
    IV. Rest 135

A BOOK OF SONNETS—
    I. The Unseen Face 138
    II. The Sweeper of the Floor . . . 138

VIOLIN SONGS—
    I. Going to Sleep 139
    II. Bed Time 139

A BOOK OF DREAMS—
    I. A piece of Gold 141
    II. "Dreaming I slept" 142

EDWARD HENRY BICKERSTETH (1825)
    Alfred H. Miles 145

FROM YEAR TO YEAR—
    I. "Come ye yourselves apart" . . . 147
    II. "The Meadow Grass" 147
    III. "My work is done" 148
    IV. "'Till He come'" 149
    V. "Peace, perfect peace" 150

HENRY SEPTIMUS SUTTON (1825—1901)
    W. Garrett Horder 151

ROSE'S DIARY—
    "The day with light its genial self engirds" 155
    "Put not on me, O Lord! this work divine" 155
    "What mean these slow returns of love?" . 156
    "O Father! I have sinn'd against Thee" . 157
    "Each day a page is of my being's book" . 157
    "Late on me, weeping, did this whisper fall" 158
    "How beautiful it is to be alive!" . . 159
    "Prayer is the world-plant's blossom" . 159
    "How beautiful our lives may be!" . . 160

INDEX.

POEMS—   PAGE

    I. The Daisy 161
    II. "Though He slay me, yet will I trust in Him" 163
    III. For the Desolate 164
    IV. A Preacher's Soliloquy and Sermon . . 165
    V. Sorrow 169
    VI. Love's Freemasonry 169
    VII. Ralph Waldo Emerson 170
    VIII. Man 172

JOHN ELLERTON (1826—1893) . *Alfred H. Miles* 173

ORIGINAL HYMNS—

    I. "God of the living" 175
    II. "Throned upon the awful Tree" . . . 176
    III. "The day Thou gavest, Lord, is ended" . 177
    IV. "Saviour, again to Thy dear name" . . 177

TRANSLATED HYMNS—

    I. "Sing Alleluia forth" 179
    II. "Welcome, happy morning" 180

RICHARD WILTON (1827—1903) *Alfred H. Miles* 181

SELECTED SONNETS—

    I. An Incident 183
    II. The Sparrow 183
    III. The Tides 184
    IV. The Well-Head 184
    V. Flamborough Lighthouse 185
    VI. The Hawthorn and the Wild Rose . . 185

RONDEAUX—

    I. "Sweet, soft and low" 186
    II. "When I am gone" 186

BALLADES—

    I. My Grandchildren at Church . . . 187
    II. The Summer of Saint Luke 188

LYRICS—

    I. Auburn 189
    II. Hymn to the Holy Spirit 190

BENEDICITE (*Selected Rondels*)—   PAGE
   I. "O all ye Works of God" . . . 191
   II. "Ye Heavens, with your encircling blue" . 191
   III. "Lightnings and Clouds" . . . 192
   IV. "O let the Earth in fair array" . . 192
   V. "Ye Hills and Mountains" . . . 193
   VI. "O all ye Green Things on the earth" . 193
   VII. "O Wells and Springs" . . . 194
   VIII. "Ye Seas and Floods" . . . 194

JOSEPH JOHN MURPHY (1827—1894) *A. B. Grosart* 195

SONNETS AND OTHER POEMS—
   I. A Thought of Stoicism . . . 197
   II. First Sorrow 198
   III. The Potter and the Clay . . . 199
   IV. Eternity 200

CHRISTINA G. ROSSETTI (1830—1894) *A H Miles* 201

TIME FLIES—
   I. "Lord Babe, if Thou art He" . . 203
   II. "Laughing Life cries at the feast" . 204
   III. "Where shall I find a white rose?" . 205
   IV. "Weigh all my faults" . . . 205
   V. "Piteous my rhyme is" . . . 206
   VI. "Young girls wear flowers" . . 207
   VII. "Golden haired, lily white" . . 207
   VIII. "Innocent eyes not ours" . . 208
   IX. "Man's life is but a working day" . 209
   X. "Have I not striven?" . . . 209
   XI. "Through burden and heat of the day" . 209
   XII. "Sorrow hath a double voice" . . 210
   XIII. "Who is this that cometh up?" . . 210
   XIV. "The goal in sight" . . . 211
   XV. "Bury Hope out of sight" . . 211
   XVI. "Behold, the Bridegroom cometh" . 212
   XVII. "The tempest over and gone" . . 213
   XVIII. "Words cannot utter" . . . 214

INDEX

	PAGE
ALEXANDER B. GROSART (1835—1899) *A. H. Miles*	215
SONGS OF DAY AND NIGHT—	
I. God Near and Far	217
II. The Everlasting Arms	218
III. He Leads Round	219
IV. The Good Die Not	221
V. God the Holy Spirit	222
VI. The Cross	223
VII. Angelic Ministry	224
VIII. The Resurrection	225
IX. If it be Possible	227
X. Indwelling—Dwelling in	228
JOHN OWEN (1836—1896) . *Alexander B. Grosart*	229
VERSE MUSINGS ON NATURE, FAITH, AND FREEDOM—	
I. Faith—1. On Defining God	231
II. What is Religion?	231
III. Where is Religion?	232
IV. What is Faith?	233
V. Life and Thought	234
II. Freedom—1. Fate and Man	236
II. The Devout Prayer	237
III. To the Future World	238
F. R. HAVERGAL (1836—1879) . *Alfred H. Miles*	239
POEMS—	
I. Consecration Hymn	241
II. A Worker's Prayer	242
III. Now and Afterward	243
IV. Adoration	244
WILLIAM HALL (1838) . . *Alfred H. Miles*	245
I. Renunciation (Selected Stanzas)	247
II. Self-Communion (Selected Stanzas)	251
III. A Bruised Reed	253
IV. Who will show us any good	253
V. Good-Night	255

		PAGE
SAMUEL JOHN STONE (1839—1900)	*Alfred H. Miles*	257
(*The Soliloquy of a Rationalistic Chicken*)		
HYMNS—		
I. "The Church's one foundation"		261
II. "Round the Sacred City gather"		263
III. "Lord of our soul's salvation"		265
IV. "Weary of earth"		266
V. "Their names are names of kings"		268
F. W. ORDE WARD (1843)	*A. H. Miles*	269
THE PRISONER OF LOVE—		
I. Christ the Outcast		271
II. The Cup		272
III. The Resurrection of the Flowers		273
IV. Summer's Parable		273
V. God and the Harvest		274
VI. Our Open Cage		275
VII. Losing and Saving		276
VIII. Spring		277
IX. Who goes Home		278
SELWYN IMAGE	*Alfred H. Miles*	279
(*Her Confirmation*)		279
POEMS AND CAROLS—		
I. A Meditation for Christmas		281
II. Gabriel and Mary		282
III. The Heavenly Host		283
AC ETIAM	*Alfred H. Miles*	285
ANNA LÆTITIA BARBAULD (1743—1825)		285
(*But are they silent all?*)		287
I. "Praise to God, immortal praise"		288
II. "Awake, my soul, lift up thine eyes"		289
THOMAS KELLY (1769—1854)		290
I. "The head that once was crowned"		290
II. "Look, ye saints, the sight is glorious"		291
HARRIET AUBER (1773—1862)		292
"Our blest Redeemer, ere He breathed"		292
JOSEPH BLANCO WHITE (1775—1839)		293
To Night		294
PHILIP PUSEY (1779—1855)		294
"Lord of our life"		294

	PAGE
THOMAS MOORE (1779—1852)	295
I "Thou art, O God, the life and light"	295
II. "Sound the loud timbrel"	296
ANN TAYLOR (GILBERT) (1782—1866)	296
"Great God, and wilt Thou condescend"	297
JANE TAYLOR (1783—1824)	296
"When daily I kneel down to pray"	298
WILLIAM JOHNSON FOX (1786—1864)	298
I. "A little child, in bulrush ark"	299
II. "'Make us a god,' said man"	300
III. "The sage his cup of hemlock quaffed"	300
ANDREW REED (1787—1862)	301
"Spirit Divine, attend our prayers"	301
CHARLOTTE ELIZABETH TONNA (*née* BROWNE) (1790—1849)	302
The Mariner's Midnight Hymn	303
JAMES EDMESTON (1791—1867)	304
I. "Lead us, heavenly Father, lead us"	304
II. "Saviour, breathe an evening blessing"	305
SAMUEL RICKARDS (1796—1865)	305
Christmas Day	306
THOMAS BINNEY (1798—1874)	307
"Eternal Light!"	308
HERBERT KNOWLES (1798—1817)	309
Lines written in Richmond Churchyard	309
MATTHEW BRIDGES (1800)	310
"Crown Him with many crowns"	311
RICHARD MASSIE (1800)	312
"O Lord, who by Thy presence"	313
JOHN REYNELL WREFORD (1800—1881)	313
"Lord, while for all mankind we pray"	314
HARRIET MARTINEAU (1802—1876)	315
I. "Arise, my soul! and urge thy flight"	315
II. "Beneath this starry arch"	316
III. "All men are equal in their birth"	316
ISAAC WILLIAMS (1802—1865)	317
I. "The child leans on its parent's breast"	318
II. At Midnight ("Away with sorrow's sigh")	319

		PAGE
JOHN HAMPDEN GURNEY (1802—1862)	. . .	320
"Lord of the harvest! Thee we hail"	.	320
HENRY JAMES BUCKOLL (1803—1871)	. . .	321
"Come, my soul, thou must be waking"	.	321
SAMUEL GREG (1804—1877)	. . .	323
I. Death ("Slowly, slowly, darkening")	. .	324
II. The Transfiguration ("Stay, Master, stay")		324
JAMES MARTINEAU (1805—1900)	. . .	325
I. "Thy way is in the deep"	. . . .	326
II. The Inward Witness ("Where is your God?")	. . . . . .	327
JOHN F. CHANDLER (1806—1876)	. . .	327
I. "'Tis for conquering kings to gain"	.	328
II. "O Jesu, Lord of heavenly grace"	.	329
GEORGE RAWSON (1807—1889)	. . .	330
I. Trust ("My Father, it is good for me")	.	330
II. "Praise ye the Lord, immortal quire"		331
EDWARD ARTHUR DAYMAN (1807—1890)	. .	332
"Sleep, thy last sleep"	. . . .	332
JOSEPH ANSTICE (1808—1836)	. . .	333
I. "Come to a desert place apart"	.	334
II. "Lord of the harvest! once again"	.	335
JOHN S. B. MONSELL (1811—1875)	. . .	335
I. "Birds have their quiet nest"	. .	336
II. God is Love, by Him upholden"	.	337
NORMAN MACLEOD (1812—1872)	. . .	338
Trust in God ("Courage, brother!")	.	339
JANE BORTHWICK (1813)	. . . . .	340
I. "Come, labour on!"	. . . .	340
II. "Jesus, still lead on"	. . . .	341
EDWARD CASWELL (1814—1878)	. . .	342
I. Swiftness of Time	. . . .	343
II. St. Bernard's Hymn	. . . .	344
I. "Jesus, the very thought of Thee"	.	344
II. "O Jesu, King most wonderful!"	.	345
III. An Evening Hymn	. . . .	346
ARTHUR PENRHYN STANLEY (1815—1881)	.	347
I. Hymn on the Transfiguration ("Master it is good to be")	. . . .	348
II. "He is gone—beyond the skies"	. .	349

	PAGE
JANE MONTGOMERY CAMPBELL (1817—1878)	351
"We plough the fields, and scatter"	351
EMILY BRONTE (1818—1848)	352
Last Lines, "No coward soul is mine"	352
ANNE BRONTE (1819—1849)	353
Last Lines, "I hope that with"	354
SIR HENRY WILLIAMS BAKER (1821—1877)	355
"The King of love my Shepherd is"	355
FRANCES POWER COBBE (1822—1904)	356
"God draws a cloud over each gleaming morn"	356
GODFREY THRING (1823—1894)	357
I. Afternoon Hymn ("The radiant morn")	358
II. The Great Calm ("Fierce raged the tempest")	358
III. "A Fortress sure is God our King"	359
HENRY TWELLS (1823)	360
"At even, ere the sun was set"	360
ADELAIDE ANNE PROCTER (1825—1864)	361
"My God, I thank Thee, who hast made"	362
WILLIAM WHITING (1825—1878)	363
"Eternal Father, strong to save"	364
LAURENCE TUTTIETT (1825)	364
"O quickly come, dread Judge of all"	365
ELIZABETH CHARLES (1827—1896)	365
I. "Never further than Thy Cross!"	366
II. "The strongest light casts deepest shades"	367
III. "Around a Table, not a Tomb"	368
FRANCES ELIZABETH COX	368
"Jesus lives! no longer now"	369
HENRY COLLINS	370
"Jesus, my Lord, my God, my all!"	370
JOHN MOULTRIE (1799—1874)	371
GERARD MOULTRIE (1829—1885)	371
Midnight Hymn of the Eastern Church	372
MARY DUNLOP MOULTRIE (1837—1866)	373

	PAGE
CATHERINE WINKWORTH (1829—1878)	373
I. The Rose of Sharon ("I know a Flower")	374
II. "O Love, who formedst me to wear"	375
III. On the Death of a Little Child	376
PHILIP STANHOPE WORSLEY (1831—1866)	377
I. "Out of the deeps"	377
II. The Two Wills ("Oft as I act")	378
RICHARD FREDERICK LITTLEDALE (1833—1890)	378
I. "From hidden source arising"	380
II. "In Paradise Reposing"	381
SABINE BARING-GOULD (1834)	381
"On the Resurrection morning"	382
FOLLIOTT SANDFORD PIERPOINT (1835)	383
The Sacrifice of Praise ("For the beauty")	384
M. B. BETHAM-EDWARDS (1836)	385
I. "God make my life a little light"	385
II. "The little birds now seek their nest"	386
THOMAS BENSON POLLOCK (1836)	387
Children's Litany (Part I.)	387
WILLIAM CHATTERTON DIX (1837)	388
I. Epiphany Hymn ("As with gladness")	388
II. Patience (Sonnet)	390
GEORGE MATHESON (1842)	390
I. "O Love that wilt not let me go"	391
II. "Gather us in, Thou Love that fillest all"	391
ADA CROSS (née CAMBRIDGE) (1844)	392
The Fourth Commandment ("The Dawn")	393
SARAH DOUDNEY	395
The Christian's "Good-night" ("Sleep on, beloved")	395
PLAN OF WORK	I
CHRONOLOGICAL ORDER OF VOLUMES	II
LIST OF AUTHORS IN EACH VOLUME	III
GENERAL INDEX OF AUTHORS	X

Edward Hayes Plumptre
to
Selwyn Image.

Edward Hayes Plumptre.

1821—1891.

OF few men of our century could it be more truly said than of Dr. Plumptre "Nihil tetigit non ornavit." This is the more remarkable when we remember the number of subjects he touched with his pen—Theology —Speculative, Exegetical, Homiletical, Translation— of the Hebrew Scriptures, of the Greek Classics, and of Dante, Biography, and Poetry including hymn writing. In each of these departments, if he did not give proof of actual genius, he certainly showed a fine taste, and the results of a finished scholarship. The part he took as a member of the Old Testament Company of Revisers is known only to those who were his co-workers, but his separately published works on the Prophets show both ample knowledge and poetic imagination. His translations of Sophocles and Æschylus still hold their place as worthy renderings of those great poets, his Dante is noteworthy not only as a translation—in parts extremely happy —but in the highest degree valuable for its introductory life and its exhaustive notes, whilst his Life of Bishop Ker has become, and is likely long to remain, the standard work on the subject.

He was born in London on the 6th of August, 1821. He was educated first at King's College, London, and afterwards at University College, Oxford. At his graduation in 1844 he took a double-first. Soon after he was elected a Fellow of Brasenose. He was ordained in 1846, and rapidly came to the front both as a Theologian and a Preacher. Amongst the more important posts he held were the following: Assistant Preacher at Lincoln's Inn, Select Preacher at Oxford, Professor of Pastoral Theology at King's College, London, Dean of Queen's College, Oxford, Prebendary of St. Paul's, Professor of New Testament Exegesis at King's College, London, Boyle Lecturer, Grinfield Lecturer on the Septuagint, Examiner in the Theological Schools at Oxford, Member of the Old Testament Revision Company, Rector of Pluckley, 1869, Vicar of Bickley, 1873, and Dean of Wells from 1881 to his death in 1891.

He married the sister of Frederick Denison Maurice. This, and similarity of pursuits and tastes, brought him into very close connection with Julius Charles Hare (who had married another sister of Maurice's), which led to Dr. Plumptre writing introductory sketches to the "Guesses at Truth" by Two Brothers (Julius Charles and Augustus William Hare), and the "Victory of Faith" by the former of these.

Dr. Plumptre's published poetical work is comprised in three volumes: "Lazarus and Other Poems" (1864); "Master and Scholar" (1866); "Things New and Old" (1884). A fourth book, "Cornua Altaris; Thoughts for the Church's Year," was announced in 1884, but never published. This would probably have contained a selection from two voluminous note-books filled with poems chiefly on Scripture subjects, which Dr. Plumptre was kind enough to place at the disposal of the present writer, and from which he drew the greater part of the poems bearing Dr. Plumptre's name in "The Poets' Bible" (1883)

His poetic work is such as we should expect from the nature, the culture, and the pursuits of such a man. Though his lifework lay chiefly in the theological region, he did not, as so many have done, regard theology apart from life by the daylight of the metaphysical thinker. He always saw the form and heard the voice of Prophet and Evangelist whilst he analysed their words. When too little was known of them from the history for this to be the case, he constructed ideal biographies, as in the case of several of the Prophets. So that the imagination was never quite shut out even from his most serious exegetical work. Then his classical training gave him great mastery of verse-forms, whilst his large classical and Biblical scholarship furnished vast stores of knowledge which he was able—easily—to cloth in poetic form. His more important poems, such as "Lazarus," "Jesus Barabbas," and others on Scripture characters are full of information, and are really studies with the added charm of being wrought into poetic form and touched with the colours of an imagination guided by the knowledge of the accurate scholar. The same remarks apply to his poems on Roger Bacon, Milton at Chalfont St. Giles, John Bunyan, etc. These may all be read as Biographic Vignettes, with the assurance that beneath every allusion there is the solid basis of fact. In his shorter poems on Scripture themes the accuracy of the scholar is everywhere present, and they are, therefore, as valuable to the seeker for truth as for the lover of poetry. In his hymns, Dr. Plumptre's thought is often better than the form of its expression. Here the scholar outweighs the poet. Indeed, the lyric is the element in which Dr. Plumptre is most deficient. With one or two exceptions, notably, "Rejoice, ye pure in heart," the most widely used of all, his hymns do not, as they should, sing themselves. The greatest poets can make bricks without straw. This Dr Plumptre cannot do. He must always have a basis of fact, and then he will not quite transfigure it as a Master would do; but he will show all its points in a lovely light. He is a scholar first and a poet afterwards. This to a generation fascinated by Impressionism may seem but faint praise. It is not intended to be. There are diversities of gifts in poetry as in everything else, and at the risk of being reckoned a Philistine, I shall say that I have found more pleasure in some of Dr. Plumptre's verse, although he does "keep one foot firm on fact ere hazarding the next step," than in many a poet who is bold enough to disregard firm foothold on the earth.

W. Garrett Horder.

LAZARUS AND OTHER POEMS.
1865.
EDWARD HAYES PLUMPTRE.

THREE CUPS OF COLD WATER.

I.

THE princely David, with his outlaw-band,
  Lodged in the cave Adullam. Wild and fierce,
With lion-like faces, and with eagle eyes,
They followed where he led. The danger pressed,
For over all the land the Philistines
Had spread their armies. Through Rephaim's vale
Their dark tents mustered thick, and David's home,
His father's city, Bethlehem, owned them lords.
'Twas harvest, and the crops of ripening corn
They ravaged, and with rude feet trampled down
The tender vines. Men hid themselves for fear
In woods or caves. The brave undaunted few,
Gathering round David, sought the mountain hold.
The sun was hot, and all day long they watched
With spear in hand and never-resting eye,
As those who wait for battle. But at eve
The eye grew dim, the lips were parched with thirst,
And from that arid rock no trickling stream
Of living water gushed. From time-worn skins
The tainted drops were poured, and fevered lips
Half-loathing drank them up. And David's soul
Was weary; the hot simoom scorched his veins;
The strong sun smote on him, and, faint and sick,
He sat beneath the shadow of the rock:
And then before his eyes a vision came,
Cool evening, meadows green, and pleasant sounds
Of murmuring fountains. Oft in days of youth,
When leading home his flocks as sunset fell,
That fount had quenched his thirst, and dark-eyed girls,
The pride and joy of Bethlehem, meeting there,

Greeted the shepherd boy, their chieftain's son
(As, bright and fair with waving locks of gold
Exulting in the flush of youth's full glow,
He mingled with their throng), and gazing, rapt
With wonder at his beauty, gave him drink.
And now the words came feebly from his lips,
A murmur half in silence, which the ear
Of faithful followers caught: "Ah! who will bring
From that fair stream, which flowing by the gate
Of Bethlehem's wall makes music in the ear,
One drop to cool this tongue?" They heard, the three,
The mightiest of the thirty, swift of foot
As are the harts upon the mountains, strong
As are the lions down by Jordan's banks;
They heard and darted forth; down rock and crag
They leapt, as leaps the torrent on its course,
Through plain and vale they sped, and never stayed,
Until the wide encampment of the foe
Warned them of danger nigh. But not for fear
Abandoned they their task. When evening fell,
And all the Philistines were hushed in sleep,
And over all the plain the full, bright moon
Poured its rich lustre, onward still they stole,
By tent fires, creeping with hushed breath, and feet
That feared to wake the echoes, till at last
They heard the babbling music, and the gleam
Of rippling moonlight caught their eager eye,
And o'er them fell the shade of Bethlehem's gate.
They tarried not. One full delicious draught
Slaked their fierce thirst, and then with anxious haste
They filled their water-urn, and full of joy,
They bore it back in triumph to their lord.
With quickened steps they tracked their path again
O'er plain and valley, up o'er rock and crag,

And as the early sunlight kissed the hills
They stood before him. He had won their hea
By brave deeds, gentle words, and stainless life,
And now they came to give him proof of love,
And pouring out the water bade him drink.
But lo! he would not taste. He heard their tale
(In few words told, as brave men tell their deeds),
And lifting up his hands with solemn prayer.
As though, he stood, a priest, before the shrine.
He poured it on the earth before the Lord.
"Far be it from me, God, that I should drink,
The slave of selfish lust, forgetting Thee,
Forgetting these my brothers. In Thine eyes
This water fresh and cool is as the blood
Of hero-souls who jeopardied their lives.
That blood I may not taste. As shrink the lips
From the hot life-stream of the Paschal Lamb,
So shrinks my soul from this. To Thee, O Lord,
To Thee I pour it. Thou wilt pardon me
For mine unkingly weakness, pardon them
For all rough deeds of war. Their noble love
Shall cover all their sins; for Thou hast claimed,
More than all blood of bulls and goats, the will
That, self-forgetting, lives in deeds like this."

So spake the hero-king, and all the host
Looked on and wondered; and those noble three,
The mightiest of the thirty, felt their souls
Knit closer to King David and to God.

II.

Through wastes of sand the train of camels wound
Their lingering way. The pilgrims, hasting on
To Mecca's shrine, were grieved and vexed at heart,
Impatient of delay. The scorching sand

Lay hot and blinding round them, and the blast
Of sultry winds, as from a furnace mouth
Brought blackness to all faces. Whirling clouds
Of white dust filled their eyes, and, falling flat,
Crouching in fear, they waited till it passed
Then, lifting up their eyes, there met their gaze
One fierce, hot glare, a waveless sea of sand.
No track of pilgrims' feet, nor whitening bones
Of camels or of asses, marked their way.
They wandered on, by sun and moon and stars
Guessing their path, not knowing where they went,
But Mecca's shrine they saw not. Day by day,
Their scant stores scantier grew. Their camels died;
No green oasis met their yearning eyes,
No rippling stream brought gladness to their hearts;
But glittering lakes that sparkled in the light,
Girt with the soft green tufts of feathery palm,
Enticed them, hour by hour, to wander on,
And, as they neared them, turned to wastes of sand.
They thirsted, and with looks of blank despair
Beheld the emptied skins. One only, borne
By Ka'ab's camel, met their wistful gaze,—
Ka'ab, the rich, the noble, he who knew
The depths of Islam,[1] unto Allah's will
Resigning all his soul. And now he showed
How out of that submission flows the strength
For noblest acts of love. That priceless store
He claimed not as his own: the "mine" and "thine"
Of selfish right he scattered to the winds,
And to his fellow-pilgrims offered all.
They shared it all alike. To Ka'ab's self
And Ka'ab's slave an equal portion came.
"Allah is great," he cried, about to drink
With thankful adoration, when a wail

Of eager craving burst from parchèd lips,
And upturned eyes with fevered anguish watched
The precious life-draught. Ka'ab heard that cry,
His eye beheld that anguish, and his heart
Was stirred with pity. Tasting not a drop,
With calm and loving look he passed the cup
To those poor dying lips, and bore his thirst,
As martyrs bear their flames. His soul had learnt,
Not Islam's creed alone that God is great:
A mightier name was written on his heart,
"God, the compassionate, the merciful;
And yielding up his will to God's, the three,
Compassion, mercy, greatness, were as one.

So ends the tale. And whether death came soon
As sleep's twin-brother, with the longed-for rest,
And clear bright streams in Paradise refreshed
The fevered thirsts of earth; or if the dawn
Revealed the distant gleam of Mecca's shrine,
And led those pilgrims on to Zemzem's fount,
We know not. This we know, that evermore,
Like living water from the flinty rock,
Gladdening the hearts of Hagar's sons, as once
God's angel helped the mother and her child,
The memory of that noble deed flows on,
And quickens into life each fainting heart,
And through long ages, in each Arab's tent
It passed into a proverb—"Ka'ab's deed
Of noble goodness:—There is none like that." [2]

III.

THE setting sun fell low on Zutphen's plain;
The fight was over, and the victory won,
And out of all the din and stir of war
They bore the flower of Christian chivalry

The life-blood gushing out.   He came, the pure,
The true, the stainless, all youth's fiery glow,
All manhood's wisdom, blended into one,
To help the weak against the strong, to drive
The Spaniard from a land which was not his,
And claim the right of all men to be free,
Free in their life, their polity, their faith.
He came, no poor ambition urging on,
But loyalty and duty, first to God,
And then to her the Virgin Queen who ruled
His guileless heart, and of a thousand good
Found him the best.   We wonder that he bowed
Before so poor an idol, knowing not
That noble souls transfer their nobleness
To that whereon they gaze, and through the veils
Of custom or of weakness reach the heart
That beats, as theirs, with lofty thoughts and true.
And now that life was ebbing.   Men had hoped
To see in him the saviour of the state
From thickening perils, one in open war
To cope with Alva, and in subtle skill,
Bating no jot of openness and truth,
To baffle all the tortuous wiles of Spain ·
And some who knew him better hoped to see
His poet's spirit do a poet's work,
With sweetest music giving voice and shape
To all the wondrous thoughts that stirred the age,
Moving the world's great heart, attracting all,
The children at their play, the old man bent
By blazing hearths, to listen and rejoice.

 And now his sun was setting.   Faint and weak
They bore him to his tent, and loss of blood
Brought on the burning thirst of wounded men,
And he too craved for water.   Brothers true,

Companions of his purpose and his risk,
Brought from the river in their helmet cup
The draught he longed for. Yet he drank it not;
That eye had fallen on another's woe,
That ear was open to another's sigh,
That hand was free to give, and pitying love,
In that sharp pain of death, had conquered self.
The words were few and simple: "Not for me;
I may not taste: He needs it more than I:"
Few as all noblest words are, pearls and gems
Of rarest lustre; but they found their way,
More than all gifts of speech or poet's skill,
To stir the depths of England's heart of hearts,
And gave to Sidney's name a brighter life,
A nobler fame through all the immortal years,
Than Raleigh's friendship, or his own brave deeds,
Or counsel's wise, or Spenser's silver notes,—
A trumpet-call to bid the heart awake,
A beacon-light to all the rising youth,
Fit crown of glory to that stainless life,
The perfect pattern of a Christian knight,
The noblest hero of our noblest age.

IV.

AND one day they shall meet before their God,
The Hebrew, and the Moslem, and the flower
Of England's knighthood. On the great white throne
The Judge shall sit, and from his lips shall flow
Divinest words: "Come, friends and brothers, come;
I speak as one whose soul has known your pangs;
Your weariness and woe were also mine;
The cry, 'I thirst,' has issued from these lips,
And I too would not drink, but bore the pain,
Yielding my will to do my Father's work,
And so that work was finished, so I learnt

The fullest measure of obedience, learnt
The wide deep love embracing all mankind,
Passing through all the phases of their woe
That I before their God might plead for all.
And thus through all the pulses of their life
I suffer when they suffer; count each deed
Of Mercy done to them as done to Me,
And one with them in sorrow and in joy,
Rejoicing in their likeness to My life,
And bearing still the burden of their sins
For which I once was offered. I was there,
The light of each man's soul, in that wild cave,
On that parched desert, on that tented field;
That self-forgetting love I owned as Mine,
And ye who, true to that diviner Light
Which triumphed over nature, freely gave
That water to the thirsty, gave to Me.

* * * * * *

[1] Islam—resignation, submission to the will of God—was proclaimed by Mahomet as the one essential religion, which had been inherited from the patriarchs, preached by the prophets, and revived by himself as its new and greatest apostle. Comp. Koran, ch. ii. and iii. (Sale's *Translation*); or ch. xci. and xcvii. (Rodwell's).

"They who set their face with resignation Godward and do what is right, their reward is with the Lord."

"When his Lord said to Abraham, 'Resign thyself to Me,' he said, 'I resign myself to the Lord of the Worlds.'"

"And this to his children did Abraham bequeath, and Jacob also, saying, 'O, my children! truly God has chosen a religion for you; so die not unless ye also be Mus'ims'" (*sc.*, resigned). (Rodwell, xci.)

[2] The story is given by Kallius in his notes to Rostgaard's translation of the collection of proverbs known as *Arabum Philosophia Popularis*, p. 57. The current form of the proverb is that Arabs, in speaking of any one whose nobleness they wish to praise, describe him as "more generous than Kalab." See also Pocock, *Hist. Arab.*, p. 344.

MASTER AND SCHOLAR.
1866.
EDWARD HAYES PLUMPTRE.
GILBOA.

I.

So life is ending, and its visions pass
    Before the inward eye,
Like soft dew falling on the tender grass,
    When all around is dry.

Through the dark night I see the ruby flush
    Of childhood's earliest day;
Through war's wild din, and battle's torrent rush,
    I hear the children play.

Yet once again I live that time of might,
    When I, and one with me
Who bore my shield, were conquerors in the fight,
    And made the aliens flee.

From crag to crag we clambered, hand in hand,
    And leapt from rock to rock;
Till from the height we looked on all the land,
    And dared the battle's shock.

I feel the faintness of that noontide heat,
    The thirst that fired the brain;
I taste the golden stream that trickled sweet,
    And brought life back again:

The fear of death is on me as of old,
    When Saul in sternness strove
An iron mantle round his heart to fold,
    And crush a father's love;

I stood as one condemned to shameful death,
    And offered up my life,
As Isaac bowed of old, with calmest breath,
    To meet the glittering knife:

When shrill and loud from warriors old and young
    There rose the awe-struck cry;
Their strong resolve through hill and forest rung,
    "This day shall no man die!"

So with my father many a month passed on,
    I smote the craven foe;
And year by year the crown of victory won,
    Requiting blow for blow:

And robes of scarlet from each plundered town,
    We brought for Israel's maids;
The ruby circlet, and the golden crown,
    Rich harvest of our raids.

So grew my soul to manhood's kingly noon,
    And all men sang my praise;
Yet darker far than night without a moon,
    Was fame's full daylight blaze.

I craved for one whose heart should beat as mine,
    My hopes and thoughts to share,
A soul to live with me the life divine,
    And half grief's burden bear.

I sought for one to be my friend and guide,
    My glory and my joy;
When lo! there stood in brightness by my side,
    The minstrel shepherd-boy.

II.

Yes, there he stood, and life's deep-hidden fountains
    Welled from my soul in one abounding flood;
The sun shone brighter on the hoary mountains,
    A sweeter music murmured through the wood.

It was not for the flush of youthful beauty,
  The golden locks that flowed like sunlight down;
Through eye's wild flash there gleamed the star of duty,
  And on his brow Truth set her kingly crown.

Strong arm was his to smite the tyrant stranger,
  Voice soft as maiden's, stirring men to tears,
A soul that knew no fear of death or danger,
  Wide thoughts of wisdom ripening with the years

Forth from his lips there flowed the song of gladness,
  His hand brought music from the soulless lyre;
And lo! the spell chased all the clouds of madness,
  Wrath passed away as wax before the fire.

Of warriors old he sang, our father's glory,
  The wonders of the nobler days of old;
And strong, deep music thrilled through all the story,
  Stirring all hearts to deeds of prowess bold.

He sang the marvels of the earth and heaven,
  The starry night, the cloud-built tent of God,
The wild, dark storm on wings of tempest driven,
  The snow-clad heights where never man has trod:

And new light streamed o'er mountain and o'er river,
  New voices mingled with the streamlet's song;
Men's hearts rose up to meet the Eternal Giver,
  The slave found freedom, and the weak grew strong.

And oh! my heart clave to him as he chanted
  The hymns that made the brain and spirit thrill;
I found the prize for which my soul had panted,
  The friend and guide of thought, and heart, and will.

I track that love throughout life's varied chances,
  And still my heart is with him to the last,
Though all our glory wane as his advances,
  His the bright future, ours the failing past.

III.

'Tis well, 'tis well, I grudge him not the glory,
    His people's love unpriced;
Long line of kings, great names renowned in story,
    The far-off, coming Christ.

I gave him, in that first bright hour of meeting,
    My robe, and sword, and shield;
And ofttimes since in every secret greeting,
    In forest or in field,

That sacrifice of self on true love's altar,
    I, of free choice, renewed;
Nor shall my spirit fail or purpose falter,
    With woman's varying mood.

I trust he loves me still, but love's requiting, . . .
    What need for that to bless?
Though he should stand a foe against me fighting,
    I should not love him less;

Though from his hand should dart the spear to slay me,
    I could not him deny;
No other love have I whereon to stay me,
    And when that fails I die:

I dream that he will give a little weeping
    Above my fameless grave;
I trust my orphaned child to his true keeping
    From shame and death to save:

So, though my lineage from the earth shall perish,
    Yet faithful to the end,
He still, through kingly state and strife, may cherish
    The memory of his friend.

    *   *   *   *   *   *

THINGS NEW AND OLD.
1884.

EDWARD HAYES PLUMPTRE.

CHALFONT ST. GILES.[1]

(FROM THOMAS ELWOOD TO WILLIAM PENNINGTON,
A.D. 1665.)

YES, he is with me now, that blind old man,
  Of whom I oft have told thee. I have sought
To save him from the city's tainted air;
And so from out the streets, whose midnight hush
Is broken by the plague-cart's bell, while death
With sweeping scythe mows down the grass of life,
I brought him hither. But a few green fields
Divide us, and at morn, and noon, and eve,
We meet as friends familiar, I to hear,
And he to speak. From pale lips eloquent
Flow golden words, and from the treasured store,
Like a wise scribe, he brings forth new and old;
Remembered words of poets and of sage
Float, like a strain of music, to his ears;
And so from out the dark clouds of the night
The moon looks forth upon his lonely path,[2]
And leads him o'er wild moor and dreary waste,
Until the day-star rises. And his joy,
When o'er him comes the breath of new-mown fields,
The fragrance of the eglantine and rose,
Or the rich sweetness which the summer rain
Draws from the bosom of the parchèd earth,
Shines, like a sunbeam o'er that sightless face,
And sound, by some strange mystery of the sense,
Seems half-transmuted into subtler waves,

And tells of form and colour.   Not for him
The golden sunset and the roseate dawn;
And yet the breath of morning, and the songs
Of lark that chants his anthems high and clear,
Bring to his soul the brightness and the glow.
He cannot see the lightning's fiery flash,
But every peal of solemn thunder sweeps
With sudden glory to the inward eye;
And lo! his soul mounts upward to the Throne
Whence issue voices mighty as the surge
Of many waters, and the emerald arch
Spans the wide vault, and thousand angels wait,
Each in his order, or go to and fro,
Serving their Master.   So each varying tone,
When the soft breeze, from out the pine-tree tops,
Calls the low murmur as of distant seas,
Or pattering of the raindrops on the eaves
Tells of the spring-tide shower, or babbling brook,
From pebbly depths and shallows in its course,
Makes clearest music,—all alike for him
Are but the notes of one vast symphony
That rises up from Nature to her God;
And each fair scene is present to his thoughts,
As once it was to sight that now is quenched.
But man is more than Nature, and his soul
Soars to yet loftier empyrean heights,
When from the ivory keys the expert's touch
Creates its wondrous world of melody,
The solemn chants which fill the lofty choir,
The madrigals which speak of youth and joy,
The rushing flood of some o'erflowing strain
That pours unbidden, man's will powerless
To start, or guide, or check it.   This his hands
Work for themselves, and I but sit and hear,

Wrapt in that cloud of music, and borne on
To heights before unknown; and yet my voice,
That too has power to stir the depths of life,
Or ringing out Great Homer's trumpet tones,
Or following Virgil's calmer, statelier tread,
Or the dread vision of the Florentine,
Or in our English speech, with psalm and hymn,
And hallelujah, such as Levites sang
Before their God, the Lord of Sabaoth,
Kindling his spirit, till the wind that sweeps
With mighty rushing wakes his soul to hear
The echoes of the anthems of the stars,
The music of the mountain and the flood.

*   *   *   *   *   *

[1] Chalfont St. Giles is memorable in English literature as the place of Milton's retirement during the great Plague of London, A.D. 1665. Thither he was taken by Thomas Elwood, one of the early disciples of William Penn, from whom this narrative of his life there is supposed to come in a letter to one of the brotherhood of Friends.

[2] "Then the remembrance of early reading came over his dark and lonely path like the moon emerging from the clouds."—Hallam: *History of Literature*, iv., p. 425, ed. 1839.

HYMNS.

EDWARD HAYES PLUMPTRE.

I.—REJOICE, YE PURE IN HEART.

REJOICE, ye pure in heart,
   Rejoice, give thanks and sing;
Your festal banner wave on high,
   The Cross of Christ your King.

Bright youth and snow-crown'd age
   Strong men and maidens meek,
Raise high your free exulting song,
   God's wondrous praises speak.

Yes onward, onward still,
   With hymn and chant and song,
Thro' gate, and porch, and columned aisle
   The hallow'd pathways throng.

With all the angel-choirs,
   With all the saints on earth,
Pour out the strains of joy and bliss,
   True rapture, noblest mirth.

Your clear Hosannas raise,
   And Hallelujahs loud,
Whilst answering echoes upward float,
   Like wreaths of incense-cloud.

With voice as full and strong
   As ocean's surging praise,
Send forth the hymns our fathers loved,
   The psalms of ancient days.

Yes, on, through life's long path,
  Still chanting as ye go,
From youth to age, by night and day,
  In gladness and in woe.

Still lift your standard high,
  Still march in firm array,
As warriors through the darkness toil,
  Till dawns the golden day.

At last the march shall end,
  The wearied ones shall rest,
The pilgrims find their Father's house,
  Jerusalem the blest

Then on, ye pure in heart,
  Rejoice, give thanks, and sing;
Your festal banner wave on high,
  The Cross of Christ your King

Praise Him who reigns on high,
  The Lord whom we adore,
Praise Father, Son, and Holy Ghost,
  One God for evermore.

II.—THINE ARM, O LORD.

THINE arm, O Lord, in days of old
  Was strong to heal and save;
It triumphed o'er disease and death,
  O'er darkness and the grave:
To Thee they went, the blind, the dumb,
  The palsied and the lame,
The leper with his tainted life,
  The sick with fevered frame;

EDWARD HAYES PLUMPTRE

And, lo, Thy touch brought life and health,
   Gave speech, and strength, and sight;
And youth renewed and frenzy calmed
   Owned Thee, the Lord of Light.
And now, O Lord, be near to bless,
   Almighty as of yore,
In crowded street, by restless couch,
   As by Gennesareth's shore.

Though love and might no longer heal
   By touch, or word, or look;
Though they who do Thy work must read
   Thy laws in Nature's book:
Yet come to heal the sick man's soul,
   Come, cleanse the leprous taint;
Give joy and peace where all is strife,
   And strength where all is faint.

Be Thou our great Deliverer still
   Thou Lord of life and death,
Restore and quicken, soothe and bless
   With Thine Almighty breath:
To hands that work and eyes that see
   Give Wisdom's heavenly lore,
That whole and sick, and weak and strong,
   May praise Thee evermore.

James Drummond Burns.

1823—1864.

This "sweet singer" was born in Edinburgh on the 18th of February, 1823. His father held the privilege of burgess-freeman, whereby this his eldest son inherited the right of being one of the hundred and eighty boys in residence in George Heriot's Hospital—an endowment answering in Scotland to Christ's Hospital of London. So early as his twelfth year he was passed to the Rector's class of the High School, though he continued a resident in the great hospital. Dr. Carson, the then rector, was a ripe scholar and effective teacher. He "took" to young Burns. In his sixteenth year (November 1837) he was transferred to the University, as one of Heriot's bursars. Sir William Hamilton and "Christopher North" (John Wilson) became his most stimulating instructors. He graduated M.A. Having completed the usual course of Presbyterian students, he proceeded, in November 1841, to the Theological Hall of the "Kirk" of Scotland, then illustrious through Welsh and Thomas Chalmers. He speedily won distinction as Essayist and strenuous debater. His first two "sessions" in the Hall were the last two of what is known in ecclesiastical history as the "Ten Years' Conflict," and the summer of 1843 saw the national Church rent into unequal halves. He threw in his lot with the

"Free Church of Scotland," and followed his old professors, and the new, to its New College. In 1845 Dr. Chalmers persuaded him to go as temporary "supply" to the vacant congregation of Dunblane —a Scottish shrine through saintly Archbishop Leighton—and this issued in his becoming its first minister. It was an arduous post, and the young pastor was of a delicate constitution and of foreboding though not at all gloomy temperament, as witness his pathetic sonnet on reaching his twenty-fifth year (p. 34). He broke down after about two years of laborious and consecrate service. He left Dunblane for Madeira. There he did noble work among the invalids and native converts. In leisure hours he cultivated an unmistakable poetic gift that had revealed itself in his early boyhood. He is found again in Dunblane in 1848, but only to complete the resignation of his church and to return to Madeira. His further stay there was brief, as a universal blight of the island's vines and other calamities scattered his congregation. In 1853 he returned to England, and, after occasional service elsewhere, was finally settled, on the 22nd of May, 1855, as minister of the Presbyterian Church of Hampstead. His fine intellect, his ripened culture, his accurate and varied scholarship, and his lovable nature found expression in sermons of an exceptionally high order, and as a corollary in a considerable body of literary work. For details on these the reader is referred to Dr. James Hamilton's *Life and Remains*—a fascinating book. Here we have only to do with him as a poet. His poetry is found (*a*) in two small volumes respectively designated "The Evening Hymn: A Book of Prayers and Hymns for

Family Use," and "Heavenly Jerusalem, or Glimpses within the Gates"; (β) a volume entitled "The Vision of Prophecy and other poems": First Edition 1854; Second 1858 (enlarged). His prose is steeped in poetry, and often surprises with exquisitely wrought word-painting—*e g.*, his description of the earthly and heavenly rainbow is worthy of Ruskin. All too soon and sorrowfully his constitutional weakness reasserted itself. In 1859 he had married inestimably, and three children brightened his home. But he had to give way. Amidst manifold tokens of his congregation's affection and thoughtfulness he removed to Mentone. At first there were gleams of hope of recovery, but they were speedily quenched. He died on the 27th of November, 1864, and was buried in Highgate Cemetery.

Two things have militated against Burns' adequate recognition as a poet of more than common genius: (α) The error in judgment of giving the leading place in title-page and book to his long blank verse poem of the "Vision of Prophecy," inasmuch as while it has felicitous lines and haunting images, it lacks inspiration as a whole; (β) "The inclusion of a number of weak and poor pieces that your chance dipper into the volume was sure to hap on. But from HUGH MILLER onward, he has been accepted as a genuine Maker (in the old sense). His splendid tribute to Wordsworth (pp. 94-116, 1858) confirms the impression left throughout, that he was his master in observation and love of Nature. His unique place as a hymn writer is recognised in Julian's Dictionary of Hymnology (*s v.*). We give examples in our selections. We shall be disappointed if these and our other selections do no send readers to the complete volumes. I close our necessarily compressed notice with Dr Julian's well-put estimate: " His poems are distinguished by vivid colouring and poetic imagination, along with directness, delicacy of execution, pensive sweetness and tenderness. Included are twenty-seven hymns and meditations, some of which rank among the very best of our modern hymns for beauty, simplicity of diction, and depth of religious feeling. His hymns and prayers alike are characterised by reverence, beauty, simplicity, and pathos." Very humble was his own self-estimate, before his volume of 1854-58:—

> "No laurel leaves, no sweet unfading flowers
> Bloom in the garden of these simple lines;
> They are but rushes woven in random hours,
> Like those some lonely shepherd-boy entwines.
> The while his fingers plait the scentless wreath,
> He finds some pleasure in his idle skill;
> At even, he leaves it withering on the heath,
> Or strews its fragments on the moorland rill."

ALEXANDER B. GROSART

POEMS.

JAMES DRUMMOND BURNS.

I.—THE VESPER HOUR.

(In Madeira.)

A ROSY light the Eastern sky is steeping,—
   The ripple on the sea has died away
To a low murmur,—and the ships are sleeping
   Each on its glassy shadow in the Bay:
The young moon's golden shell over the hill
Trembles with lustre, and the trees are still.

The air grows clearer, and her amice blue
   The gentle Twilight hath about her cast,
And from her silver urn she sprinkles dew:
   Silence and Sleep, twin sisters, follow fast
Her soundless sandals, and where'er she goes
Day-wearied Nature settles to repose.

Hark! the clear bell from that tall convent-tower
   Hath sounded,—and, or e'er its echoes die,
Another chime hath rung the vesper hour,—
   A farther and a fainter makes reply;
Till far and near the soft appeal to prayer
With music fills the undulating air.

Ye sweet-voiced bells, ring on! Though at your call
   I may not breathe in prayer a creature's name,
Yet on my heart more touching memories fall,
   And ye remind me of a holier claim,—
His, whose undrooping eye alone can keep
Watch over His belovèd as they sleep.

II.—THE CHILD SAMUEL.

HUSH'D was the evening hymn,
   The temple-courts were dark;
The lamp was burning dim
   Before the sacred ark;
When suddenly a voice divine,
Rang through the silence of the shrine.

The old man, meek and mild,—
   The priest of Israel—slept;
His watch, the temple-child,—
   The little Levite—kept;
And what from Eli's sense was seal'd
The Lord to Hannah's son reveal'd.

Oh give me Samuel's ear!
   The open ear, O God!
Alive and quick to hear
   Each whisper of Thy word;
Like him to answer at Thy call,
And to obey Thee first of all.

Oh give me Samuel's heart!
   A lowly heart that waits
Where in Thy house Thou art,
   Or watches at Thy gates,
By day and night—a heart that still
Moves at the breathing of Thy will.

Oh give me Samuel's mind!
   A sweet unmurmuring faith,
Obedient and resign'd
   To Thee, in life and death;
That I may read with child-like eyes
Truths that are hidden from the wise.

III.—HUMILITY.

O! LEARN that it is only by the lowly
    The paths of peace are trod;
If thou would'st keep thy garments white and holy,
    Walk humbly with thy God.

The man with earthly wisdom high uplifted
    Is in God's sight a fool;
But he in heavenly truth most deeply gifted
    Sits lowest in Christ's school.

The lowly spirit God hath consecrated
    As His abiding rest;
And angels by some patriarch's tent have waited,
    When kings had no such guest.

The dew that never wets the flinty mountain,
    Falls in the valley free;
Bright verdure fringes the small desert-fountain,
    But barren sand the sea.

Not in the stately oak the fragrance dwelleth
    Which charms the general wood,
But in the violet low, whose sweetness telleth
    Its unseen neighbourhood.

The censer swung by the proud hand of merit
    Fumes with a fire abhorred;
But Faith's two mites, dropped covertly, inherit
    A blessing from the Lord.

Round lowliness a gentle radiance hovers,
    A sweet unconscious grace;
Which, even in shrinking, evermore discovers
    The brightness on its face.

Where God abides, Contentment is and Honour,
    Such guerdon Meekness knows;
His peace within her, and His smile upon her,
    Her saintly way she goes.

Through the straight gate of life she passes stooping,
    With sandals on her feet;
And pure-eyed Graces, hand in hand come trooping,
    Their sister fair to greet.

The angels bend their eyes upon her goings,
    And guard her from annoy;
Heaven fills her heart with silent overflowings
    Of its perennial joy.

The Saviour loves her, for she wears the vesture
    With which He walked on Earth;
And through her child-like glance, and step, and gesture,
    He knows her heavenly birth.

He now beholds this seal of glory graven
    On all whom He redeems;
And in His own bright City, crystal-paven,
    On every brow it gleams.

The white-robed saints, the throne-steps singing under,
    Their state all meekly wear;
Their praise wells up from hidden springs of wonder
    That grace has brought them there.

IV.—THE FOOTSTEPS OF THE FLOCK.

NOT always, Lord, in pastures green
    The sheep at noon Thou feedest,
  Where in the shade they lie
  Within Thy watchful eye:
Not always under skies serene
    The white-fleeced flock Thou leadest.

On rugged ways, with bleeding feet,
  They leave their painful traces;
    Through deserts drear they go,
    Where wounding briers grow,
And through dark valleys, where they meet
  No quiet resting-places.

Not always by the waters still,
  Or lonely wells palm-hidden,
    Do they find happy rest,
    And, in Thy presence blest,
Delight themselves, and drink their fill
  Of pleasures unforbidden.

Their track is worn on Sorrow's shore,
  Where windy storms beat ever—
    Their troubled course they keep,
    Where deep calls unto deep;
So going till they hear the roar
  Of the dark-flowing river.

But wheresoe'er their steps may be,
  So Thou their path be guiding,
    O be their portion mine!
    Show me the secret sign,
That I may trace their way to Thee,
  In Thee find rest abiding.

Slowly they gather to the fold,
  Upon Thy holy mountain,—
    There, resting round Thy feet,
    They dread no storm nor heat,
And slake their thirst where Thou hast rolled
  The stone from Life's full fountain.

V.—THE BIRD AND THE BEE.

THE bird is your true Poet. I have seen him,
   When the snow wrapped his seeds, and not a crumb
Was in his larder, perch upon a branch,
And sing from his brave heart a song of trust
In Providence, who feeds him though he sows not,
Nor gathers into barns. Whate'er his fears
Or sorrows be, his spirit bears him up;
Cares ne'er o'ermaster him, for 'tis his wont
To stifle them with music. Out of sight
He buries them in the depths of his sweet song,
And gives them a melodious sepulture.

   He teaches me philosophy,—yea, more,
He leads me up to Faith. Your busy Bee
No favourite is of mine. There is no music
In that monotonous hum. To me it seems
A trumpet, which the little Pharisee
Sounds, that the common people of the field
May well regard his industry, and mark
How he improves the sunshine. Even that song
Dies with the flowers; for when the dreary days
Of Winter come, he folds his wing to lie
In his luxurious halls, and there amidst
His magazines of daintiest food, and vaults
Brimming with luscious amber-coloured wine,
The spiritless sluggard dreams away his hours;
Or if he wake, 'tis but to gorge himself
In solitude, with the rich cloying fare
Of an exclusive feast. His hospitality
No stranger ever shares. Heedless he sees
His mates of Summer droop and starve before
His frozen gates. He revels deep within,
Without they die: yet the small misanthrope
Shall guard his treasures with a surly sting!

SONNETS.

JAMES DRUMMOND BURNS.

I.—PRESENTIMENT.

HAST thou not felt when journeying to the place
   Whence some clear prospect might before thee lie,—
  Some gleam of beauty,—to reward the eye,
For long dull leagues of dreary interspace,
A strange desire to mend thy lagging pace,
   Which still grew stronger as the scene drew nigh,
   Till one could fret at the necessity
Which bound him in the senses' strict embrace?
Such is the inward yearning of the soul
   Towards the vision of the Infinite
When Time's thick folded mists at last unroll;
It strives to cast aside each earthly bond,
   And scale the ridge between it and the light
Of God that sleeps on blessèd lands beyond.

II.—REASON AND FAITH.
Psalm lxxiii. 16, 17.

HOW many are the mysteries that lie
   Along life's winding way, and vex the mind
   With restless speculation, vague and blind:
In vain doth Reason hold her torch on high,
To trace the round of calm Infinity,
   In all its sapphire clearness; in the gloom
   She gropes, until she stumbles o'er a tomb;
Earth's roof of cloud to her is all the sky.
   But Faith, while in the temple-court she keeps
   Her midnight watch, sees up the azure deeps
God's name in starry cipher written fair,—
   The vision of His Wisdom, Power, and Love,
   Serenely throned these drifting mists above,
Revealed unto the upward gaze of Prayer.

III.—MY FIRST BIRTHDAY IN A FOREIGN LAND.
(Written at the Age of Twenty-Five.)

BEHIND my wandering steps, the busy hands
   Of Time build up the moments into years,
And noiselessly, from these fast-dropping sands,
   The temple of my mortal life he rears.
   Alas! to me too surely it appears
A weak devoted structure, which commands
No prospect of continuance, and stands
   On a most tottering base. But Thou these fears,
O God, canst turn to hopes, that when the frail
   Tent of the spirit shrivels into dust,
One of the many mansions shall be mine,
Eternal in the Heavens. So through the vale
   Of Life I go my way with lowly trust,
Contented heart, and will resigned to Thine!

IV.—MEMORY OF A DEAR FRIEND.

MY grief pursues me through the Land of Sleep,
   It winds into the secret of my dreams,
   And shapes their shadowy pomp. When Fancy seems
To charm my fever'd spirit into deep
Forgetfulness, the restless Thought will creep
   From its dim ambush, startling that repose,
   And glooms and spectral terrors round me close,
Like iron walls I may not overleap.
And then I seem to see thy face again,
   But not, belovèd! as thou wert and art,
And, with thy sweet voice tingling in my brain,
   From this great agony of fear I start,
To feel the slow throb of habitual pain,
   And undull'd anguish grasping at my heart.

V.—IMAGINATION.

NOT seldom will the sun, when westering slow,
   Turn his bright eye upon a fronting train
   Of clouds, and from the mists and falling rain
Weave suddenly his broad and gorgeous bow.
The stainless air puts on a purple glow,
   The beauteous secrecies of light are plain,
   And from these stripes the swimming vapours gain
More splendour than the orient skies can show.
Such is Imagination, and the power
   Which peoples Nature with its glorious dreams;
Which sprinkles everywhere its golden shower,
   And to the fine-eyed poet, in what seems
His vacant but his visionary hour,
   Tints every cloud with mild auroral gleams.

VI.—BY THE SEA-SIDE.

RUN in, glad waves, scoop'd in transparent shells,
   Which catch soft lights of emerald ere they break;
Let the small ripple fret the sand, and make
The faintest chime of music, such as dwells
Far down within the sea-conch's murmuring cells,—
   While, hovering o'er the spray, the white birds wet
   Their wings, and shouting fishers draw the net
To land, and far sails glitter on the swells.
'Tis bliss to rest, the while these soft blue skies
   Breathe over Earth their benison of peace,
To feel these lovely forms enchant the eyes,
   And grow into the mind by slow degrees,—
Till, breathless as a woodland pool, it lies,
   And sleeps above its sleeping images.

VII.—EVENING PICTURE.

OVER the hill-edge ripples the warm light,—
   One level ray along the sprouting vines
  Gleams like a seraph's spear. The dusky lines
Of the far woods grow shapeless on the height,
Where the slow mists fold up their fleeces white,
   Now flecked with purple O'er that cloud of pines
  The sky to clearest spirit of air refines,
And a star settles trembling on the sight.
Cool winds are rustling downwards to the seas,
   To worn, home-faring men benignly given.
From the soft glooms of church-encircling trees,
   Fast darkening in the shadows of the even,
The small bells sprinkle pensive cadences,
   And Earth is peacefully atoned with Heaven!

VIII.—GREAT BRITAIN.
(From Sonnets on finding the North-West Passage.)

DESPOND not, Britain! Should this sacred hold
   Of Freedom, still inviolate, be assailed,
  The high, unblenching spirit which prevailed
In ancient days is neither dead nor cold :
Men are still in thee of heroic mould,—
   Men whom thy grand old sea-kings would have hailed
  As worthy peers, invulnerably mailed,
Because by duty's sternest law controlled.
Thou yet shalt rise, and send abroad thy voice
   Among the nations, battling for the right,
In the unrusted armour of thy youth ;
And the oppressed shall hear it and rejoice,
   For on thy side is the resistless might
Of Freedom, Justice, and Eternal Truth !

Cecil Frances Alexander.

1823—1895.

CECIL FRANCES ALEXANDER, second daughter of Major John Humphreys, of Miltown House, Co. Tyrone, Ireland, was born in the year 1823. Her principal volumes of verse are: "Verses for Holy Seasons" (1846); "Hymns for Little Children" (1848); "Narrative Hymns for Village Schools" (1853); "Poems on Subjects in the Old Testament" (Part I., 1854, Part II, 1857); "Hymns Devotional and Descriptive (1858); and "The Legend of the Golden Prayers, and other Poems" (1859); besides which she contributed to numerous hymn-books and collections of sacred verse, including the "Lyra Anglicana" and "Hymns Ancient and Modern." She married Dr. Alexander, afterwards Bishop of Derry, in the year 1847, and died on the 12th of October, 1895.

Though chiefly known as a writer of hymns for children, Mrs. Alexander's verse displays powers which under greater restraint would have been even more successful upon a higher plane. A sense of the sublime, and an eye for the picturesque, and especially for colour, associated with an easy command of language, and an ear for rhyme and rhythm, are constantly in evidence; and in her lyric, "The Burial of Moses," have produced a poem which does not seem to fall short of the great subject of which it treats. This is high praise indeed, but the poem bids fair to become a classic. Though not written especially for children, it appeals alike to young and old. A little child of six years of age known to the writer, after hearing it read, declared with enthusiasm that it was the grandest poem she had ever heard. Older critics will scarcely challenge the use of the word "grand" in this connection. Unfortunately in others of her poems Mrs. Alexander did not exercise the same restraint. "The Lonely Grave," the opening stanzas of which include the following picturesque verse—

> The s range-shaped flowers of gorgeous dyes,
> Unmoved by any wandering breeze,
> Look out with their great scarlet eyes,
> An . watch him from the giant trees—

begins well, but it is much too long, and, like others of Mrs. Alexander's longer poems, becomes tedious before it concludes. Some of her hymns and shorter poems, however, have attained wide acceptance, securing a position which they seem well qualified to retain.

ALFRED H. MILES.

HYMNS FOR CHILDREN.

CECIL FRANCES ALEXANDER.

1—EVERY MORNING THE RED SUN.

EVERY morning the red sun
   Rises warm and bright;
But the evening cometh on,
   And the dark, cold night;
There's a bright land far away,
Where 'tis never-ending day.

Every spring the sweet young flowers
   Open bright and gay,
Till the chilly autumn hours
   Wither them away:
There's a land we have not seen,
Where the trees are always green.

Little birds sing songs of praise
   All the summer long,
But in colder, shorter days
   They forget their song.
There's a place where Angels sing
Ceaseless praises to their King.

Christ our Lord is ever near
   Those who follow Him;
But we cannot see Him here,
   For our eyes are dim:
There is a most happy place,
Where men always see His Face.

Who shall go to that fair land ?
    All who do the right :
Holy children there shall stand,
    In their robes of white ;
For that Heaven so bright and blest,
Is our everlasting rest.

II.—THERE IS A GREEN HILL FAR AWAY

THERE is a green hill far away
    Without a city wall,
Where the dear Lord was crucified,
    Who died to save us all.

We may not know, we cannot tell
    What pains He had to bear,
But we believe it was for us
    He hung and suffered there.

He died that we might be forgiven,
    He died to make us good,
That we might go at last to Heaven,
    Saved by His precious blood.

There was no other good enough
    To pay the price of sin ;
He only could unlock the gate
    Of Heaven, and let us in.

O dearly, dearly, has He loved,
    And we must love Him too,
And trust in His redeeming blood,
    And try His works to do.

HYMNS AND SACRED POEMS.

CECIL FRANCES ALEXANDER

I.—EARTH AND HEAVEN.

THE roseate hues of early dawn,
   The brightness of the day,
The crimson of the sunset sky,
   How fast they fade away!

Oh, for the pearly gates of Heaven,
   Oh, for the golden floor,
Oh, for the Sun of Righteousness
   That setteth nevermore!

The highest hopes we cherish here,
   How fast they tire and faint;
How many a spot defiles the robe
   That wraps an earthly saint!

Oh, for a heart that never sins,
   Oh, for a robe washed bright,
Oh, for a voice to praise our King,
   Nor weary day or night!

Here faith is ours, and heavenly hope,
   And grace to lead us higher;
But there are perfectness, and peace,
   Beyond our best desire.

Oh, by Thy love and anguish, Lord!
   Oh, by Thy life laid down,
Oh, that we fall not from Thy grace
   Nor cast away our crown.

II.—TOUCHED WITH A FEELING OF OUR INFIRMITIES.

When, wounded sore, the stricken soul
    Lies bleeding and unbound,
One only hand, a piercèd hand,
    Can salve the sinner's wound.

When sorrow swells the laden breast,
    And tears of anguish flow,
One only heart, a broken heart,
    Can feel the sinner's woe.

When penitence has wept in vain,
    Over some foul, dark spot,
One only stream, a stream of blood,
    Can wash away the blot.

Jesus, Thy blood can wash us white;
    Thy hand bring sure relief;
Thy heart is touched with all our joys,
    And feeleth for our grief.

Uplift Thy bleeding hand, O Lord,
    Unseal that cleansing tide;
We have no shelter from our sin
    But in Thy wounded side.

III.—THE BURIAL OF MOSES.

"And He buried him in a valley in the land of Moab, over against Beth-Peor: but no man knoweth of his sepulchre unto this day."—DEUT. xxxiv. 6.

BY Nebo's lonely mountain,
   On this side Jordan's wave,
In a vale of the land of Moab
   There lies a lonely grave;
And no man knows that sepulchre,
   And no man saw it e'er,
For the angels of God upturned the sod,
   And laid the dead man there.

That was the grandest funeral
   That ever pass'd on earth;
But no man heard the trampling,
   Or saw the train go forth—
Noiselessly as the daylight
   Comes back when night is done,
And the crimson streak on ocean's cheek
   Grows into the great sun;

Noiselessly as the spring-time
   Her crown of verdure weaves,
And all the trees on all the hills
   Open their thousand leaves;
So without sound of music,
   Or voice of them that wept,
Silently down from the mountain's crown
   The great procession swept.

Perchance the bald old eagle
  On grey Beth-Peor's height,
Out of his lonely eyrie
  Looked on the wondrous sight;
Perchance the lion stalking
  Still shuns that hallowed spot,
For beast and bird have seen and heard
  That which man knoweth not.

But when the warrior dieth,
  His comrades in the war,
With arms reversed and muffled drum,
  Follow his funeral car;
They show the banners taken;
  They tell his battles won,
And after him lead his masterless steed,
  While peals the minute-gun.

Amid the noblest of the land
  Men lay the sage to rest,
And give the bard an honour'd place
  With costly marble dress'd,
In the great minster transept,
  " Where lights like glories fall,
And the organ rings, and the sweet choir sings
  Along the emblazon'd wall

This was the truest warrior
  That ever buckled sword;
This, the most gifted poet
  That ever breath'd a word.
And never earth's philosopher,
  Traced with his golden pen
On the deathless page truths half so sage
  As he wrote down for men.

And had he not high honour,—
    The hill-side for a pall,
To lie in state, while angels wait
    With stars for tapers tall;
And the dark rock pines, like tossing plumes,
    Over his bier to wave,
And God's own hand, in that lonely land,
    To lay him in the grave?

In that strange grave without a name,
    Whence his uncoffin'd clay
Shall break again—O wondrous thought!—
    Before the Judgment Day;
And stand, with glory wrapped around,
    On the hills he never trod;
And speak of the strife, that won our life,
    With the Incarnate Son of God.

O lonely grave in Moab's land!
    O dark Beth-Peor's hill!
Speak to these curious hearts of ours,
    And teach them to be still.
God hath His mysteries of grace,
    Ways that we cannot tell;
He hides them deep, like the hidden sleep
    Of him He loved so well.

IV.—RUTH.

IN the land of Bethlehem Judah
  Let us linger, let us wander;
Ephrath's sorrow, Rachel's pillar,
  Lieth in the valley yonder;
And the yellow barley harvest
Floods it with a golden glory.
Let us back into the old time,
Dreaming of her tender story,
Of her true heart's strong devotion,
From beyond the Dead Sea water,
From the heathen land of Moab—
Mahlon's wife, and Mara's daughter.

  On the terebinth and fig-tree
Suns of olden time are shining,
And the dark leaf of the olive
Scarcely shows its silver lining;
For still noon is on the thicket,
Where the blue-neck'd pigeons listen
To their own reproachful music;
And the red pomegranates glisten.
As a queen a golden circlet,
As a maid might wear a blossom,
So the valley wears the cornfields
Heaving on her fertile bosom:
And the round grey hills stand o'er them,
All their terraced vineyards swelling,
Like the green waves of a forest,
Up to David's royal dwelling

Lo! the princely-hearted Boaz
Moves among his reapers slowly,
And the widow'd child of Moab
Bends behind the gleaners lowly;
Gathering, gleaning as she goeth
Down the slopes, and up the hollows,
While the love of old Naomi,
Like a guardian angel, follows;
And he speaketh words of kindness,
Words of kindness calm and stately,
Till he breaks the springs of gladness
That lay cold and frozen lately,
And the love-flowers, that had faded
Deep within her bosom lonely,
Slowly open as he questions,
Soon for him to blossom only,—
When that spring shall fill with music,
Like an overflowing river,
All his homestead, and those flowers
Bloom beside his hearth for ever.
Mother of a line of princes,
Wrought into that race's story,
Whom the Godhead, breaking earthward,
Mark'd with an unearthly glory.

Still he walks among the reapers:
The long day is nearly over,
And the lonely mountain partridge
Seeks afar his scanty cover;
And the flocks of wild blue pigeons,
That had glean'd behind the gleaner,
Find their shelter in the thicket;
And the cloudless sky grows sheener

With a sudden flush of crimson,
Steeping in a fiery lustre
Every sheaf-top in the valley,
On the hill-side every cluster.

Slowly, slowly fade, fair picture,
Yellow lights and purple shadows,
On the valley, on the mountain,
And sweet Ruth among the meadows.
Yet delay, true heart, and teach us,
Pausing in thy matron beauty,
Care of elders, love of kindred,
All unselfish thought and duty.
Linger, Boaz, noble-minded!
Teach us, haughty and unsparing,
Tender care for lowlier station,
Kindly speech, and courteous bearing.
Still each softest, loveliest colour,
Shrine the form beloved and loving,
Heroine of our hearts' first poem,
Through our childhood's dreamland moving
When the great old Bible open'd,
And a pleasant pastoral measure,
As our mothers read the story,
Fill'd our infant hearts with pleasure.

W. Walsham How.

1823—1897.

WILLIAM WALSHAM HOW was born at Shrewsbury on the 13th of December, 1823, and was a son of William Wybergh How, solicitor and banker of that town. He was educated at Shrewsbury and Wadham College, Oxford, matriculating in 1840, and going into residence in 1841. Originally intending to follow the legal profession, he changed his views while at Oxford, and proceeded after graduating to the Divinity School at Durham, where he studied under Dr. Jenkyns. He was ordained in 1846, and accepted a Curacy at Kidderminster, and subsequently at (Holy Cross) Shrewsbury. In 1851 he was appointed Rector of Whittington, near Oswestry, where he remained until 1879, when he was presented with the living of St. Andrews Undershaft, and made Bishop Suffragan of East London, with the title of Bishop of Bedford. Here he had charge of the three popular rural deaneries of Hackney, Stepney, and Spitalfields, Tottenham being added at a later date. He was select preacher at Oxford 1868-9, examining chaplain to the Bishop of Lichfield 1878-9, and lecturer on pastoral work at Cambridge 1883, and special preacher 1884. He was made D.D. of Oxford in 1886, and was translated to the See of Wakefield on its creation in 1888.

An anonymous volume of verse, published many years ago, was Mr. How's first appeal to the public as a poet. Of this a new and enlarged edition appeared in 1886, which volume, with a book of fifty-four hymns, published while Bishop of Bedford, forms the main substance of his poetic work. The Bishop's poems show a true feeling for nature, a keen sympathy with suffering and sorrow, power of pathos, and sense of humour. The first is abundantly demonstrated in "Shelsley Beauchamp and the First Spring Day," the second in "Poetry and the Poet," the third in "The Boy Hero" and "Gentleman John," and the fourth in "The Three Prelates" and "A Puzzling Question." Of the shorter poems which are alone available for quotation in a work like this, "Converse," p. 52, shows the observation of the poet's eye; "Stars and Graves," p. 51, the poet's mind grappling with the problems of life and death; "Pasce Verbo, Pasce Vita," p. 53, the practical nature of his religion; and "A Starlit Night by the Sea-Shore," p. 54, his sense of the brotherhood of human relationships. Some of the Bishop's hymns have become universal favourites, and others deserve much wider use than they have received. He died on August the 10th, 1897.

ALFRED H. MILES.

POEMS.

W. WALSHAM HOW.

I.—STARS AND GRAVES.

1847.

> "Solemn before us
> Veiled, the dark portal,
> Goal of all mortal —
> Stars silent rest o'er us,
> Graves under us silent."
>   GOETHE. *Tr.* CARLYLE.

THE poet scanned with mighty awe
 The mystery of Man;
He spake the strange things that he saw,
 And thus it ran:—

"The silent stars are overhead,
 The silent graves below:
A dream between—how quickly fled!—
 Is all we know.'

He pointed up—he pointed down—
 The witnesses were there.
O'er the between a veil was thrown
 He could not tear.

The Preacher saw the hand he raised,
 And heard the words he spake;
And in his soul with grief amazed
 A fire outbreak.

"Poet," he cried, "the things we see
 They are not all we know;
The web of thy philosophy
 I rend it so!"—

He pointed with his eager hand
 Behind and then before,—
And there, and there, for ever stand
 Two wonders more.

"The silent stars sing out with mirth,
  The graves with grass are green:—
Christ cometh twice upon the earth;—
  We live between!"

II.—CONVERSE.

(PENMAENMAWR.)
1867.

TWO friends sat wrapped in converse low and grave,
  Heart opened unto heart, hand linked in hand,
Hearing, yet hearing not, the pulsing wave
  Beat on the shadowy strand;

Gazing in frequent pause with dreaming eye
O'er the wide silver sea into the West;
Making sweet silences, when faint words die,
  And loving hearts take rest;

Sweet silences, that strangers never know,
Between the murmured words, that, like a dream,
Wander amid the past scenes dim and low,—
  Oh, how far off they seem!

"Words following silence, silence following words,
So sped the golden sunset, till the land
Grew dimmer, and the last white flock of birds
  Flashed on the glimmering sand.

Then all at once upstreamed in rippling flow
Of silent rosy waves a second sea,
Surging across all heaven, a trancing show
  Of gorgeous pageantry.

The feathered cloudlets filled the plains of air,
Ranged by the soft wind's delicate marshalling,
Till you could fancy angel armies there,
  Nought seen but burnished wing.

Then more low converse till the last rose paled:—
But oh! if earth may bear such peace and love,
What shall the converse be when earth has failed
    And spirits meet above!"

III.—"PASCE VERBO, PASCE VITA."
—St. Bernard

LO! this one preached with fervent tongue;
    The world went forth to hear;
Upon his burning words they hung,
    Intent, with ravished ear.

Like other lives the life he led,
    Men spake no word of blame:
And yet, unblest, unprofited,
    The world went on the same.

Another came, and lived, and wrought,
    His heart all drawn above;
By deeds, and not by words, he taught
    Self-sacrificing love.

No eager crowds his preaching drew;
    Yet one by one they came;
The secret of his power they knew,
    And caught the sacred flame.

And all around, as morning light
    Steals on with silent wing,
The world became more pure and bright
    And life a holier thing.

Ah! Pastor, is thy heart full sore
    At all this sin and strife?
Feed with the Word, but ah! far more
    Feed with a holy life.

IV.—A STARLIT NIGHT BY THE SEA-SHORE
[Suggested by Matthew Arnold's "Self-dependence."]

O GREAT Stars, aflame with awful beauty!
   O great Sea, with glittering heaving breast!
Stars, that march all calm in lines of duty;
   Sea, that swayest to stern law's behest;—

Mighty in your unimpassioned splendour,
   Ye are filling all my puny soul
With the longing this vexed self to render
   Wholly to calm Duty's sure control.

It were restful so to let the ruling
   Of the mightier law sway all the life,
Eager will and passionate spirit schooling,
   Till unfelt the pains of lesser strife.

Yet, O Stars, your quivering shafts unheeding
   On these tangled human sorrows smite;
Merciless Stars! that on hearts crushed and bleeding
   Pour the sharp stings of your bleak cold light.

Yet, O Sea, that glittering breast is heaving,
   All unconscious of the life it rears,
Shouting in the mirth of its bereaving,
   Laughing o'er a thousand widows' tears.

No! I ask not for a life high lifted
   O'er the changeful passions of mankind,
Undistracted, self-contained, and gifted
   With a force to feebler issues blind.

Rather fill my soul to overflowing
   With the tide of this world's grief and wrong;
Let me suffer; though it be well knowing
   Suffering thus, I am not wholly strong.

Let what grandeur crown the life of others,
   Let what light on lone endurance shine;
I will set myself beside my brothers,
   And their toils and troubles shall be mine!

HYMNS.

W. WALSHAM HOW.

I.—*JESUS AT THE DOOR.*

"Behold, I stand at the door, and knock."—Rev. iii. 20.

O JESU, Thou art standing
   Outside the fast-closed door,
In lowly patience waiting
   To pass the threshold o'er.
Shame on us, Christian brothers,
   His name and sign who bear,
Oh, shame, thrice shame, upon us,
   To keep Him standing there !

O Jesu, Thou art knocking;
   And lo! that Hand is scarred,
And thorns Thy Brow encircle,
   And tears Thy Face have marred.

O love that passeth knowledge
   So patiently to wait !
O sin that hath no equal
   So fast to bar the gate !

O Jesu, Thou art pleading
   In accents meek and low—
"I died for you, My children,
   And will ye treat Me so ?"

O Lord, with shame and sorrow
   We open now the door :
Dear Saviour, enter, enter,
   And leave us nevermore.

II.—O GOD, ENSHRINED.

"And when I saw Him, I fell at His feet as dead."—
Rev. i. 17.

O GOD, enshrined in dazzling light
    Above the highest sphere,
My soul is filled with awe to feel
    That Thou art present here.

Thine Eye is as a lamp of fire,
    And in its searching flame
I see myself, all stained with sin,
    And bow my head with shame.

But, O my God, Thy Son hath died!
    And from the dust I rise,
And from myself and all my sin
    To Thee I lift mine eyes.

My sins are dark, but over all
    Thy burning love I see;
And all my soul is full of praise,
    And worships only Thee.

III.—OFFERTORY.

"All things come of Thee, and of Thine own have we given Thee."—1 Chron. xxix. 14.

WE give Thee but Thine own,
    Whate'er the gift may be;
All that we have is Thine alone,
    A trust, O Lord, from Thee.

May we Thy bounties thus
    As stewards true receive,
And gladly, as Thou blessest us,
    To Thee our first-fruits give.

Oh! hearts are bruised and dead;
And homes are bare and cold;
And lambs for whom the Shepherd bled
Are straying from the fold!

To comfort and to bless,
To find a balm for woe,
To tend the lone and fatherless,
Is Angels' work below.

The captive to release,
To God the lost to bring,
To teach the way of life and peace,—
It is a Christ-like thing.

And we believe Thy word,
Though dim our faith may be,—
Whate'er for Thine we do, O Lord,
We do it unto Thee.

IV.—THE NEW JERUSALEM.

'The kingdom of God is within you."—St. Luke xvii. 21.

THE City paved with gold,
  Bright with each dazzling gem!
When shall our eyes behold
The new Jerusalem?
Yet lo! e'en now in viewless might
Uprise the walls of living light!

The kingdom of the Lord!
It cometh not with show·
Nor throne, nor crown, nor sword,
Proclaim its might below.
Though dimly scanned through mists of sin,
The Lord's true kingdom is within!

The gates of pearl are there
In penitential tears :
Bright as a jewel rare
Each saintly grace appears :
We track the path saints trod of old,
And lo ! the pavement is of gold !

The living waters flow
That fainting souls may drink ;
The mystic fruit-trees grow
Along the river's brink :
We taste e'en now the water sweet,
And of the Tree of Life we eat.

Not homeless wanderers here
Our exile songs we sing ;
Thou art our home most dear,
Thou city of our King !
Thy future bliss we cannot tell,
Content in Thee on earth we dwell.

Build, Lord, the mystic walls !
Throw wide the unseen gates !
Fill all the golden halls,
While yet Thy triumph waits !
Make glad Thy Church with light and love,
Till glorified it shines above !

William Alexander.

1824.

THE RIGHT REV. WILLIAM ALEXANDER, D.D. D.C.L., Bishop of Derry and Raphoe, was born at Londonderry on the 13th of April, 1824. He was educated at Tunbridge School, and at Exeter and Brasenose Colleges, Oxford, where he graduated with classical honours in 1847. He won the sacred poem prize in 18— with his poem "The Death of Jacob," and was appointed to recite the congratulatory ode to Lord Derby on his installation as Chancellor in the Sheldonian Theatre in 18— He competed unsuccessfully for the chair of Poetry at Oxford in 1867. Having held several appointments, he was nominated to the Deanery of Emly in 1864, and appointed Bishop of Derry and Raphoe in 1867. He was select preacher at Oxford 1870-2 and 1882, Cambridge 1872-92, Dublin 1879 He was also Bampton lecturer 1876.

Dr. Alexander's poetic work is comprised in the volume "St. Augustine's Holiday and other Poems," published in 1887. His verse is picturesque, and shows a love of Nature as she reveals herself to spiritual insight. Even the more illusive aspects of natural phenomena, the changes that pass the ordinary eye without observation, are full of spiritual significance to the poet's mind, and these subtleties of observation he seems able, by a corresponding delicacy of treatment, to recall and perpetuate. "A

Sea Gleam" and "Very Far Away" will evidence this. A love of the legend and some power of narrative are shown in the title poem and others of the volume, but the delicacy of perception and touch already referred to forms perhaps the chief charm of the poet's verse.

ALFRED H. MILES.

POEMS

WILLIAM ALEXANDER.

I.—A SEA GLEAM.

'TWAS a sullen summer day;
  Skies were neither dark nor clear,
  Heaven in the distance sheer
Over sharp cliffs sloped away—
  Ocean did not yet appear.

Not as yet a white sail shimmer'd,
  Not with full expanse divine
  Did the great Atlantic shine;
Only very far there glimmer'd
  Dimly one long tremulous line.

In the hedge were roses snow'd
  Or blush'd o'er by summer morn,
  Right and left grew fields of corn,
Stretching greenly from the road—
  From the hay a breath was borne.

Not of small sweet wild rose twine,
  Not of young corn waving free,
  Not of clover fields thought we;
Only to that dim bright line
  Looking, cried we, "'Tis the Sea."

In life's sullen summer day
  Lo! before us dull hills rise,
  And above, unlovely skies
Slope off with their bluish grey
  Into some far mysteries.

Love's sweet roses, hope's young corn,
  Green fields whisper'd round and round
  By the breezes landward bound
(Yet, ah! scalded too and torn
  By the sea winds), there are found.

And at times in life's dull day,
   From the flower, and the sod,
   And the hill our feet have trod
To a brightness far away,
   Turn we saying, "This is God."

II.—VERY FAR AWAY.

ONE touch there is of magic white,
   Surpassing southern mountain's snow,
That to far sails the dying light
   Lends, where the dark ships onward go
Upon the golden highway broad
That leads up to the isles of God.

One touch of light more magic yet,
   Of rarer snow 'neath moon or star
Where, with her graceful sails all set,
   Some happy vessel seen afar,
As if in an enchanted sleep
Steers o'er the tremulous stretching deep.

O ship! O sail! far must ye be
   Ere gleams like that upon ye light:
O'er golden spaces of the sea,
   From mysteries of the lucent night,
Such touch comes never to the boat
Wherein across the waves we float.

O gleams more magic and divine,
   Life's whitest sail ye still refuse,
And flying on before us shine
   Upon some distant bark ye choose.
—By night or day, across the spray,
That sail is very far away.

III.—CHRIST ON THE SHORE.

IN the silence of the morning,
  Of the morning grey and clouded,
    Mist enshrouded,
On the shore of Galilee,
Like a shape upon a column,
    Sad and solemn
  Christ is standing by the sea,
In the silence of the morning.

On the waters cold and misty,
  Like a rock, its dark back lifting
    Through the drifting
  Vapours, heaves the fisher's boat.
Still through grey-fog hood and mantle
    That most gentle
  Watcher looketh where they float
On the waters cold and misty.

Hearts are waiting, eyes are weeping,
  Comes a voice, a susurration;
    Tribulation
  Melteth, melteth like the mist;
Yet, like music rich and olden
    Hiding golden
  Words, that sweet voice hideth Christ
From the hearts that wait, and weep Him
In another morning silence,
  When a greyer fog falls dreary
    And we weary
  With the sea's beat evermore,
Cometh One, and pale and wounded,
    Mist-surrounded,
  Looketh from another shore
In another morning silence.

Other waters cold and misty
  On the wet sands grandly singing,
    Bear a swinging
    Little bark call'd Life by men;
While the bark is swinging slowly,
    That most Holy
    Watcher looks: light silvers then
On the waters cold and misty.

Hearts are waiting, eyes are weeping,
  Falls a voice, O sweet but broken!
    Falls a token
    Light bedimm'd with blinding mist.
Take us where there are no ocean's
    Wild commotions;
    Where we shall not know, O Christ!
Weary hearts, or tear-wet eyelids.

IV.—A FINE DAY IN HOLY WEEK.

THERE is a rapturous movement, a green growing
    Among the hills and valleys once again,
And silent rivers of delight are flowing
    Into the hearts of men.

There is a purple weaving on the heather,
  Night drops down starry gold upon the furze,
Wild rivers and wild birds sing songs together,
    Dead nature breathes and stirs.

Is this the season when our hearts should follow
  The Man of Sorrows to the hills of scorn?
Must not our pilgrim grief be scant and hollow
    On such a sunny morn?

Will not the silver trumpet of the river
  Wind us to gladsomeness against our will?
The subtle eloquence of sunlight shiver
    What sadness haunts us still?

If I might choose these notes should all be duller,
    That silver trump should fail in Passion week;
The mountain-crowning sky wear one pale colour,
    Pale as my Saviour's cheek.

And day and night there should be one slow raining,
    With mournful plash, upon the moor and moss,
And on the hill one tree, its bare arms straining;
    Bare as my Saviour's cross.

Nay, if my heart were sorrowful exceeding,
    Its pulses big with that divinest woe,
These natural things would only set it bleeding
    To think it should be so—

To think that guilty and degraded Nature
    Could look as joyful as she looketh now,
When the warm blood has dropp'd from her Creator
    Upon her branded brow.

V.—THE BIRTHDAY CROWN.

IF aught of simple song have power to touch
  Your silent being, O ye country flowers,
    Twisted by tender hands
    Into a royal brede,

O hawthorn, tear thou not the soft white brow
Of the small queen upon her rustic throne,
    But breathe thy finest scent
    Of almond round about.

And thou, laburnum, and what other hue
Tinct deeper gives variety of gold,
    Inwoven lily, and vetch
    Bedropp'd with summer's blood,

I charge you wither not this long June day!
Oh, wither not until the sunset come,
    Until the sunset's shaft
    Slope through the chestnut tree;

Until she sit, high-gloried round about
With the great light above her mimic court—
    Her threads of sunny hair
      Girt sunnily by you.

What other crown that queen may wear one day,
What drops may touch her forehead not of balm,
    What thorns, what cruel thorns,
      I will not guess to-day.

Only, before she is discrown'd of you,
Ye dying flowers, and thou, O dying light,
    My prayer shall rise—" O Christ !
      Give her the unfading crown.

" The crown of blossoms worn by happy bride,
The thorny crown o'er pale and dying lips,
    I dare not choose for her—
      Give her the unfading crown !"

SONNETS.

WILLIAM ALEXANDER.

ST. JOHN AT PATMOS.

I.

WHAT be his dreams in Patmos? O'er the seas
    Looks he toward Athens, where the very fall
  Of Grecian sunlight is Platonical?
Or, peradventure, towards the Cyclades,
The Delian earth-star, ray'd with laurel trees—
    From ribbon'd baskets where Demeter threw
    Flowers the colour of the country blue
Oat-garlanded in Paros—or where bees
Humming o'er Amalthæa, who fed Zeus
    With goat-milk, goldenly the forest starr'd,
While rosy purple apples full of juice
    Laugh'd in the grassy horn—where, Naxosward,
Flush'd Dyonysus, driven o'er the brine,
Ivied the mast, and cream'd the crimson wine.

II.

Not fancies of the soft Ionian clime,
    Nor thoughts on Plato's page, that greener grow
    Than do the plane-trees by the pleasant flow
Of the Ilissus in the summer time,
Came to the Galilean with sweet chime.
    Blanch'd in the blaze of Syrian summers lo!
    He gazes on Gennesareth, aglow
Within its golden mountain cup sublime.
The sunset comes. Behind the Roman tower
    The dark boat's circled topsails shift and swell,
The tunick'd boatmen dip their nets an hour,
    And the sun goeth down on Jezreel.
Quench'd is the flickering furnace of the dust,
The mountains branded as with red gold dust.

III.

But ere heaven's cressets burn along its plain,
   The Master comes. And as a man, all night
   Lull'd in a room full fronting ocean's might,
First waking sees a whiteness on his pane,
A little dawning whiteness, then again
   A little line insufferably bright
   Edging the ripples, orbing on outright
Until the glory he may scarce sustain;
And as a mighty city far-off kenn'd
   Although the same, from each new height and glen
   Looks strangely different to the merchantmen,
Who in long files towards its ramparts wend;—
   So to St. John's deep meditative eye,
   That Nature grew to God's own majesty.

William Josiah Irons.

1812—1883.

WILLIAM JOSIAH IRONS was the son of Joseph Irons, preacher and hymn-writer (1785-1852). Joseph Irons was a personal friend of the Rev. John Newton, and attended his ministry at St. Mary-Woolnoth, of which parish William Josiah Irons became rector in 1872. After the death of Newton, Joseph Irons seceded from the Church of England, and became the pastor of a Nonconformist Church at Sawston, and later of one meeting at the Grove Chapel, Camberwell, London. He was a powerful preacher, and sometimes addressed his congregation in eloquent and poetical blank verse. For the use of his own people he published a book of original hymns, which was used as a supplement to the psalms and hymns of Dr. Watts. This book, first published in 1816 under the title "Zion's Hymns," was enlarged from time to time, until in 1827 it contained six hundred and eleven original hymns. Many of these hymns are vigorous and expressive, but their strong Calvinistic flavour has limited their use, and very few have passed into other collections. The following hymn may be taken as a sample, though many are less pronounced in doctrine :—

> The God of heav'n maintains
> His universal throne;
> In heav'n, and earth, and hell, He reigns,
> And makes His wonders known.

His counsels and decrees
  Firmer than mountains stand;
He will perform whate'er He please,
  And none can stay His hand.

All worlds His will controls,
  And His eternal mind
Fixes the destiny of souls;
  Takes this, leaves that behind.

Jacob by grace He sav'd,
  Nor gives a reason why;
But Esau's heart He left deprav'd;
  And who shall dare reply?

What, if the potter take
  Part of a lump of clay,
And for himself a vessel make,
  And cast the rest away?

Who shall resist his will?
  Or say, "What doest thou?"
Jehovah is a sovereign still,
  And all must to Him bow.

My soul shall still adore
  My God in all His ways;
His sov'reignty I can't explore,
  But I will trust His grace.

Besides his hymns Joseph Irons published "Nymphas. Bride and Bridegroom communing. A Paraphrastic Exposition of the Song of Solomon in Blank Verse" (1840); "Judah, the Book of Psalms paraphrased in Spiritual Songs for Public Worship" (1847); and "Calvary," a poem in blank verse.

William Josiah Irons was born at Hoddesdon, Herts, on the 12th of September, 1812, and was educated privately, and at Queen's College, Oxford, where he graduated B.A. in 1833. Two years later he took Holy Orders, and became Curate of St. Mary Newington. In 1837 he was appointed Incumbent of St. Peter's, Walworth, and afterwards successively Vicar of Barkway, Incumbent of Brompton, Rector of Wadingham, and Rector of St. Mary-Woolnoth (1872). He received the degree of D.D. in 1854. He was Bampton Lecturer in 1870, and in this connection produced his most important prose work, the "Bampton Lectures" on "Christianity as taught by St. Paul." He was also Prebendary of St. Paul's Cathedral. He published many sermons, letters, and pamphlets in connection with the ecclesiastical controversies of his time, and many of his hymns were first published in sheet form, and afterwards collected into his own and other hymn-books.

Of hymnological works he published a "Metrical Psalter" in 1857, to which he added an "Appendix" in 1861; also "Hymns for use in Church" (1866), and "Psalms and Hymns for the Church" (1873). The first two of these books contained hymns by various writers, but the "Psalms and Hymns for the Church" contained only original hymns and translations. Several editions of this work were called for, and additions were made from time to time, until the edition of 1883 contained three hundred and eight original hymns.

According to Julian, "the principal object of this last work was to supply special hymns on the Collects, Epistles, and Gospels, and for Advent and Lent, together with special hymns for the Festivals; and this to a great extent Dr Irons was enabled to accomplish. His versions of individual psalms are directly from the Hebrew line for line.

Many of Dr. Irons' hymns are very fine, and deserve much wider use than they have obtained. Julian places them in the very front rank of modern hymns, and with good reason. Few modern writers have produced so many really fine hymns, and it is to be regretted that modern compilers have not made more extensive use of them.

ALFRED H. MILES.

PSALMS AND HYMNS FOR THE CHURCH.
1883.

WILLIAM JOSIAH IRONS.

I.—EVENING HAS COME.

EVENING has come, once more the veil of night
    Is drawn around us by the hand Divine;
Yet both alike, the darkness and the light,
    The evening and the morning, Lord, are Thine.

Sweet is the silent hour which Thou hast given,
    For nature asks some pause, as in distress;
Eternal life is only known in heaven,
    There man can live and know no weariness.

And yet, in all the unconscious world around,
    There is no pause, only the spirit waits,
Like traveller for some mountain-city bound,
    Tarrying before the dawn without the gates.

Our moral life stands still awhile, as though
    Probation were suspended all night long:
Thought comes at times and says it is not so—
    Some work goes on, that we may rise more strong.

O Lord, we live and move and rest in Thee!
    The darkness is not dark if Thou be there;
When "the day dawns and all the shadows flee,"
    Then shall true life begin in purer air:

And we shall know Thee, dwelling evermore
    In light no eye hath seen, nor yet can see;
And FATHER SON and SPIRIT there adore,
    One glorious GOD, Eternal TRINITY.

II.—HAIL, HOLY REST!

HAIL, holy rest! calm herald of that day
   When all the toils of time shall pass away;
First gift of God, as life on earth began,
We welcome thee, O Sabbath made for man!

Lord of the Sabbath, lift our hearts to Thee,
That in Thy light we now may all things see;
By Thee created, loved, redeemed, and blest,
In Thee alone is everlasting rest.

Now on the way to our eternal home,
To thee, true Sabbath of our souls, we come;
In all our path, though countless mercies shine,
The glory and the brightness, Lord, are Thine.

If in the cool of day we find Thee near,
Thy voice awakes no dark foreboding fear;
We hear Thy step in every rustling breeze,
Thy shadow glances from the waving trees.

Our land enjoys her Sabbaths, Lord, and still
Thy "peace on earth" breathes soft from vale to hill
Yet lives the hope, wherever man hath trod,
"A rest remaineth for the sons of God!"

Rest, rest for laden souls whose prayers arise,
And in Thy name find access to the skies;
Rest in absolving love, while we confess,
Since Thou canst cleanse from all unrighteousness.

And most before Thine altar as we bow,
And in Thy presence feel Thy mercy now;
The Father, Son, and Spirit we adore,
And find "this is our rest for evermore."

III.—LO, SIGNS IN SUN, AND MOON, AND STARS.

LO, signs in sun, and moon, and stars,
   And on the earth distress and fear,
With sound of elemental wars,
   Telling "the Son of Man" is near.

Things quickly coming on the earth,
   Find their dread augury in the sky;
O children of the heavenly birth,
   "Look up, redemption draweth nigh."

Behold the early fig-trees' bloom,
   And verdure spangling all the land:
The future bursting from the womb,
   Saying, "the Kingdom is at hand."

For when we see that rising day,
   No warning voices shall be stilled,
Nor shall His Israel pass away,
   "Until Christ's words be all fulfilled."

Then help us, Lord, to know Thy signs,
   Mark every line the evening bears,
Ready to meet Thy bright designs,
   "Lest that Day take us unawares."

So, "Son of Man," while tarrying here,
   Watch we the clouds with steadfast eyes,
Until Thy glory shall appear,
   "The Sun of Righteousness arise."

IV.—CLOUDS AROUND THE MOUNTAINS.

CLOUDS around the mountains breaking,
   Bring the morning's solemn sigh;
Murky lights the distance streaking,
   Warn us of the reddening sky.
      Be ye ready,
For the Day of God is nigh.

Through the earth and o'er the ocean,
   Angel armies go before;
Voices, in the dread commotion,
   Echo—"time shall be no more."
     Be ye ready,
For the Judge is at the door.

Lo the Son of Man appearing,
   With the starry sign unfurled;
Heaven is gazing, earth is fearing,
   At the terrors round Him hurled.
     Be ye ready,
For "He comes to judge the world."

Now, O Saviour, new-create us!
   By Thy grace touch every heart;
Now from sinners separate us,
   Let us not from Thee depart.
     Make us ready,
To be with Thee as Thou art.

Saints and angels high in glory
   Brighter crowns than ours will wear;
May we cast ourselves before Thee,
   Praising Thee that we are there!
     In their anthems,
All Thy ransomed ones may share.

"Come, ye blessèd!" THINE own greeting,
   And our FATHER's loving call;
With the SPIRIT's voice repeating,
   "Blessèd," blessèd are they all,
     Who in glory,
At their Father's footstool fall.

V.—MOTHER MINE, WHY HAST THOU BORNE ME?

[From the Greek.—A meditation of S. Gregory, Naz.]

MOTHER mine, why hast thou borne me,
   Given me toilsome thorny life?
Was thine own lot clear from sorrow—
   Didst thou succumb in the strife?
Was it love that brought me hither,
   In men's varying paths to roam,
Tilling fields, or crossing ocean,
   Chasing, fighting for their home?
Would'st thou I had poet's glory?
   Wore the athlete's laurel-crown?
Say'st thou, "God shall be thy portion,"
   Though earth's sorrows cast thee down?—
Yet disease and powerless effort
   Force the agonising tear;
Joyful might I quit these sufferings,
   Mother mine, why am I here!
Even when to God aspiring,
   Words relieve not half my mind;
Sacred glimpses flash upon me,
   God the Trinity I find;
Yet how quickly all escapes me,
   Like the lightning from the sky,
Shining round us brightly, swiftly,
   Vanished ere we fix our eye.
Could I hold Thee, Lord,—that vision,
   TRINAL Good of heaven and earth!—
Then I might rejoice in being,
   And no longer blame my birth:
Save, O save me, Word Eternal!
   Raise me hence to life above:
There, pure minds shall circle round Thee,
   Where no cloud shall hide Thy love.

VI.—IS NOT THIS OUR KING AND PROPHET?

"Is not This our King and Prophet?"—
  Ring Hosannas, wave the palm,
Let the children from the temple
  Echo back the people's psalm;
"Blessèd is the Son of David,"
  Blessèd is the Christ of God,
Welcome to the hill of Sion,
  Deck the pathway, strew the sod!

"Meek and lowly One," He cometh,
  And the anthem greets His ears;
Lo the city lies before Him,
  But He sees it through His tears;
Looking from the Mount of Olives,
  Towers and marble temple rise;—
Is thy peace, O well-loved Salem,
  "Hid for ever from thine eyes"?

Sees He now, in solemn vision,
  Calvary "without the gate"?
Israel fallen—"house and city
  Left unto her desolate"?
Yes, O Saviour all-enduring!
  Thou wast watching every heart—
Which would love Thee, which forsake Thee,
  Which would do the traitor's part.

Pity, Lord, man's hollow praises,
  Then or now, which greet Thee thus;
"By Thy Cross, and by Thy Passion,"
  O have mercy yet on us!
Now Thou reignest with the Father
  And the Spirit evermore;
Lord, look down upon Thy servants,
  Who repent, and would adore.

VII.—O SILENT NIGHT.

O SILENT Night, O darkness of the dead!
   A few hours since, and Jesus full of grace
Sat with His chosen, blessed the mystic Bread,
   And poured the Cup, and joined the Hymn of praise
Where now are they who sat around?—Is John
   Tending the lonely Mother in His stead?
Is Judas, who betrayed the Holy One,
   "Gone to his place"? and have the rest all fled?
Is Peter weeping?—are "His brethren" gone?
What was that word—"the Shepherd I will smite,
The sheep shall all be scattered far" to-night?—
   He saw, He knew it all, and He is Dead.

VIII.—HE LOVED HIS OWN UNTO THE END

"HE loved His own unto the end,"
   And asked their love;
He said, "I call you each My friend,
And not My servant; and I send
     One from above,
Who shall reveal such grace and truth to you
As in My sojourn here ye never knew."

"But why depart?" they cry, "why will
     To leave us here?
Thou sayest that Thou dost love us still:
Can it be love if thus Thou fill
     Our cup of fear?
O Master, Master, should'st Thou now depar
All sorrow needs must overwhelm our heart"

Yet it is love: He said, "I go;
     For could I stay,
Your earth-bound thoughts would never know
Love's fullest mysteries, which flow
     From Me alway;

My human heart might linger with you yet,
But now affections must on heaven be set.

"You could not know Me more, unless
    My Spirit came
And taught the ways of righteousness,
How sin and judgment to confess,
    How learn to blame
All clinging to inferior things of earth,
Blind to the glory of your heavenly birth.

"My peace I leave with you, but not
    As this world gives;
My Spirit comes to you, yet what
He teaches shows no earthly lot:
    He ever lives,
The world must learn. I hear the Father's call
Away from earth!—Awhile I leave you all.

"Arise! let us go hence." He rose,
    And, as He spake,
Calmly He moved, as one who knows
The coming onset of his foes.
    The night winds shake
With distant sounds, as through the olive grove
"Let us depart" is echoed from above.

IX.—PAUSE NOW, AND THINK.

PAUSE now, and think, O Christian soul!
    Is Christ a shadowy name?
Say, wilt thou give to Him that whole
    Being, for which He came?
Ask of thyself: "Whose Son is He?"
    Is He of earth or heaven?
And art thou a co-heir to be
    Of hopes that He has given?

Pause now, and think, O Christian soul
  What is the Christ to thee?
A dim idea, to console
  In some extremity?
A Name to win thee man's respect,
  The praise of flesh and blood?
If so, thou art not His elect,
  And not the child of God.

For God on high claims all our love,
  "Him only shalt thou serve,"
His mansions wait for thee above,
  If here thou wilt not swerve.
On earth He sent His Son to show
  The one true heavenward way,
And thou must follow Him to know
  God's everlasting day.

Dwell thou in God, and God in thee,
  So mayest thou know the Son:
The I in them, and Thou in Me,
  "That they in Us be one."
His penitents begin that joy,
  His saints that bliss fulfil;
And angels there find sweet employ,
  Obedient to His Will.

O pause, then, doubtful Christian soul!
  Think what a heaven is thine,
If thou wilt break from earth's control,
  And own thy Christ divine.
Nor hesitate to make thy choice,
  Nor "tempt thy God," Who still
Waits, with the angels to rejoice
  Over man's conquered will.

X.—O ALL-SURPASSING SPLENDOUR!

O ALL-SURPASSING Splendour!—one alone
   Of earthly race hath seen that vision fair;
The present God, the rainbow round the throne,
   And the elect, descending through the air,
His Tabernacle,—He their glorious light;
For in His presence there can be no night.

"All New,"—a higher world than had been made
   In the past-workings of omnipotence,
Wills without sin,—Earth's precious stones displayed
   Tell faintly some Divine magnificence
Of that regenerate sphere, the pure abode
For sons and daughters of the Immortal God.

Those gates of pearl, those walls of burning light,
   Those twelve foundations, with apostles' names,
That golden pavement, burnished clear and bright,
   Those mystic cherub wings with outspread flames,
The Tree of Life, by God's own river laved,
Sustaining all the "nations of the saved."

Ah, we sink down oppressed,—we cannot bear
   The contact now of that high element!
We must be changed, and pass this lower air,
   To learn Thy wonders, God Omnipotent.
Lord of our world to come, Thy piercing light
Transfigures all things to our longing sight.

And as we look through the dim-vistaèd years,
   Watching Thee from Thy pure Incarnate Birth;
Vision on vision of Thy form appears,
   Thou Who art fairer than the sons of earth;
And if we faint,—it is but for Thy sake,
To "Jesus only" would our souls awake.

Aubrey de Vere.

1814—1902.

The general poetry of Mr. Aubrey de Vere is represented in Vol. IV. of The Poets and the Poetry of the Century, where it is introduced by a biographical and critical article from the pen of Mr. Mackenzie Bell. For biographical and bibliographical particulars the reader is referred to that article, while his attention is here invited to some of the religious verse which entitles Mr. de Vere to representation among the Sacred Poets.

Reverence and awe—essential characteristics of the devotional spirit—are strongly marked in Mr. de Vere's religious verse; and short as some of his religious poems are, they seem to reproduce the very atmosphere of devotion from which they evidently sprung. Take, for example, the following lines on "The Divine Presence":—

> All but unutterable Name!
>   Adorable, yet awful sound!
> Thee can the sinful nations frame
>   Save with their foreheads to the ground?
>
> Soul-searching and all-cleansing Fire;
>   To see Thy countenance were to die:
> Yet how beyond the bound retire
>   Of Thy serene immensity?
>
> Thou mov'st beside us, if the spot
>   We change—a noteless, wandering tribe;
> The orbits of our life and thought
>   In Thee their little arcs describe.

In the dead calm, at cool of day,
   We hear Thy voice, and turn, and flee :—
Thy love outstrips us on our way !
   From Thee, O God, we fly—to Thee.

A Wordsworthian and a poet of nature, Mr. de Vere carries the devotional spirit with him among the hills and valleys of his love, and quite naturally, when most at home with nature, is nearest to nature's God. Witness the lines on "Spring" and "Spring Thoughts," given in the following pages. The parallels of nature and life, too, which are so perennial a source of inspiration to the poet, are tenderly present to his eyes and thoughts, as evidence the following "Lines" :—

   The lights o'er yonder snowy range,
     Shine yet intense, and tender;
   Or, slowly passing, only change
     From splendour on to splendour.

   Before the dying eyes of day
     Immortal visions wander;
   Dreams prescient of a purer ray,
     And morn spread still beyond her.

   Lo ! heavenward now those gleams expire,
     In heavenly melancholy,
   The barrier-mountain, peak, and spire,
     Relinquishing them slowly.

   Thus shine, O God ! our mortal powers,
     While grief and joy refine them—
   And when in death they fade, be ours
     Thus gently to resign them !

ALFRED H. MILES.

POEMS.

AUBREY DE VERE.

I.—SPRING.

ONCE more, through God's high will and grace,
   Of hours that each its task fulfils,
Heart-healing Spring resumes its place
   The valley through, and scales the hills.

Who knows not Spring? who doubts when blows
   Her breath, that Spring is come indeed?
The swallow doubts not; nor the rose
   That stirs, but wakes not; nor the weed.

Once more the cuckoo's call I hear;
   I know, in many a glen profound,
The earliest violets of the year
   Rise up like water from the ground.

The thorn, I know, once more is white;
   And far down many a forest dale,
The anemones in dubious light
   Are trembling like a bridal veil.

By streams released that surging flow
   From craggy shelf, through sylvan glades,
The pale narcissus, well I know,
   Smiles hour by hour on greener shades.

The honey'd cowslip tufts once more
   The golden slopes;—with gradual ray
The primrose stars the rock, and o'er
   The wood-path strews its milky way.

I see her not—I feel her near,
  As charioted in mildest airs
She sails through yon empyreal sphere,
  And in her arms and bosom bears

That urn of flowers, and lustral dews,
  Whose sacred balm, on all things shed,
Revives the weak, the old renews,
  And crowns with votive wreaths the dead.

II.—SPRING THOUGHTS.

WHO feels not, when the Spring once more
  Stepping o'er Winter's grave forlorn
With winged feet, retreads the shore
  Of widowed earth, his bosom burn?

As ordered flower succeeds to flower,
  And May the ladder of her sweets
Ascends, advancing hour by hour
  From scale to scale, what heart but beats?

Some Presence veiled, in fields and groves,
  That mingles rapture with remorse;
Some buried joy beside us moves,
  And thrills the soul with such discourse

As they, perchance, that wondering pair
  Who to Emmaus bent their way,
Hearing, heard not. Like them our prayer
  We make—"The night is near us—Stay!"

With Paschal chants the churches ring:
  Their echoes strike along the tombs:
The birds their hallelujahs sing:
  Each flower with floral incense fumes.

Our long-lost Eden seems restored;
    As on we move with tearful eyes
  We feel through all the illumined sward
    Some upward-working Paradise.

III.—SENSE, FAITH, AND GLORY.

THREE worlds there are:—the first of Sense—
    That sensuous earth which round us lies;
  The next of Faith's Intelligence:
    The third of Glory in the skies.

  The first is palpable, but base:
    The second heavenly, but obscure;
  The third is star-like in the face—
    But ah! remote that world as pure!

  Yet, glancing through our misty clime,
    Some sparkles from that loftier sphere
  Make way to earth; then most what time
    The annual spring flowers appear.

  Amid the coarser needs of earth
    All shapes of brightness, what are they
  But wanderers, exiled from their birth,
    Or pledges of a happier day?

  Yea, what is Beauty, judged aright,
    But some surpassing, transient gleam;
  Some smile from heaven, in waves of light,
    Rippling o'er life's distempered dream?

  Or broken memories of that bliss
    Which rushed through first-born Nature's blood
  When He who ever was, and is,
    Looked down, and saw that all was good?

IV.—MARTHA AND MARY.

"O SISTER! leave you thus undone
    The bidding of the Lord;
Or call you this a welcome? Run
    And deck with me the board."
Thus Martha spake: but spake to one
    Who answered not a word:
        For she kept ever singing,
          "There is no joy so sweet,
        As musing upon one we love
          And sitting at His feet!"

"O Sister! must thy hands alone
    His board and bath prepare?
His eyes are on you! raise your own:
    He'll find a welcome there!"
Thus spake again, in loftier tone,
    That Hebrew woman fair.
        But Mary still kept singing,
          "There is no joy so sweet,
        As musing upon Him we love
          And resting at His feet."

Coventry Patmore.

1823—1896.

Coventry Patmore, born at Woodford, Essex, on the 23rd of July, 1823, takes his place among the general poets in Vol. V. of The Poets and the Poetry of the Century, where examples of his best work are introduced by a critical and biographical article from the pen of Dr. Garnett. "The Angel in the House," the work with which the poet's name is most popularly associated, is dealt with in that connection, and the particulars there given need not be repeated here. In "The Unknown Eros" volume, published in 1877, there are, however, a number of poems dealing with national and religious subjects, which entitle the poet to representation in any work dealing with the sacred poetry of his time. Of these the poem "The Toys," given in the following pages, is perhaps the choicest example, as it is not marred, as some of the other poems in that volume are, by "religious and political controversy," conducted in a "polemical spirit." It is only necessary to place Mr. Patmore's appeals to patriotism side by side with those of Wordsworth to see how they fall short of the dignity with which it is possible to treat religiously political themes. "The Toys" has no such drawback. It is human, and as such has an infinitely wider basis of appeal than that of the religious sectary or the political partisan. It is written by a father who has learnt something of the fatherhood of God from his own fatherly relationship, and who realises that "Like as a father pitieth his children, so the Lord pitieth them that fear Him." Coventry Patmore died on the 26th of November, 1896.

ALFRED H. MILES.

THE TOYS.

COVENTRY PATMORE.

MY little son, who look'd from thoughtful eyes,
    And moved and spoke in quiet grown-up wise,
Having my law the seventh time disobey'd,
I struck him, and dismiss'd
With hard words and unkiss'd;
His Mother, who was patient, being dead.
Then, fearing lest his grief should hinder sleep,
I visited his bed.
But found him slumbering deep,
With darken'd eyelids, and their lashes yet
From his late sobbing wet.
And I, with moan,
Kissing away his tears, left others of my own;
For, on a table drawn beside his head,
He had put, within his reach,
A box of counters and a red-vein'd stone,
A piece of glass abraded by the beach
And six or seven shells,
A bottle with bluebells,
And two French copper coins, ranged there with
    careful art,
To comfort his sad heart.

So when that night I pray'd
To God, I wept, and said:
Ah, when at last we lie with trancèd breath,
Not vexing Thee in death,
And Thou rememberest of what toys
We made our joys,

How weakly understood
Thy great commanded good,—
Then, Fatherly not less
Than I whom Thou hast moulded from the clay,
Thou'lt leave Thy wrath, and say,
"I will be sorry for their childishness."

Francis Turner Palgrave.

1824—1897.

IN Vol. V. of THE POETS AND THE POETRY OF THE CENTURY a selection of the general poetry of Mr. Francis Turner Palgrave is given, with a prefatory notice by Mr. H. J. Gibbs. The general selection there presented is here supplemented by examples of Mr. Palgrave's religious verse, to which a few bibliographical and other particulars may be added.

The eldest son of Sir Francis Turner Palgrave, the historian, the subject of this sketch, was born at Great Yarmouth on the 28th of September, 1824, and was educated at the Charterhouse School and Balliol College, Oxford. He graduated in 1847, taking a first in Classics, and was elected to a fellowship at Exeter College. In 1885 he succeeded Professor Shairp in the Chair of Poetry at Oxford. He was Vice-Principal, under Dr. Temple (afterwards Bishop of London and later Archbishop of Canterbury), of Kneller Hall Training College for Schoolmasters from 1850 to 1855, and afterwards successively Secretary to Lord Granville and Assistant Secretary to the Committee of the Privy Council on Education.

Mr. Palgrave published "Idyls and Songs" (1854); "Hymns" (1867); "Lyrical Dreams" (1871); "A Lyric Garland" (1874); "The Vision of England" (1881); "Amenophis and other Poems" (1892). Besides these original works Mr. Palgrave has also edited the "Poems of Arthur Hugh Clough, with a Memoir" (1862); "The Golden Treasury" (1864); "Shakespeare's Songs and Sonnets" (1865); "Scott's Poems" (1866); "The Children's Treasury of Lyrical Poetry" (1875); "Chrysomela: a Selection from the Poems of Herrick" (1877); "Keats" (1884), and "Wordsworth" (1885); besides a volume of original "Essays on Art" (1866); and two stories, "Preciosa" (1852), and "Five Days' Entertainment at Wentworth Grange" (1868).

The following selections are taken from the volume "Amenophis and other Poems, Sacred and Secular" (1892), a volume which contains a number of pieces "printed (with revision) from the series published in 1870," together with others which "appeared dispersedly." Francis Turner Palgrave died on the 24th of October, 1897.

ALFRED H. MILES.

AMENOPHIS AND OTHER POEMS.
1892.
FRANCIS TURNER PALGRAVE.

I.—AT EPHESUS

> ... Vidi un veglio solo
> Venir dormendo con la faccia arguta

OF those that saw Him, when
   On common earth He trod
The life of man with men,
   I only, only, breathe,
Who lean'd upon His breast, and knew that He was God.

   As some strange thing that lies
   Surviving all his kind,
   I, 'neath the radiant skies,
   Crawl baby-weak once more,
Stranded upon my hundred years of life, and blind.

   And as that beast could tell
   Of old incredible shapes
   That peopled lake and dell;
   Seas, where rocks climb the sky,
And azure ice-hills where the parch'd Sahara gapes:—

   So John can testify,
   Alone of living men,
   By seeing of the eye
   And hearing of the ear,
That very God as man breathed, died, and rose again.

   It was the time foreshown;
   Like a new sun o'er earth,—
   Beyond all wonders known
   Wonder most wonderful,—
The Well-Belovèd came, the Babe of heavenly birth.

He did the deeds, He spoke
The words past human wit:
Then gently slipp'd the yoke
Of flesh, and went to God;—
And we our treasure found, only when losing it.

Yet, though the Word withdrew,
The Paraclete remain'd;
Christ's nearness oft we knew;
Enough to guide our life
From thought of how He spoke, and how He loved, we gain'd

And once, 'tis said, o'er one
As though born out of time
The glory-vision shone,
Journeying Damascus-way;
Who lived in Christ, and died in some far westward clime

Of breathing witnesses
Survives now none but I;
Who heard the Master bless
The bread and wine of life;
Saw Him and touch'd, betwixt the sepulchre and the sky.

—But though the faith of Sight
By natural law must fail,
A heavenlier higher light
Upon the soul will dawn;
The unseen outshine the seen; the faith of Faith prevail.

The things of sense are much;
But more the things of mind:
What we but see or touch
Less real, durable, true,
Than that invisible all-sustaining Life behind:

As one of Athens taught
In his own ethnic way,
That all things here were nought
But shadowy images
Of forms that in the eternal Wisdom living lay.

When these dim eyes are closed,
Children! Remember well
The word that John imposed
With his last lips on you,—
To walk henceforth by faith, and grasp the invisible.

What if no more the Lord
Before the last dread day
Be seen, yet shall His word
Its might and music keep;
Shall find fit echo in the heart of heart for aye.

As, in due transit, by
The milestone-years ye go,
Though star-like fix'd on high
The cross and He thereon
Down Time's gray avenue further, fainter, show:—

If then the Lord delays,
O yet ye need not fear,
Faint hearts of latter days!
Time cannot touch the love
To which a thousand years but one brief hour appear.

As age on age unrolls,
If faith her light withdraw
From present-bounded souls
Who only dare believe
What they themselves have seen, or hold or Nature's la\

Or those who will not raise,
E'en as they cry for light,
Their heads o'er life's hot haze,
Nor care to see the stars,
Mute witnesses for God, nor dawning after night :—

Yet oft in that dark hour
When first the unseen is felt,
The Word will come in power,
The so-far-off draw nigh,
Christ's living love the long doubt-frozen bosom melt.

—O living Love, so near
On earth, so near above,
In Thy good time appear,
Take all Thy children home,—
Who love, yet know Thee not;—who, faithful, bow, and love

—My little children true!
Before these lips are dumb
They leave this word for you,—
Love one another! And
Again, Love one another! . . . Enough; He calls; I come

II.—AN INCIDENT AT MENDRISIO.
April 23, 1886.

Ἄφετε τὰ παιδία ἔρχεσθαι πρός Με—

IT was the Day, the sad, the good,
   The Day thrice-blest, when He,
The Love uniting God with Man,
   Hung on the Tree :—

And where within the transept wide
   A vacant space was made,
With reverent touch the village hands
   His Image laid;

Not such as old Donato wrought:
   Yet this rude craftsman's heart
With deeper passion stamp'd the wood
     Than finer art.

And all the Italian throng was there,
   Bronze-wrinkled crone, and maid,
Fathers with sons; the lame, the blind,
     Where Christ was laid.

They knelt for prayer; they kiss'd for love
   Their Saviour's riven Side,
The Hands, the Feet, the bleeding Heart
     For us Who died.

But in the throng what part has she,
   The little maiden sweet,
Who climbs and trembles to the Cross
     With fervent feet?

Like her, the Blessèd Virgin Child
   Who clomb the Temple-stair,
God given, given back to God,
     Pure, sacred, fair.

—With kisses fast and close, herself
   Upon the Face she throws;
The innocent breath with love is warm,
     Sweet as the rose.

Ah, darling! though thine infant heart
   Outrun thy knowledge dim,
E'en on God's throne that eager love
     Is dear to Him.

III.—ON THE LOVE OF CHILDREN.

TO that green hill, the shepherds' haunt,
    Why speed the children's feet?
And who the Youth that sits alone,
The clamorous flock to greet?

His hands are laid above their heads,
Their faces at His knee:
His looks are looks of love; yet seem
Something beyond to see.

The simple townsmen cross the hill
And bid the throng away,
" Nor press around the stranger youth,
Nor by the fold delay."

As one who smiles and wakes, He lifts
A child upon His knee:
"God's kingdom is of such as these;
So let them come to Me."

—Ah, Lord and Christ! Thy perfect heart
No fond excess could touch!
But man's best strength is feebleness,
And we may love too much!

Yet maim'd the man, or poor in blood,
Who glows not with delight
Whene'er the little ones go by
In casual daily sight;

Or when the child at mother's knee,
His altar, lisps a prayer,
And perfect faith, and utter love,
And Christ Himself, is there

Or when the little hands are clasp'd
To beg some baby grace,
And all the beauty of the dawn
Comes rose-red o'er the face;

Or when some elder one from sport
Her smaller sister wiles,
And two bright heads o'ershade the book;
Half study, and half smiles.

—Ah, Lord and Christ! Thy perfect heart
No fond excess could touch!
Yet when that innocence we see,
How can we love too much?

They twine around our heart of hearts;
Their spell we seek in vain;—
Go, ask the linnet why he sings,—
He can but sing again!

To winter-life their bloom and breath
Renew a later spring,
O dewy roses of the dawn,
Fresh from God's gardening!

Earth's treasures waste with use; but Thine,
O Lord! by lessening grow;
From love's pure fount the more we take,
The more the waters flow.

How should we prize the things unseen,
Not prizing what we see?
How turn away Thy little ones
Without forbidding Thee?

The Shepherd wills not we should stint
Or count our kisses o'er;
Nor bids us love His lambs the less,
But Him Who loves them, more.

IV.—HYMN TO OUR SAVIOUR.

CHRIST Who art above the sky
   Teach me how to live and die!
Thou hast sent me here to be
Born of human-kind like Thee:
Born to walk the flinty road
Which Thy crimson'd footsteps trode;
Clear mine eyes to track them right,
Leading upwards to the light.

Pure as snow from taint of wrong,
Thou hast known temptation strong;
Tried and burst the snares that lie
Set to lure us from the sky:
Thou wilt aid me firm to stand
When the tempter is at hand;
Thou wilt draw my thoughts to Thee,
And the demon-sin will flee.

When I slip, my frailty spare;
Saviour, save me from despair!
By the mercy-gate Thou art,
Vision of the Bleeding Heart,
Gazing with thorn-circled face
Human-eyed on all the race:
If I kneel before the gate,
Thou wilt never cry "Too late!"

If in vain my strength has toil'd;
Hopes defeated; purpose foil'd;
If the light of life be dim,
  Waning mind, and wither'd limb;
'If my dear ones leave me lone,
Be Thou here when all are gone;
Thou hast known what anguish is,
Thou canst turn my tears to bliss.

In the day of doubt and gloom,
Let Thy mercy-message come,
O'er my fever'd soul below
Falling soft as snow on snow;
"Though the mother smile no more
"On the baby that she bore;
"Bride by bridegroom be forgot,
"Yet will I forsake thee not."

Though far off in light, by me
Nearer than earth's nearest be:
By the love that brought Thee down;
By the bitter cross and crown;
By Thy shepherd-care to save
All Thy flock from font to grave;
Aid me here to live and die,
Christ Who art above the sky!

V.—CHRISTUS CONSOLATOR.

Σὺν Χριστῷ—πολλῷ μᾶλλον κρεῖσσον

HOPE of those that have none other,
Left for life by father, mother,
All their dearest lost or taken,
Only not by Thee forsaken;
Comfort Thou the sad and lonely,
Saviour dear, for Thou canst only.

When hell's legions darken o'er us,
Wiles and smiles of sin before us,
When the wrongs we wrought uncaring
Smite us with the heart's despairing;
Souls in sorrow lost and lonely,
Help us, Lord! for Thou canst only.

By the days of earthly trial,
By Thy friend's foreknown denial,

By Thy cross of bitter anguish,
Leave not Thou Thy lambs to languish:
Fainting in life's desert lonely
Thou canst lead the wanderers only.

Sick with hope deferr'd, or yearning
For the never-now-returning,
When the glooms of grief o'ershade us,
Thou hast known, and Thou wilt aid us!
To Thine own heart take the lonely,
Leaning on Thee, only, only.

VI.—THE GARDEN OF GOD.

CHRIST in His heavenly garden walks all day,
  And calls to souls upon the world's highway;
Wearied with trifles, maim'd and sick with sin,
Christ by the gate stands, and invites them in.

—"How long, unwise, will ye pursue your woe?
Here from the throne sweet waters ever go:
Here the white lilies shine like stars above:
Here in the red rose burns the face of Love.

"'Tis not from earthly paths I bid you flee,
But lighter in My ways your feet will be:
'Tis not to summon you from human mirth,
But add a depth and sweetness not of earth.

" Still by the gate I stand as on ye stray:
Turn your steps hither: am not I the Way?
The sun is falling fast; the night is nigh:
Why will ye wander? Wherefore will ye die

" Look on My hands and side, for I am He:
None to the Father cometh, but by Me:
For you I died; once more I call you home:
I live again for you: My children, come!"

VII.—A HYMN OF REPENTANCE.

WHEN low on life's horizon, sunk from heaven,
   The sun goes down, and night collects on high,
And grisly shapes of sin, as clouds storm-driven,
   In sad procession move against the sky,
      Lord, who can bear to die?
        But Thou say'st, No;
        Not so; not so:—
Though in death's twilight terror take thee,
I will not leave thee or forsake thee.

They pass, the sins of youth, once loved, now loathèd,
   In Passion's purple hues and folly dyed;
The sins of age, with leper whiteness clothèd;—
   The lust, the lie, the selfishness, the pride:
      Who may such sight abide?
        But Thou say'st, No;
        Not so; not so:—
Though dark remorse and shame o'ertake thee,
I will not leave thee or forsake thee.

O Lord and Judge, when from Thy mouth the sentence
   Flames, and with prostrate knee and downcast eyes
We sigh before the Throne our late repentance,
   How should the spirit hope for wings to rise
      To Heaven's own Paradise?
        But Thou say'st, No;
        Not so; not so;—
To Him Who bled for man betake thee;
He will not leave thee or forsake thee.

Thrice-holy Child, Who, pure from pure proceeding,
   By Mary's side in gifts and graces grew;
Thou Who for our sake once hung pale and bleeding,
   Wilt Thou exact from me the penance due,
      Whose sins Thy death renew?

>   But Thou say'st, No;
>   Not so; not so;—
> Close to My wounded side I take thee;
> I will not leave thee or forsake thee.

VIII.—DEATH AND THE FEAR OF IT.

LORD! How fast the minutes fly
'Twixt us and the hour we die!
Days are weeks before we know;
Weeks to months untimely grow;
And behind each glad New Year
Death his ambush sets more near.

Death!—by whomsoever heard,
'Mongst all words most fearful word!
—Quit each thing familiar here!
Face to face with God appear!
Change no mortal tongue can tell:—
All's in that one syllable!

Hour of dread farewells to be!
Faces more than life to me;
Little lips that beg me stay;
Tears I shall not wipe away;
Faithful hand, yet clasp'd in mine:—
Death Triumphant!—all is thine!

Author of man's mystic lot,
God, Thy ways as ours are not:
Thou hast destined us to be
Seized by death, yet safe in Thee:
Love Immortal casting out
Feverish fear, and freezing doubt.

—In the spaces of the night,
In the depths of dim affright,
Jesus, with our trials tried,
Do not Thou forsake my side!
Childlike on Thy faithful breast
Hold my heart, and bid me rest.

Like a sword above my head
Death is hanging by a thread;
Yet, O gracious Lord on high,
Surely Thou wilt hear my cry,
By Thy life laid down for me
Turning death to victory!

Only this can light the grave,
Thou hast died:—and Thou wilt save:—
Thou by lying low in earth
Hast assured our second birth,
Bidding in the sunless tomb
Amaranthine roses bloom.

If the spirit shivering shrink
From annihilation's brink,
Through the soul like sunshine come,
—"Death is but another womb:
Born through woe to human breath,
Ye are born to God through death."

—Nearer than the nearest by,
Be beside me when I die!
With Thy strength my weakness nerve
Ne'er through fear from faith to swerve;
So, Death's storm-vex'd portal past,
Safe in Thee to sleep at last.

IX.—I AM THE RESURRECTION AND THE LIFE.

DARK World, rejoice! The day-spring
  Has broke, more bright than when
The star-crown'd Angel chorus
  Sang God's good news to men,—
    The Lord of Life e'en now
      From Death's dim prison
      This third day risen,
    With victory on His brow—Risen!

O day that seal'd for ever
  The hope of hopes to man!
Made Death himself the gateway
  To life's immortal span!
    That brimm'd with quickening light
      The soul's grave-prison,
      Whence He had risen,
    God's Daystar in His might—Risen!

For all the million millions
  Whirl'd on this roving ball
Since man's creation-morning,
  One Lord hath died, for all;
    God, yet still Man, He springs
      From Death's dim prison,
      In glory risen,
    With healing on His wings—Risen!

But most who mourn their dearest
  Through desolate silent years,
Loved with what utter longing,
  And wept for with what tears—
    For them the Love that died
      Unbars life's prison:—
      They see Christ risen,
    The loved ones at His side—Risen!

Walter Chalmers Smith.

1824.

WALTER CHALMERS SMITH was born at Aberdeen on the 5th of December, 1824. He was educated at the grammar school and the university of his native city, and afterwards studied theology at Edinburgh. His first ministerial charge was in London, at the Free Scotch Church in Chadwell Street, Islington, where he was ordained in 1850. In 1858 he became minister of Orwell, Kinross-shire, where he remained three years, removing thence to the Free Roxburgh Church, Edinburgh, and three years later to the Free Tron Church, Glasgow. In 1876 he returned to Edinburgh, and became pastor of the Edinburgh Free High Church.

From 1860 to 1893 Dr. Smith published the following volumes of verse: "The Bishop's Walk" (1860); "Hymns of Christ and the Christian Life' (1867); "Olrig Grange" (1872); "Borland Hall" (1874); "Hilda; among the Broken Gods" (1878); "Raban; or, Life Splinters" (1880); "North Country Folk" (1883); "Kildrostan" (1884); "Thoughts and Fancies for Sunday Evenings" (1887); "A Heretic and other Poems" (1891); "Selections from the Poems of Walter C. Smith" (1893).

The most popular of these works have been "Olrig Grange" and "Hilda; among the Broken Gods," which have both passed through several editions.

Dr. Smith's poetry is full of living interest, due to the fact that the problems discussed are those which reach down to the depths of our nature—in which therefore all who think must be interested. These are handled with ample knowledge, and in the main with great fairness, even to ideas with which the writer does not agree. There is not the deep psychological insight, nor the power of flashing light on obscure problems which arrest the reader of Robert Browning's poetry; but there is some of that power of looking at things out of the eyes of others, which is probably the most wonderful characteristic of Robert Browning's mind. But if Dr. Smith moves along lower levels, and does not tackle such subtle questions as Browning did, for the ordinary reader he has this great advantage, that all is written with absolute clearness. Browning's name stands for hard thinking, Dr. Smith's for pleasant reading, which leaves the reader with a deeper sympathy for, and better understanding of, the troubles and perplexities of men and women.

Dr. Smith and Dr. George MacDonald—both Aberdonians—have much in common in thought and feeling; but their manner of apprehending and of setting forth truth differs greatly. Dr. MacDonald's way is that of the mystic—a quality of which I find none in Dr. Smith. His poems are "marked by richness of thought, creative imagination and lyrical charm, although unequal and not seldom careless in construction." His longer poems would be more effective if the characters did not take so long in their self-revelations of thought and feeling. He sets forth vividly and often pathetically the inner struggles which form the real tragedies of these modern days. In the lyrics which are scattered over his longer poems there is the true poetic note.

Although Dr. Smith's work has a claim to a place among that of the general poets, there is a certain fitness in his being placed among the sacred poets, since the strongest force in his poetry is the religious one, so that, even in what may be called his secular poetry, the most vital parts grow out of his theologic thought or religious feeling. In this respect he is like the other poet of Aberdeenshire, George MacDonald, who says himself, that he would not care either to write poetry or tell stories if he could not preach in them—but then there is preaching and preaching; and if all preaching were of the living sort we get from these two Aberdonians, the name would carry a higher meaning than it usually does.

Dr. Smith sees clearly enough that the springs of life lie in the religious part of man's nature, so that even in "Kildrostan," which is a crofter's story, and deals with questions that are Social, the most powerful passages are concerned with religion. In "Olrig Grange," which is a love story, there is no more effective portion than the picture of the mother, orthodox in doctrine, but utterly worldly at heart. Whilst in "Hilda; among the Broken Gods" religion is presented as it is seen out of many eyes—by Claud Maxwell, poet; Hilda, saint wife; Winifred Urquhart, materialist; Luke Spratt, evangelist; Rev. Elphinstone Bell, priest; just as in "The Ring and the Book," by Robert Browning, the same tragedy is set forth as it appeared to all who were in any way connected with it. "A Heretic," which, as its name implies, is concerned with the new movement of thought on religious questions so characteristic of our age, tells the story of one cast out from the Kirk for heresy, but whose beautiful Christian character demonstrated the vitality of his religion.

The following lines from this poem are at once an illustration of the truth they set forth and of the poet's method:—

> But one man like a tree shall stand,
>   Leafing and fruiting year by year,
> And cling to his little patch of land,
>   And cast a shade for the lazy steer,
> With no more change than the passing breeze
>   Makes when it tosses the creaking bough;
> And prosperous, plentiful, full of ease,
>   To-morrow he shall be the same as now.
> Another shall flow like a freshening stream,
>   Flashing there where the sunbeam flies,
> Eddying here in a brooding dream,
>   And all its life in its movement lies;
> This the law of his being strange,
> Ever he grows by flux and change.
> What would you? Nature will have her way;
> Will mend by night what you mar by day,
> And laugh at the man who would say her Nay.
> Tree cannot pluck up its roots and go,
> Restless stream cannot cease to flow,
> Each must obey the high Law given
> To the things of earth by the Lord of Heaven.

In "North Country Folk," one of the least known, but in our judgment one of the best pieces of work from his pen, there are three pictures of "Parish Pastors" belonging to different schools of Presbyterianism in Scotland. These are drawn with a masterly hand, and show how under the same creed and within the same ecclesiastical forms individual character and preference will assert themselves. We know not where to look for fresher or more delightful pictures in verse of Scottish life than in this volume.

In "Olrig Grange" there are many incisive bits of character description. Here is one of Thorold—the hero of the poem:—

> Trained for a priest, for that is still the pride
> And high ambition of the Scottish mother,
> There was a kind of priestly purity
> In him, and a deep undertone of awe
> Ran through his gayest fancies, and his heart
> Reached out its sympathies, and laid fast hold
> On the outcast, the unlovely, and alone
> I' the world. But being challenged at the door
> Of God's high Temple to indue himself
> With armour that he had not proved, to clothe
> With articles of ready-made Belief
> His Faith inquisitive, he rent the Creed
> Trying to fit it on, and cast it from him;
> Then took it up again, and found it worn
> With age, and riddled by the moth, and rotten
> Therefore he trod it under foot, and went
> Awhile with only scant fig-leaves to clothe
> His naked spirit, longing after God,
> But more for knowledge panting than for faith.
> The Priest was left behind; the hope of Glory
> Became pursuit of Fame, and yet a light
> From heaven kept hovering always over him,
> Like twilight from a sun that had gone down.

In "Kildrostan"—the most dramatic of his works—with a striking plot there is a description, with both humorous and pathetic touches of a religious gathering of Crofters, of which Tremain, an unbelieving Cynic, thus speaks:—

"Why should I not
Enrich my soul with all experiences
Of life and passion to be moulded duly
Into pure forms of art? I came to see
The Christian superstition, where I heard
The thing was really living. Up in town
'Tis but a raree show of surplices,
And albs and copes and silver candlesticks,
And droning repetitions; poor survivals
Of the old Pagan Cult; or else it is
A small dissenting shop where they retail
Long yards of worn-out logic, or an ounce
Of bitter morals with a syllabub
Of sentiment. But this is different.
I could almost have fancied I was back
With Cyril in the Abrandrian desert
And throngs of howling, unwashed monks who hunted
A Neo-Platonist; only your factor
Is no philosopher."

But to give a single speech like this is little better than offering a brick to represent a building. In the following pages, however, a more extended attempt is made to represent the several volumes of the poet by characteristic selections.

Readers of Dr. Smith's works may not find the high ethereal spirit of the great Masters of Song, but they will find touching stories of life—"metrical novelettes," as Edmund Clarence Stedman calls them—and descriptions of many types of character given with much of the insight of the poet.

W. GARRETT HORDER.

HYMNS.

1867.

WALTER CHALMERS SMITH.

I.—EARTH WAS WAITING.

"When the fulness of the time was come, God sent forth His Son, made of a woman."—GAL. iv. 4.

EARTH was waiting, spent and restless,
   With a mingled hope and fear;
And the faithful few were sighing,
   "Surely, Lord, the day is near;
The desire of all the nations,
   It is time He should appear."

Still the gods were in their temples,
   But the ancient faith had fled;
And the priests stood by their altars
   Only for a piece of bread;
And the Oracles were silent,
   And the Prophets all were dead.

In the sacred courts of Zion,
   Where the Lord had His abode,
There the money-changers trafficked,
   And the sheep and oxen trod;
And the world, because of wisdom,
   Knew not either Lord or God.

Then the spirit of the Highest
   On a virgin meek came down,
And He burdened her with blessing,
   And He pained her with renown;
For she bare the Lord's Anointed
   For His cross and for His crown.

Earth for Him had groaned and travailed,
   Since the ages first began ;
For in Him was hid the secret
   That through all the ages ran—
Son of Mary, Son of David,
   Son of God, and Son of Man.

II.—LORD, I WOULD CHOOSE

"Mary hath chosen that good part."—LUKE x. 42.

LORD, I would choose the better part
   Which none may take away from me ;
Let me not fret with anxious heart,
   But sit at peace, and hold with Thee
Communion sweet here at Thy feet

There be that love Thee well and true,
   And yet they vex their souls with care ;
For still much service they will do,
   And many needless vessels bear,
And they with such are cumbered much.

They love Thee, Lord, and Thy good word,
   Yet of Thy joy they stint their heart,
And grudge the peace Thou dost accord
   To them that choose the better part ;
And, idly faint, they make complaint.

The one thing needful let me do,
   Nor let my service cumber me ;
Who serve the Lord must hold in view
   They need Him more than needeth He ;
Who serve Him best in Him too rest.

So would I rest, Lord, at Thy feet,
   And learn of Thee, and look above ;
Doing the service that is meet,
   But free to worship and to love,
And find increase of grace and peace.

OLRIG GRANGE.
1872
WALTER CHALMERS SMITH.
(Selected Lines)
LOQUITUR THOROLD.

I.

But my Faith is not gone, although
   At times it seems to fade away.
I would I were as long ago;
   I cling to God, and strive to say,
   The devil and all his reasons Nay:
But in the crucible of thought
Old forms dissolve, nor have I got,
   Or seem to wish, new moulds of clay
To limit the boundless truth I sought.

Can the great God be aught but vague,
   Bounded by no horizon, save
What feeble minds create to plague
   High Reason with? We madly crave
   For definite truth, and make a grave,
Through too much certainty precise,
And logical distinction nice,
   For all the little Faith we have,
Buying clear views at a terrible price.

Too dear, indeed, to part with Faith
   For forms of logic about God,
And walk in lucid realms of death,
   Whose paths incredible are trod
   By no soul living. Faith's abode
Is mystery for evermore;
Its life to worship and adore,
   And meekly bow beneath the rod,
When the day is dark, and the burden sore.

II.

My sun sinks without clouds or fears;
   No spectral shadows gather round
The gateway of the endless years,
   Where we, long blindfold, are unbound,
   And lay our swathings on the ground,
To face the Eternal. So I rest
Peacefully on the Strong One's breast,
   Even though the mystery profound
Ever a mystery be confessed.

My old doubts?—Well, they no more fret,
   Nor chafe and foam o'er sunken rocks.
I don't know that my Faith is yet
   Quite regular and orthodox;
   I have not keys for all the locks,
And may not pick them. Truth will bear
Neither rude handling, nor unfair
   Evasion of its wards, and mocks
Whoever would falsely enter there.

But all through life I see a Cross,
   Where sons of God yield up their breath:
There is no gain except by loss,
   There is no life except by death,
   There is no vision but by Faith,
Nor glory but by bearing shame,
Nor justice but by taking blame;
   And that Eternal Passion saith,
"Be emptied of glory and right and name."

RABAN; OR, LIFE SPLINTERS.
1880.
WALTER CHALMERS SMITH.

WORK AND SPIRIT.

IS it the work that makes life great and true?
   Or the true soul that, working as it can,
Does faithfully the task it has to do,
   And keepeth faith alike with God and man?

Ah! well; the work is something; the same gold
   Or brass is fashioned now into a coin,
Now into fairest chalice that shall hold
   To panting lips the sacramental wine:

Here the same marble forms a cattle-trough
   For brutes by the wayside to quench their thirst,
And there a god emerges from the rough
   Unshapely block—yet they were twins at first.

One pool of metal in the melting pot
   A sordid, or a sacred thought inspires;
And of twin marbles from the quarry brought
   One serves the earth, one glows with altar-fires.

There's something in high purpose of the soul
   To do the highest service to its kind;
There's something in the art that can unroll
   Secrets of beauty shaping in the mind.

Yet he who takes the lower room, and tries
   To make his cattle-trough with honest heart,
And could not frame the god with gleaming eyes,
   As nobly plays the more ignoble part.

And maybe, as the higher light breaks in
   And shows the meaner task he has to do,
He is the greater that he strives to win
   Only the praise of being just and true.

For who can do no thing of sovran worth
   Which men shall praise, a higher task may find
Plodding his dull round on the common earth,
   But conquering envies rising in the mind.

And God works in the little as the great
   A perfect work, and glorious over all—
Or in the stars that choir with joy elate,
   Or in the lichen spreading on the wall

NORTH COUNTRY FOLK.
1883.
WALTER CHALMERS SMITH.

A CRY FROM THE MERSE.

"They have heard evil tidings; there is sorrow on the sea."—JER. xlix. 23.

HALF o' us drooned in the Firth!
   Hearses at ilk ither door!
No a hale heart in the toon,
   No a dry e'e on the shore!
No a hooss but has its dead,
   Father, or cousin, or brither!
For nane o' us stands by himsel',
   We are a' sib to ilk ither.

My Janet was wedded to Jake,
   George was my brither-in-law,
Elsie was promised to Will—
   An' noo they're a' dead an' awa';
Drooned within sight o' their hames,
   Throttled richt doon to their graves,
Wi' the screams o' their wives an' the weans
   Mixed up wi' the crash o' the wa

Lord God, what does it mean?
   They were a' brave lads an' true,
And what can this misery bring
   O' profit tae us or you?
My head gangs roon when I think
   Hoo the sea lay calm in the bay,
Till it had them a' weel in its grip,
   An' took the brave lads for a prey.

Lord, keep me frae sin if ye can :
    I canna be sure what I do ;
There's Elsie sits dazed-like an' dumb,
    And Janet moans a' the day through ;
I try tae keep hauds o' Thee, Lord,
    But a' that I get for my pains
Is tae drift farther into the dark
    'Mid the wail o' the women an' weans.

Oh, the folk are a' kind in their way,
    Baith gentle an' simple, nae doot ;
An' ready wi' pity an' prayers,
    An' siller if siller wu'd do't !
But prayers winna bring the lads back,
    An' pity feels almost like mockin',
An' a' the fine gowd i' the lan'
    Winna sowder the heart that is broken.

The bairnies are greetin' a' day,
    An' the women are moanin' a' nicht,
An' the bread winna gang doon oor throats,
    An' the Book doesna bring ony licht ;
An' though there's nae hope in oor hearts,
    We gang an' glower lang at the sea,
An' scan weel the rig o' ilk boat,
    An' then we come hame like tae dee.

Half o' us drooned i' the Firth !
    A' o' us drooned in despair !
Bairns cryin', "Daddie, come hame,"
    As their mithers are rivin' their hair !
An' where there's a corpse they are glad,
    For the sea has the maist in her maw ;
An' I watna weel what's tae come neist—
    But, Lord, if ye'd just tak' us a'.

THOUGHTS AND FANCIES.
1887.
WALTER CHALMERS SMITH.

I.—ONE THING I OF THE LORD DESIRE.

ONE thing I of the Lord desire—
   For all my way hath miry been—
Be it by water or by fire,
   O make me clean.

Erewhile I strove for perfect truth,
   And thought it was a worthy strife;
But now I leave that aim of youth
   For perfect life.

If clearer vision Thou impart,
   Grateful and glad my soul shall be;
But yet to have a purer heart
   Is more to me.

Yea, only as the heart is clean
   May larger vision yet be mine,
For mirrored in its depths are seen
   The things divine.

I watch to shun the miry way,
   And stanch the spring of guilty thought
But, watch and wrestle as I may,
   Pure I am not.

So wash Thou me without, within;
   Or purge with fire, if that must be;
No matter how, if only sin
   Die out in me.

II.—BE STILL.

BE still, and know He doeth all things well,
   Working the purpose of His holy will,
And if His high designs He do not tell
   Till He accomplish them—do thou be still.

Why should'st thou strive and fret and fear and doubt,
   As if His way, being dark, must bode thee ill?
If thine own way be clearly pointed out,
   Leave Him to clear up His, and be thou still.

Was ever yet thy trust in Him misplaced?
   And hoping in Him, did He not fulfil
The word on which He caused thee to rest,
   Though not as thou had'st thought, perchance? Be s

What if the road be rough which might be smooth?
   Is not the rough road best for thee, until
Thou learn by patient walking in the truth
   To trust and hope in God, and to be still?

A little faith is more than clearest views;
   Would'st thou have ocean like a babbling rill?
God without mystery were not good news;
   Wrestle not with the darkness, but be still.

Be still, and know that He is God indeed
   Who reigns in glory on His holy hill,
Yet once upon the Cross did hang and bleed,
   And heard the people raging—and was still.

III.—O'ER LAND AND SEA.

O'ER land and sea love follows with fond prayers
   Its dear ones in their troubles, griefs, and cares;
      There is no spot
On which it does not drop this tender dew,
Except the grave, and there it bids adieu,
      And prayeth not.

Why should that be the only place uncheered
By prayer, which to our hearts is most endeared,
   And sacred grown?
Living, we sought for blessings on their head;
Why should our lips be sealed when they are dead,
   And we alone?

Idle? their doom is fixed? Ah! who can tell?
Yet, were it so, I think no harm could well
   Come of my prayer:
And O the heart, o'erburdened with its grief,
This comfort needs, and finds therein relief
   From its despair.

Shall God be wroth because we love them still,
And call upon His love to shield from ill
   Our dearest, best,
And bring them home, and recompense their pain,
And cleanse their sin, if any sin remain,
   And give them rest?

Nay, I will not believe it. I will pray
As for the living, for the dead each day.
   They will not grow
Less meet for heaven when followed by a prayer
To speed them home, like summer-scented air
   From long ago.

Who shall forbid the heart's desires to flow
Beyond the limit of the things we know?
   In heaven above
The incense that the golden censers bear,
Is the sweet perfume from the saintly prayer
   Of trust and love.

A HERETIC AND OTHER POEMS.
1891.
WALTER CHALMERS SMITH.
I.—CREEDS.

AH! these old creeds
   Who can believe them to-day?
Yet were brave deeds
Inspired by them once, too; and they
   Made men of heroic mould
   In the great fighting ages of old.

  Is it the wounds
Which science has given? or the sap
   On critical grounds,
Which has brought about their mishap?
   Nay, these touched not a vital spot,
   Though they brag of the wreck they have wrought.

  But the spirit has risen
From the hard, narrow letter which kept
   Men's thoughts in a prison,
Where they struggled or languished or slept;
   And now we can soar high above
   All the creeds but the Credo of Love.

  They are things of the past,
Survivals, and now out of date;
   The men were not cast
In our moulds, who endured such a weight,
   So linked and compact: let them go,
   They who wore them had no room to grow.

  All too complete,
They were subtly and skilfully wrought
   With logic neat;
But they are not in touch with our thought;
   And they will not allow they have found
   Any spot where they have not sure ground.

They are ever so far
From the days we are living in now,
From our work and our war,
And the thoughts that are aching our brow;
    And yet though they be but part true,
    Vain to patch up the old, or make new.

Creed-making now
In these latter ages of time
Would yield stuff, I trow
Thin and loose as a small poet's rhyme—
    Tags and thrums, hints and guesses, no more
    With a deep, settled doubt at the core.

What not to believe,
That now is the stage we are at;
And how shall we weave
Any faith to live on out of that?
    There must go to the making of creeds
    Sure hearts, girded up for high deeds.

But ours is an age
Of unmaking, taking things down:
For the warfare we wage
We must swarm from the fortified town,
    And spread out to find air and room
    Beyond the old walls and their gloom.

Yet we have faith
In the Right and the True and the Good,
And in Him whose last breath
Was the prayer of a pitiful mood,
    Which smites the meek spirit with awe,
    And with Love, the true life of all Law.

II.—THE VISION OF GOD.

O THE silences of heaven,
  How they speak to me of God,
Now the veil in twain is riven
  That concealed where He abode!
Yet its clouds were once around Him,
  And I sought Him in despair,
And never there I found Him,
  Till I brought Him with me there.

Not the optic glass revealed Him,
  No mechanical device
Pierced the darkness that concealed Him
  With a vision more precise:
Only lowliness can merit
  That His secret He should tell
Only spirit seeth spirit,
  And the heart that loveth well.

Never till His love hath found thee,
  Shall the cloud and mist depart;
Vain to seek Him all around thee,
  Till He dwell within thy heart.
Not without thee, but within thee
  Must the oracle be heard,
As He seeketh still to win thee,
  And to guide thee by His word.

When I found Him in my bosom,
  Then I found Him everywhere,
In the bud and in the blossom,
  In the earth and in the air;
And He spake to me with clearness
  From the silent stars that say,
As ye find Him in His nearness,
  Ye shall find Him far away

George MacDonald.

1824.

GEORGE MACDONALD was born at Huntley, Aberdeenshire, on the 10th of December, 1824, and was educated at the parish school of Huntley and King's College, Aberdeen. His general poetry is represented in Volume V. of this work, where he is treated as one of the general poets. Much of his verse, however, is devoted to religious subjects, and it is impossible to omit a selection of it from a volume dealing specifically with sacred and didactic poetry. The reader is referred to Volume V. for a critical article on George MacDonald's poetry from the pen of Dr. Japp, and it will be found that the leading characteristics of the poet's verse as there indicated become intensified when he is dealing with exclusively religious subjects. These are a combination of simplicity and mysticism which finds some parallel in the poetry of Blake—the outlook of a natural and childlike eye, suggesting an infinitude of parallels and parables to the seer's vision. Besides this, there is in Dr. MacDon ld's poetry the beating of an intensely human h art, which finds in human relationships and experiences innumerable illustrations and interpretations of the nature and discipline of the Divine Father.

These characteristics are happily illustrated by two single stanza poems included with others under the title of "Motes in the Sun." What could be more Blake-like in its opening lines, and what more MacDonald-like in its close and in the whole as a union of the natural and the spiritual, than the lines entitled "Waiting"?

> Lie, little cow, and chew thy cud,
>   The farmer soon will shift thy tether;
> Chirp, linnet, on the frozen mud,
>   Sun and song will come together;
> Wait, soul, for God, and thou shalt bud,
>   He waits thy waiting with his weather.

The Divine love as interpreted by the intensely human heart of the poet has many illustrations throughout his works, of which the lines entitled "Forgiveness" may be given here:—

> God gives His child upon his slate a sum—
>   To find eternity in hours and years;
> With both sides covered, back the child doth come,
>   His dim eyes swollen with shed and unshed tears;
> God smiles, wipes clean the upper side and nether,
> And says, "Now, dear, we'll do the sum together!"

So much of Dr. MacDonald's poetry would be proper to this volume that selection is difficult. "The Disciple," "The Gospel Women," and "Parables" might all be quoted from; but we have confined our selection to "Organ Songs," "Violin Songs," "A Book of Sonnets," and "A Book of Dreams."

ALFRED H. MILES.

ORGAN SONGS.

GEORGE MACDONALD.

I.—I KNOW WHAT BEAUTY IS.

I KNOW what beauty is, for Thou
   Hast set the world within my heart;
   Of me Thou madest it a part;
I never loved it more than now.

I know the Sabbath afternoons;
   The light asleep upon the graves;
   Against the sky the poplar waves;
The river murmurs organ tunes.

I know the spring with bud and bell;
   The hush in summer woods at night;
   Autumn, when leaves let in more light;
Fantastic winter's lovely spell.

I know the rapture music gives,
   Its mystery of ordered tones;
   Dream-muffled soul, it loves and moans,
And, half-alive, comes in and lives.

And verse I know, whose concord high
   Of thought and music lifts the soul
   Where many a glimmering starry shoal
Glides through the Godhead's living sky.

Yea, Beauty's regnant All I know—
   The imperial head, the thoughtful eyes;
   The God-imprisoned harmonies,
That out in gracious motions go.

But I leave all, O Son of man,
  Put off my shoes, and come to Thee,
  Most lovely Thou of all I see,
Most potent Thou of all that can!

As child forsakes his favourite toy,
  His sisters' sport, his new-found nest;
  And, climbing to his mother's breast,
Enjoys yet more his late-left joy—

I lose to find. On fair-browed bride
  Fair pearls their fairest light afford;
  So, gathered round Thy glory, Lord,
All glory else is glorified.

II.—LONGING.

MY heart is full of inarticulate pain,
  And beats laborious. Cold ungenial looks
Invade my sanctuary. Men of gain,
  Wise in success, well-read in feeble books
No nigher come, I pray: your air is drear;
'Tis winter and low skies when ye appear.

Beloved, who love beauty and fair truth,
  Come nearer me; too near ye cannot come;
Make me an atmosphere with your sweet youth;
  Give me your souls to breathe in, a large room;
Speak not a word, for, see, my spirit lies
Helpless and dumb; shine on me with your eyes.

O all wide places, far from feverous towns;
  Great shining seas; pine forests; mountains wild;
Rock-bosomed shores; rough heaths, and sheep-
    cropt downs;
  Vast pallid clouds; blue spaces undefiled—
Room! give me room! give loneliness and air—
Free things and plenteous in your regions fair!

White dove of David, flying overhead,
  Golden with sunlight on thy snowy wings,
Outspeeding thee my longing thoughts are fled
  To find a home afar from men and things;
Where in his temple, earth o'erarched with sky,
God's heart to mine may speak, my heart reply.

O God of mountains, stars, and boundless spaces,
  O God of freedom and of joyous hearts,
When Thy face looketh forth from all men's faces,
  There will be room enough in crowded marts!
Brood Thou around me, and the noise is o'er,
Thy universe my closet with shut door.

Heart, heart, awake! The love that loveth all
  Maketh a deeper calm than Horeb's cave.
God in thee, can His children's folly gall?
  Love may be hurt, but shall not love be brave?—
Thy holy silence sinks in dews of balm;
Thou art my solitude, my mountain-calm!

III.—I WOULD I WERE A CHILD.

I WOULD I were a child,
  That I might look, and laugh, and say, My Father!
And follow Thee with running feet, or rather
  Be led through dark and wild!

How I would hold Thy hand,
My glad eyes often to Thy glory lifting!
Should darkness 'twixt Thy face and mine come
    drifting,
  My heart would but expand.

If an ill thing came near,
I would but creep within Thy mantle's folding,
Shut my eyes close, Thy hand yet faster holding,
  And soon forget my fear.

O soul, O soul, rejoice!
Thou art God's child indeed, for all thy sinning;
A poor weak child, yet His, and worth the winning
   With saviour eyes and voice.

Who spake the words? Didst Thou?
They are too good, even for such a giver:
Such water drinking once, I should feel ever
   As I had drunk but now.

Yet sure the Word said so,
Teaching our lips to cry with His, Our Father!
Telling the tale of him who once did gather
   His goods to him, and go!

Ah, Thou dost lead me, God!
But it is dark and starless, the way dreary;
Almost I sleep, I am so very weary
   Upon this rough hill-road.

Almost! Nay, I *do* sleep;
There is no darkness save in this my dreaming;
Thy fatherhood above, around, is beaming;
   Thy hand my hand doth keep.

With sighs my soul doth teem;
I have no knowledge but that I am sleeping;
Haunted with lies, my life will fail in weeping;
   Wake me from this my dream.

How long shall heavy night
Deny the day? How long shall this dull sorrow
Say in my heart that never any morrow
   Will bring the friendly light?

Lord, art Thou in the room?
Come near my bed; oh, draw aside the curtain!
A child's heart would say *Father*, were it certain
That it would not presume.

But if this dreary sleep
May not be broken, help Thy helpless sleeper
To rest in Thee; so shall his sleep grow deeper—
For evil dreams too deep.

Father! I dare at length;
My childhood sure will hold me free from blaming:
Sinful yet hoping, I to Thee come, claiming
Thy tenderness, my strength.

IV.—REST.

1.

WHEN round the earth the Father's hands
   Have gently drawn the dark;
Sent off the sun to fresher lands,
   And curtained in the lark;
'Tis sweet, all tired with glowing day,
   To fade with fading light,
To lie once more, the old weary way,
   Upfolded in the night.

If mothers o'er our slumbers bend,
   And unripe kisses reap,
In soothing dreams with sleep they blend,
   Till even in dreams we sleep.
And if we wake while night is dumb,
   'Tis sweet to turn and say,
It is an hour ere dawning come,
   And I will sleep till day.

II.

There is a dearer, warmer bed,
   Where one all day may lie,
Earth's bosom pillowing the head,
   And let the world go by.
There come no watching mother's eyes;
   The stars instead look down;
Upon it breaks, and silent dies,
   The murmur of the town.

The great world, shouting, forward fares:
   This chamber, hid from none,
Hides safe from all, for no one cares
   For him whose work is done.
Cheer thee, my friend; bethink thee how
   A certain unknown place,
Or here or there, is waiting now,
   To rest thee from thy race.

III.

Nay, nay, not there the rest from harms,
   The slow composèd breath!
Not there the folding of the arms,
   The cool, the blessèd death!
That needs no curtained bed to hide
   The world with all its wars;
No grassy cover to divide
   From sun and moon and stars.

It is a rest that deeper grows
   In midst of pain and strife;
A mighty, conscious, willed repose,
   The death of deepest life

To have and hold the precious prize
   No need of jealous bars;
But windows open to the skies,
   And skill to read the stars.

IV.

Who dwelleth in that secret place,
   Where tumult enters not,
Is never cold with terror base,
   Never with anger hot.
For if an evil host should dare
   His very heart invest,
God is his deeper heart, and there
   He enters in to rest.

When mighty sea-winds madly blow,
   And tear the scattered waves,
Peaceful as summer woods, below
   Lie darkling ocean caves:
The wind of words may toss my heart,
   But what is that to me!
'Tis but a surface storm—Thou art
   My deep, still, resting sea.

A BOOK OF SONNETS.

GEORGE MACDONALD.

I.—*THE UNSEEN FACE.*

"I DO beseech Thee, God, show me Thy face
"Come up to Me in Sinai on the morn!
Thou shalt behold as much as may be borne."
And on a rock stood Moses, lone in space.
From Sinai's top, the vaporous, thunderous place,
God passed in cloud, an earthy garment worn
To hide, and thus reveal. In love, not scorn,
He put him in a clift of the rock's base,
Covered him with his hand, his eyes to screen—
Passed—lifted it : his back alone appears!
Ah, Moses, had he turned, and hadst thou seen
The pale face crowned with thorns, baptized with tear
The eyes of the true man, by men belied,
Thou hadst beheld God's face, and straightway died.

II.—*THE SWEEPER OF THE FLOOR.*

METHOUGHT that in a solemn church I stood.
Its marble acres, worn with knees and feet,
Lay spread from door to door, from street to street.
Midway the form hung high upon the rood
Of Him who gave His life to be our good ;
Beyond, priests flitted, bowed, and murmured meet,
Among the candles shining still and sweet.
Men came and went, and worshipped as they could—
And still their dust a woman with her broom,
Bowed to her work, kept sweeping to the door.
Then saw I, slow through all the pillared gloom,
Across the church a silent figure come :
"Daughter," it said, "thou sweepest well my floor!"
It is the Lord! I cried, and saw no more.

VIOLIN SONGS.

GEORGE MACDONALD.

I.—GOING TO SLEEP.

LITTLE one, you must not fret
   That I take your clothes away;
Better sleep you so will get,
   And at morning wake more gay—
     Saith the children's mother.

You I must unclothe again,
   For you need a better dress;
Too much worn are body and brain;
   You need everlastingness—
     Saith the heavenly father.

I went down death's lonely stair;
   Laid my garments in the tomb;
Dressed again one morning fair;
   Hastened up, and hied me home—
     Saith the elder brother.

Then I will not be afraid
   Any ill can come to me;
When 'tis time to go to bed,
   I will rise and go with Thee—
     Saith the little brother.

II.—BED TIME.

"COME, children, put away your toys;
   Roll up the kite's long line;
The day is done for girls and boys—
   Look, it is almost nine!
Come, weary foot, and sleepy head,
Get up, and come along to bed."

The children, loath, must yet obey;
  Up the long stair they creep;
Lie down, and something sing or say
  Until they fall asleep,
To steal through caverns of the night
Into the morning's golden light.

We, elder ones, sit up more late,
  And tasks unfinished ply,
But, gently busy, watch and wait—
  Dear sister, you and I,
To hear the Father, with soft tread,
Coming to carry us to bed.

A BOOK OF DREAMS.

GEORGE MACDONALD.

I.—A PIECE OF GOLD.

III.

A PIECE of gold had left my purse,
   Which I had guarded ill;
I feared a lack, but feared yet worse
   Regret returning still.

I lifted up my feeble prayer
   To Him who maketh strong,
That thence no haunting thoughts of care
   Might do my spirit wrong.

And even before my body slept,
   Such visions fair I had,
That seldom soul with chamber swept
   Was more serenely glad.

No white-robed angel floated by
   On slow, reposing wings;
I only saw, with inward eye,
   Some very common things.

First rose the scarlet pimpernel
   With burning purple heart;
I saw within it, and could spell
   The lesson of its art.

Then came the primrose, childlike flower.
   And looked me in the face;
It bore a message full of power,
   And confidence, and grace.

And breezes rose on pastures trim
  And bathed me all about;
Wool-muffled sheep-bells babbled dim,
  Or only half spoke out.

Sudden it closed, some door of heaven,
  But what came out remained;
The poorest man my loss had given
  For that which I had gained!

Thou gav'st me, Lord, a brimming cup
  Where I bemoaned a sip;
How easily Thou didst make up
  For what my fault let slip!

What said the flowers? what message new
  Embalmed my soul with rest?
I scarce can tell—only they grew
  Right out of God's own breast.

They said, to every flower He made,
  God's thought was root and stem—
Perhaps said what the lilies said
  When Jesus looked at them.

II.—DREAMING I SLEPT.

v.

DREAMING I slept. Three crosses stood
  High in the gloomy air;
One bore a thief, and one the Good;
  The other waited bare.

A soldier came up to the place,
  And took me for the third;
My eyes they sought the Master's face,
  My will the Master's word.

He bent His head; I took the sign,
   And gave the error way;
Gesture nor look nor word of mine
   The secret should betray.

The soldier from the cross's foot
   Turned. I stood waiting there:
That grim, expectant tree, for fruit
   My dying form must bear.

Up rose the steaming mists of doubt,
   And chilled both heart and brain;
They shut the world of vision out,
   And fear saw only pain.

"Ah me, my hands! the hammer's blow!
   The nails that rend and pierce!
The shock may stun, but, slow and slow,
   The torture will grow fierce.

"Alas, the awful fight with death!
   The hours to hang and die!
The thirsting gasp for common breath!
   The weakness that would cry!"

My soul returned: "A faintness soon
   Will shroud thee in its fold;
The hours will bring the fearful noon;
   'Twill pass—and thou art cold.

"'Tis His to care that thou endure,
   To curb or loose the pain;
With bleeding hands hang on thy cure—
   It shall not be in vain."

But, ah, the will, which thus could quail,
  Might yield—oh, horror drear!
Then, more than love, the fear to fail
  Kept down the other fear.

I stood, nor moved. But inward strife
  The bonds of slumber broke:
Oh! had I fled, and lost the life
  Of which the Master spoke.

Edward Henry Bickersteth.

1825.

EDWARD HENRY BICKERSTETH, D.D., Bishop of Exeter, was the son of the Rev. Edward Bickersteth, sometime Secretary of the Church Missionary Society, and Rector of Watton, Herts, whose "Christian Psalmody," published in 1833, had great influence upon the progress of Christian song. Edward Henry Bickersteth was born at Islington in the month of January 1825, and was educated at Trinity College, Cambridge, where he graduated B A. with honours 1847, M.A. 1850 Taking Holy Orders, he became successively Curate of Banningham, Norfolk, and Christ Church, Tunbridge Wells; Rector of Hinton-Martell, 1852; Vicar of Christ Church, Hampstead, 1855; Dean of Gloucester, and Bishop of Exeter, 1885.

Bishop Bickersteth published "Poems" (1849); "Water from the Well-Spring" (1852); "The Rock of Ages" (1858); "Commentary on the New Testament" (1864); "Yesterday, To-day, and For Ever" (1867); "The Spirit of Life" (1868); "The Two Brothers and other Poems" (1871); "The Master's Home Call" (1872); "The Reef and other Parables" (1873); "The Shadowed House, and the Light Beyond" (1874); "Songs of the House of Pilgrimage" (undated); and "From Year to Year" (1883). He also edited several hymnals, the most important of which was "The Hymnal Companion to the Book of Common Prayer" (1870).

Of his original poems Bishop Bickersteth's "Yesterday, To-day, and For Ever" is the principal, though his choicest verses will be found in the volume "From Year to Year." The former work is a blank-verse poem of twelve books, describing the death of a Christian and his visions and experiences in the other world. The poem contains many fine descriptions, and has been very popular, more than fifteen editions having been called for. Of his shorter poems some have been widely used as hymns. Julian says: "His thoughts are usually with the individual, and not with the mass: with the single soul and his God, and not with the vast multitude bowed in adoration before the Almighty. Hence, although many of his hymns are eminently suited to congregational purposes, and have attained to a wide popularity, yet his finest productions are those best suited for private use." The following selections from the volume "From Year to Year" will amply bear out this criticism, and justify their place in this volume.

ALFRED H. MILES

FROM YEAR TO YEAR.
1883.
EDWARD HENRY BICKERSTETH.

I.—COME YE YOURSELVES APART.

COME ye yourselves apart and rest awhile,
   Weary, I know it, of the press and throng,
Wipe from your brow the sweat and dust of toil,
   And in My quiet strength again be strong

Come ye aside from all the world holds dear
   For converse which the world has never known,
Alone with Me and with My Father here,
   With Me and with My Father not alone.

Come, tell Me all that ye have said and done,
   Your victories and failures, hopes and fears.
I know how hardly souls are wooed and won:
   My choicest wreaths are always wet with tears.

Come ye, and rest: the journey is too great,
   And ye will faint beside the way and sink:
The bread of life is here for you to eat,
   And here for you the wine of love to drink.

Then, fresh from converse with your Lord, return
   And work till daylight softens into even:
The brief hours are not lost in which ye learn
   More of your Master and His rest in heaven.

II.—THE MEADOW GRASS.

THE meadow grass is green and blithe,
   With gold and purple hues besprent;
It recks not of to-morrow's scythe,
   Rich in its lavish bloom and scent;
The sun is warm, the evening gay,
Who speaks of aught but life to-day?

The jocund world is borne along
   By troops of rosy-figur'd hours,
Its path of merriment and song
   Still garlanded with new-cut flowers;
And all her children seem to say,
To-morrow will be as to-day.

But standing from the throng apart
   There are who drink of sorrow's springs,
And answer to their bleeding heart
   That heart's persistent questionings,
" Is there no harvest far away
Of seed we sow in tears to-day?"

Listen, the world's melodious chime
   Grows faint and fainter year by year,
And things to come are shadowing time,
   And soon the Master will be here:
God grant us crown'd by Him to say,
Eternity is ours to-day.

III.—MY WORK IS DONE.

"MY work is done, I lay me down to die,
   Weary and travel-worn I long for rest,
Speak but the word, dear Master, and I fly,
   A dove let loose, to nestle in Thy breast."
     "Not yet, My child, a little longer wait,
     I need thy prayerful watch at glory's gate!"

"But, Lord, I have no strength to watch and pray;
   My spirit is benumb'd, and dim my sight;
And I shall grieve Thy watchful love, as they
   Who in the garden slept that Paschal night."
     "My child, I need thy weakness hour by hour
     To prove in Me, thy strengthlessness is power."

"Not for myself alone I urge the suit;
  But loved ones lose for me life's priceless bloom,
And tender, patient, uncomplaining, mute,
  Wear out their joyance in my darken'd room."
    "Enough, My child, I need their love to thee:
    Around thy couch they minister to Me."

"It is enough, dear Master; yea, Amen,
  I will not breathe one murmur of reply,
Only fulfil Thy work in me, and then
  Call me and bid me answer,—'Here am I.'"
    "My child, the sign I waited for is given,
    Thy work is done, I need thee now in heaven.

IV.—"TILL HE COME."

"TILL He come," Oh, let the words
  Linger on the trembling chords;
Let the little while between
In their golden light be seen;
Let us think how heaven and home
Lie beyond that "Till He come."

When the weary ones we love
Enter on their rest above,
Seems the earth so poor and vast,
All our life-joy overcast?
Hush, be every murmur dumb:
It is only, "Till He come."

Clouds and conflicts round us press;
Would we have one sorrow less?
All the sharpness of the cross,
All that tells the world is loss,
Death, and darkness, and the tomb,
Only whisper, "Till He come."

    See the fast of love is spread,
    Drink the wine, and eat the bread:
    Sweet memorials,—till the Lord
    Call us round His heavenly board;
    Some from earth, from glory some,
    Severed only "Till He come."

V.—PEACE, PERFECT PEACE.

PEACE, perfect peace, in this dark world of sin?
    The blood of Jesus whispers peace within.

Peace, perfect peace, by thronging duties press'd?
To do the will of Jesus, this is rest.

Peace, perfect peace, with sorrows surging round?
On Jesus' bosom naught but calm is found.

Peace, perfect peace, with loved ones far away?
In Jesus' keeping we are safe and they.

Peace, perfect peace, our future all unknown?
Jesus we know, and He is on the throne.

Peace, perfect peace, death shadowing us and ours?
Jesus has vanquished death and all its powers.

It is enough: earth's struggles soon shall cease,
And Jesus call us to heaven's perfect peace.

Henry Septimus Sutton.

1825—1901.

HENRY SEPTIMUS SUTTON was born at Nottingham in 1825. His father, Richard Sutton, was a bookseller and newspaper proprietor in that town. Thus the boy was surrounded from his earliest days with books, and needed no other library than his father's shop—where he spent most of his leisure, and where he browsed on the ample fare—often totally oblivious of the flight of time. Arrived at the suitable age, he was articled to a surgeon, and for some years studied medicine; but the passion for literature at length drew him away from the study of the human body and the remedies for its ailments; he gave up all idea of the Physician's calling, and turned to the Press as his life employment.

In 1847 he published a little book called "The Evangel of Love." This was in prose. In the following year he issued his first poetical work—a tiny volume, which he dedicated to his father. One of his friends has said of this book: "It was not sent forth to the multitude. It was only a still, small voice intended for the ears of poets, and dreamers, and religious mystics. It fulfilled its mission. The world let it pass; but chosen souls, slowly and only here and there, caught it up, silently received its message, and placed it amongst their choicest treasures."

In 1854 Mr. Sutton put forth a volume of philosophical theology called "Quinquenergia," but in this was included a series of poems of rare quality called "Rose's Diary," on which more than on any others his fame as a poet will rest.

It was the publication of "The Evangel of Love" which probably determined both his life work and the place where it should be accomplished. This book fell under the eye of Ralph Waldo Emerson, and won from him high commendation, and led to a lifelong friendship. Emerson brought Mr. Sutton's work under the notice of Alexander Ireland of Manchester, who induced him to accept employment upon one of the leading newspapers of that city, where he continued to reside, and where he followed the career of a journalist.

In 1886 he was persuaded to allow the two series of poems already named to be republished together, with a few written since. Emerson declared that this little volume contained pieces worthy of the genius of George Herbert. Its author has indeed been classed with the saintly poet of Bemerton and Henry Vaughan. There seems to me a certain truth in such classification; he *is* like those well-known poets, but I am not sure whether the points of difference are not more and greater than the points of likeness. Mr. Sutton is far more of the mystic, and his mysticism is of a deeper kind than these earlier poets. Bronson Alcott said of Mr. Sutton's theological book already referred to: "This is truly an original and mystic book, the work of a profound religious genius, combining the remarkable sense of William Law with the subtlety of Behmen and the piety of Pascal. The author is one of the few Englishmen I would go far to meet." *There* seems to me the clue to Mr. Sutton's poetry. It has more that is akin to the great mystics than to poets of the quaint type of Herbert and Vaughan. I shall, I fear, astonish, and, perhaps, shock some readers when I say that Mr. Sutton had a deeper religious nature than either Herbert or Vaughan. No one doubts Herbert's goodness; but too often his quaintness is mistaken for depth. Some of our editors of sacred anthologies seem willing to sacrifice nearly everything on the altar of quaintness—that is a quality not to be despised, but it is surely second to far-reaching vision of truth and passionate love to the Invisible God. For my part, I find far more points of likeness in Mr. Sutton's poems to certain of Miss Rossetti's; but even here there is a difference, accounted for by the fact that though both of them were mystics they were reared in vastly different schools of theological belief. But in spite of this I think I could put side by side poems from these two poets which at heart strike the selfsame note—another illustration of how the really mystic mind overleaps, through its clear vision of God, all sundering doctrines concerning His Nature.

It may here be added, as a proof of this, that Miss Rossetti greatly admired Mr. Sutton's poems (and, indeed, introduced them to Professor Palgrave, who included some of them in his "Treasury of Sacred Song"), whilst another deeply religious man, and one of the profoundest thinkers of our age, Dr. James Martineau, though belonging to a school of theological thought widely separated both from Miss Rossetti and Mr. Sutton, said of "Rose's Diary": "It has long been to me as the presence of a tender and faithful friend. Nay, so sacred is my feeling towards it, that on learning of the promise of a new volume, I almost dreaded to see it, lest it should change by a single shade the complexion of a love so clear and warm, and am half relieved to find that the book now issued derives its main character from poems which have so long missed the permanent form and wide influence due to their rare beauty."

But whilst Mr. Sutton was probably most at home in deeply religious verse, he also showed capacity of a high kind for descriptive verse. The little poem "The Daisy" is as accurate and quaintly picturesque as anything of the kind we possess. In "A Preacher's Soliloquy and Sermon" he is far nearer Herbert than in the poems of "Rose's Diary", whilst the very brief poem "Sorrow" could scarcely be surpassed for conciseness and suggestiveness. "Ralph Waldo Emerson" is a noble tribute to a noble character. Some of the verses are not only finely descriptive of the man, but wrought with the strength of a master-hand. This is especially so in the second and seventh stanzas.

This is enough to introduce a little-known poet to the many readers of this series. I shall be surprised if the extracts given do not send many to the little volume from which they have been taken.

Henry Septimus Sutton died early in May, 1901.

W. GARRETT HORDER.

ROSE'S DIARY.
1850.
HENRY SEPTIMUS SUTTON.

VI.
JUNE.

The day with light its genial self engirds;
The trees are glad with fluty voices dear:—
"Thou art my God!"—When I say o'er those words,
I see a light beyond the day, and hear
Voices far richer than the songs of birds.

Mine eyes with happy tears then overswim;
The thoughts I have are sweetest that can be;
My mind's a cup with love above the brim;
Fine incense circles round whate'er I see;
In every sound I hear a holy hymn.

Thou art my God! Thou, Father, Thou my Friend;
My Saviour Thou, the eternal Lord of all!
O thought which doth all other thought transcend,
Beneath whose stress well may I prostrate fall
In love and wonder which should know no end!

VIII.
SEPTEMBER.

Put not on me, O Lord! this work divine,
For I am too unworthy, and Thy speech
Would be defrauded through such lips as mine.
I have not learn'd Thee yet, and shall I teach?
O choose some other instrument of Thine!

The great, the royal ones, the noble saints,
These all are Thine, and they will speak for Thee.
No one who undertakes Thy words but faints;
Yet, if that man is saintly and sin-free,
Through him Thou wilt, O Lord! self-utter'd be.

But how shall I say anything, a child,
Not fit for such high work,—oh how shall I
Say what in speaking must not be defiled?
And yet, and yet, if I refuse to try,
The light that burns for mine own life will die.

X.
NOVEMBER.

What mean these slow returns of love; these days
Of wither'd prayer; of dead unflowering praise?
These hands of twilight laid on me to keep
Dusk veils on holy vision? This most deep,
Most eyelid-heavy, lamentable sleep?

Lo, time is precious as it was before;
As sinful, sin; my goal as unattain'd;
And yet I drowse, and dream, and am not pain'd
At God far off as ever heretofore,—
At sin as flagrant as of old, or more.

Dear Lord, what can I do? I come to Thee:
I have none other helper. Thou art free
To save me, or to kill. But I appeal
To Thine own love which will not elsewise deal
Than prove Thyself my help, Thy will my weal.

Wake, wake me, God of love! and let Thy fire
Loosen these icicles and make them drop
And run into warm tears; for I aspire
To hold Thee faster, dearer, warmer, nigher,
And love and serve Thee henceforth without stop.

XI.
DECEMBER.

O Father! I have sinn'd against Thee,—done
The thing I thought I never more should do.
My days were set before me, light all through,
But I have made them dark, it is too true,
And drawn dense clouds between me and my Sun.

Forgive me not, for grievous is my sin;
Yea, very deep and dark. Alas! I see
Such blackness in it, that I may not be
Forgiven of myself,—how then of Thee?—
Vile, vile without; black, utter black within.

If my shut eyes should dare their lids to part,
I know how they must quail beneath the blaze
Of Thy love's greatness. No: I dare not raise
One prayer to look aloft, lest I should gaze
On such forgiveness as would break my heart.

XVI.
NOVEMBER.

Each day a page is of my being's book,
And what I do is what I write therein;
And often do I make sad blots of sin;
And seldom proves the writing quite akin
To what my heart beforehand undertook.

Daily I turn a fresh leaf, and renew
My hope of now at last a nobler page;
But presently in something I engage
That looks but poorly on a calm review,
And leaves my future a mean heritage.

So leaf on leaf, once clean, is turn'd and gone,
And the dark spots show through, and I grow sad,
And blush, and frown, and sigh. And, if I had
A million pages yet to write upon,
Perhaps the millionth would be just as bad.

What shall I do? Some new leaves, even yet,
May be before me. And perhaps I may
Write, even yet, some not ignoble day.
Alas! I do not know;—I cannot say.—
What is it to feel living?—I forget.

XVIII.
February.

Late on me, weeping, did this whisper fall:—
"Dear child, there is no need to weep at all.
Why go about to grieve and to despair?
Why weep now through thy future's eyes, and bear
Vainly to-day to-morrow's load of care?

"Mine is thy welfare. Ev'n the storms fulfil,
On those who love Me, none but My decrees.
Lightning shall not strike thee against My will;
And I, thy Lord, can save thee when I please
From quaking earth and the devouring seas.

"Why be so dull, so slow to understand?
The more thou trustest Me, the more can flow
My love, and thou, a jewel in My hand,
Shalt richer be; whence thou canst never go
So softly slipping, but that I shall know.

"If thou should'st seem to slip,—if griefs and pains
And death assail,—for thee there yet remains
My love, which lets them, and which surely will
Thee reinstate where thou a place shalt fill
Inviolate, for ever steadfast still."

"Father!" (I said) "I do accept Thy word.
To perfect trust in Thee now am I stirr'd
By the dear gracious saying I have heard."
And, having said this, fell a peace so deep
Into my heart, what could I do but weep?

XXI.
MAY.

How beautiful it is to be alive!
To wake each morn as if the Maker's grace
Did us afresh from nothingness derive
That we might sing "How happy is our case!
How beautiful it is to be alive!"

To read in God's great Book, until we feel
Love for the love that gave it; then to kneel
Close unto Him Whose truth our souls will shrive,
While every moment's joy doth more reveal
How beautiful it is to be alive.

Rather to go without what might increase
Our worldly standing, than our souls deprive
Of frequent speech with God, or than to cease
To feel, through having wasted health or peace,
How beautiful it is to be alive.

Not to forget, when pain and grief draw nigh,
Into the ocean of time past to dive
For memories of God's mercies, or to try
To bear all sweetly, hoping still to cry
"How beautiful it is to be alive!"

Thus ever towards man's height of nobleness
Strive still some new progression to contrive;
Till, just as any other friend's, we press
Death's hand; and, having died, feel none the less
How beautiful it is to be alive.

XXII.
JUNE.

Prayer is the world-plant's blossom, the bright flower,
A higher purpose of the stem and leaves;—
Or call it the church-spire, whose top receives
Such lightning calm as comforts, not aggrieves,
And with it brings the fructifying shower.

Prayer is the hand that catcheth hold on peace;—
Nay, 'tis the very heart of nobleness
Whose pulses are the measure of the stress
Wherewith He doth us, we do Him, possess:
If these should fail, all our true life would cease.

Who live in prayer a friend shall never miss;
If we should slip, a timely staff and kind
Placed in our grasp by hands unseen shall find;
Sometimes upon our foreheads a soft kiss,
And arms cast round us gently from behind.

XXIII.
July.

How beautiful our lives may be, how bright
In privilege, how fruitful of delight!
For we of love have endless revenue;
And, if we grieve, 'tis not as infants do
That wake and find no mother in the night.
They put their little hands about, and weep
Because they find mere air, or but the bed
Whereon they lie; but we may rest, instead,
For ever on His bosom, Who doth keep
Our lives alike safe, when we wake, and sleep.
And lo! all round us gleam the angelic bands,
Swift messengers of Providence all-wise,
With frowning brows, perhaps, for their disguise,
But with what springs of love within the eyes,
And what strong rescue hidden in the hands!
And our lives may in glory move along,
First, holy-white, and then with goodness fair
For our dear Lord to see;—the keenest thong
Of all that whips us, welcome: and the air
Our spirits breathe, self-shaped into a song.

POEMS.

HENRY SEPTIMUS SUTTON.

I.—THE DAISY.

A GOLD and silver cup
   Upon a pillar green,
Earth holds her Daisy up
   To catch the sunshine in;—
A dial-plant, set there
   To show each radiant hour;—
A field-astronomer,
   A sun-observing flower;—

A little rounded croft
   Where wingèd kine may graze;—
A golden meadow soft,
   Quadrille-ground for young fays;—
A fenced-in yellow plot
   With pales milk-white and clean,
Each tipt with crimson spot
   And set in ground of green.

The children with delight
   To meet the Daisy run;
They love to see how bright
   She shines upon the sun.
Like lowly white-crown'd queen
   She graciously doth bend,
And stands with quiet mien
   The little children's friend.

Sometimes the Daisy's seen,
   A simple rustic maid,
In comely gown of green,
   And pure white frill array'd,
Dreaming, like one in mood
   Of hope by fancy spun,
Awaiting to be wooed,
   And willing to be won.

The dandy Butterfly,
   All exquisitely dress'd,
Before the Daisy's eye
   Displays his velvet vest;
In vain is he array'd
   In all that gaudy show;
What need hath rustic maid
   Of such a foppish beau?

The vagrant Bee but sings
   For what he gets thereby,
Nor comes, excepts he brings
   His pocket on his thigh;
Then let him start aside
   And woo some wealthier flower
The Daisy's not his bride,
   She hath no honey-dower.

The Gnat, old back-bent fellow,
   In frugal frieze-coat drest,
Seeks on her carpet yellow
   His tottering limbs to rest;
He woos her with eyes dim,
   Voice thin, and aspect sage;—
What careth she for him?
   What mate is youth for age?

Upon her head she lifts,
    Where they can best be seen,
Her little golden gifts
    In white-fringed basket green
Still ready to be met
    In every passing hour,
The little children's pet,
    Their ever-faithful flower.

II—"THOUGH HE SLAY ME, YET WILL I TRUST IN HIM."

WHAT if I perish, after all,
    And lose this life, Thy gracious boon?
Let me not fear that I shall fall
    And die too soon.

I cannot fall till Thou dost let,
Nor die, except at Thy command.
Low let me lie, my Father, yet
    Beneath Thy hand.

'Tis good to think, though I decrease
Thou dost not, Lord, decrease with me;
What matters it that I must cease,
    Since Thou must be?

The life thou willedst me I use
To thank Thee for that gracious will;—
If I must lose it, I would choose
    To thank Thee still.

No more might I lift prayerful eyes,
Or sway a tongue to grateful tones;
Yet should a noise of praise still rise
    Even from my bones.

III—FOR THE DESOLATE.

WHEN, though no loving accents fall
   In snows upon thy parched brow,
Yet others unto others call
   To give the kiss or breathe the vow;
Then let thy love for them beguile
   The self-love that would in thee rise,
And bid a softly-welling smile
   Warm once again thy frozen eyes.

When o'er thy brain the passion flows
   And rolls into thine eyes its tears,
Because thy soul no solace knows
   Of answering hopes and answering fears.
Then dash thy tears down as they swell,
   And give thy grief a strong control,
And with a stern derision quell
   The rising anguish of thy soul.

When thy lone dreams sweet visions see
   And loving looks upon thee shine,
And loving lips speak joys to thee
   That never, never may be thine;
Then press thy hand hard on thy side,
   And force down all the swelling pain;
Trust me, the wound, however wide,
   Shall close at last, and heal again.

Think not of what is from thee kept;
   Think, rather, what thou hast received:
Thine eyes have smiled, if they have wept;
   Thy heart has danced, if it has grieved.
Rich comforts yet shall be thine own,
   Yea, God Himself shall wipe thine eyes;
And still His love alike is shown
   In what He gives, and what denies.

IV.—A PREACHER'S SOLILOQUY AND SERMON.

The Soliloquy.

WHAT wealth to earth our God hath given!
   What growing increment for heaven!
Men, women, youth, and children small,
I thank the good God for you all!

Not always was it mine to give
Such high regard to all who live;
Time was, I know, when I could go
   Along the streets and scarcely see
The presences my God did show
   So lavishly to me.
Around my steps,—before, behind,—
   They His creative power declared;
I only heeded them, to find
   The easiest path, as on I fared.
And even the innocent little ones,
Of value high o'er stars and suns,—
Evangelists, by Heaven's decree,
Commission'd truths to teach to me
   That elsewise I had never known,—
They seem'd young foreigners to be,
   They never seem'd mine own.
How could I be so dull and blind?
How dared I slight God's humankind?

I know ye nothing care for me;—
   Each to each deep mysteries,
We cannot guess what we may be
   Except by what a glance can seize.

Perchance we never met before,
   Meet now the first and final time,
Yet are ye mine, over and o'er,
   That, haply, I may help you climb
To Jesus, up the mount divine.
Oh might such high success be mine!
Fain would I couch your vision dim;
Fain would I lead you up to Him!

Nay, nay, I cannot yield up one—
   No little child, no youth, no man;
I cannot say, Depart from me;
   I cannot say, Begone, begone,
     I have no part in thee.
No part? But how? Do I not love you?
   Is not this title still more strong
Than if I'd bought you all with gold?—
Love strenuous flies, a spirit above you;
   Try to escape, it will outfly you,
   It will embrace, ay, and defy you
To break away its gentle hold.
Because God's love is swift and strong,
Therefore ye all to me belong.

Why do I dare love all mankind?
Tis not because each face, each form
   Is comely, for it is not so;
Nor is it that each soul is warm
   With any Godlike glow.
Yet there's no one to whom's not given
Some little lineament of heaven,
Some partial symbol, at the least, in sign
Of what should be, if it is not, within,
Reminding of the death of sin
   And life of the Divine.

There was a time, full well I know,
When I had not yet seen you so;
   Time was, when few seem'd fair;
But now, as through the streets I go,
There seems no face so shapeless, so
     Forlorn, but that there's something there
     That, like the heavens, doth declare
     The glory of the great All-fair;
And so mine own each one I call;
And so I dare to love you all.

Glory to God, who hath assign'd
To me this mixture with mankind!
Glory to God, that I am born
   Into a world, whose palace-gates
So many royal ones adorn!
   Heaven's possible novitiates,
With self-subduing freedom free,
Princely ye are, each one, to me,
   Each of secret kingly blood,
Though not inheritors as yet
   Of all your own right royal things,
For it were folly to forget
     That they alone are queens and kings
       Who are the truly good.
Yet are ye angels in disguise,
   Angels who have not found your wings;
  see more in ye than ye are
   As yet, while earth so closely clings;
As through a cloud that hides the skies
   Undoubting science hails a star
Not to be seen by other eyes,
   Yet surely among things that are,

So the dense veil of your deformities
    Love gives me power away to pull.
Alas! why will ye not from sin arise,
    And be Christ's beautiful?

The Sermon.

Ho! every one that thirsts, draw nigh, draw nigh!
The drink I offer, Christ's own words supply.
Ho! every one that thirsts not, thirst, I cry;
Why will ye still neglect to drink,—and die?
See, here are living wells; why will ye scorn?
Ye unborn, why refuse ye to be born?
I call you to repent, oh hear my call!
Doth my voice reach you, through the stiff cere-clothes
That do enshroud and wrap you up withal?
Doth my shout come, a whisper in your ears,
As sounds might, travell'd from far distant spheres,
Into the ravell'd windings of a cave?
O then turn down those cerements of the grave
    From round about your ears;
Let my voice be as thunder, let it roll
    Into each wakening soul;
Come forth, O Lazarus! when I say so
Deem me a way where through Christ's mandates flow,
And let each buried one attend, and know
The stone is roll'd away; Christ calls to him below.
Come forth, O Lazarus! when I say so,
Let where it lists His Holy Spirit blow,
Until each Lazarus comes forth, and know
Christ only waits to say—Loose him, and let him go!
His voice delights to set all prisoners free;
His blood, His truth, makes all sin white as wool;
Oh hear! Oh wash you, cleanse you, and so be
    Christ's own, Christ's beautiful!

V.—SORROW.

THE flowers live by the tears that fall
   From the sad face of the skies,
And life would have no joys at all
   Were there no watery eyes.

Love thou thy sorrow: grief shall bring
   Its own excuse in after years:—
The rainbow!—see how fair a thing
   God hath built up from tears.

VI.—LOVE'S FREEMASONRY.

Written, as I think,
In some secret ink;
Yet the meaning, found,
Will prove good and sound.

"AH, if to know the sign she fail,"
   He said, "Woe, Woe!" and he grew pale.
The sign was made; but not a trace
Of knowing was upon her face.

As if death's mouth, the grave, had spoke,
His blood its law of flowing broke,
And he felt twist in every vein,
Snake-like, a nerve of swollen pain.

There wrestled he, standing apart
To force it back unto the heart,
If haply to a running flood
It might dissolve, of living blood.

O life in death and death in life!
O torturing, damn'd, yet conquering strife
For yet, years afterwards, made whole,
He held the sceptre of his soul.

And lo! with faces all elate
With such a joy, so deep, so great,
That its most dear, most sweet, and chief
Resemblance was to glorious grief,

They stood in voiceless transport round,
Naught owing to articulate sound;
But a soft music forth doth press
And swells, and falls, from all their dress:

For, as their nature stands above
The power of tongue to tell their love,
God makes from forth their garments' hem
Music go out and speak for them.

These looked, and loved him with their eyes
Filled with pass-words from Paradise;
"And evermore," he sang, "the sign
Given, swift-answered, proves them mine!"

"Ah, Lord," he said, "I did but seek
To bless with love a maiden meek;
A maiden given a royal, free,
Most god-like gift,—but not to me.

"I and my staff, wherein amassed
Was all my wealth, this Jordan passed;
'Tis Thou who mak'st me here to stand
Augmented to a twofold band."

VII.—RALPH WALDO EMERSON.
1849.

AS robe majestic down a statue flows,
So noble thought down Emerson. Withal,
Such sweetness went, you even might suppose,
Spite of that bearing dignified and tall,
A woman's gentle heart beat under all;

For while no prayers his constancy could shake,
No storm avail his spirit's barque to make
From anchor of his settled purpose break,
His every action could not but confess
The tempering of ingrained tenderness.

Yet, while our young souls loved him, 'twas agreed
Amongst us that this man, though ever apt
For kind deed, and in self so little wrapped,
Almost too high for love was; had indeed
Of no man's love or admiration need.

And yet he, loving, liked to be beloved;
And if at times it might appear he moved
Austerely calm and cold, that was because
Grand hearts may not transcend their nature's laws
Either to beat more quickly or to pause.

There was the genial waiting on his friend
That friendship loves to feel. Absence would send
As much pain, as much pleasure presence lend
To him as one could wish; but the control
Was over all of a self-mastered soul.

Therefore in our brief intercourse was mixed,
With strangeness, intimacy; and a feud
There came our awe and confidence betwixt;
And moods of his there were that must be viewed
Like gated ways where none might dare intrude.

One foolish man, by his sweet mien betrayed,
An undue freedom took. Swift silence played
Like lambent lightning round, and on us fell
Awe of the great majestic soul that well
Knew, still or speaking. how to be obeyed.

So have I seen in festive season go
A summer barque, laugh-lightened, 'neath the flow
Of waving flags, the while, in their sweet pride,
On deck the youths and maidens gaily glide
With motions by sweet music justified.

Sudden, o'er sunken rock, harsh grates the keel;
From every mouth the merry laughter dies;
The founts of music freeze; astonished eyes
Gaze wide on eyes astonished; and all feel
The fears proud hearts indignantly conceal.

But, no new shock confirming what each dreads,
Again the music melts and flows; its threads
The dance reweaves; over each mouth there spreads
The young vermilion laughter; and once more
The fluttering flags wave wind-filled as before.

VIII.—MAN.

MAN doth usurp all space,
    Stares thee in rock, bush, river, in the face.
Never yet thine eyes beheld a tree;
'Tis no sea thou seest in the sea,
'Tis but a disguisèd humanity.
To avoid thy fellow, vain thy plan;
All that interests a man is man.

John Ellerton.

1826—1893.

JOHN ELLERTON was born in London on the 16th of December, 1826, and was educated at Trinity College, Cambridge. Taking Holy Orders, he became Curate of Eastbourne, and successively Vicar of Crewe Green 1860, Rector of Hinstock 1872, of Barnes 1876, and of White Roding 1886. He published "Hymns for Schools and Bible Classes" 1859, and acted as co-editor with Bishop How in the production of "Church Hymns," published by the Society for Promoting Christian Knowledge in 1871, ten years later publishing his "Notes and Illustrations of Church Hymns" (1881). In 1888 he collected his scattered poems, and published them in a small volume, entitled "Hymns, Original and Translated," from which volume the following selections are taken. His principal prose works are "The Holiest Manhood" (1882) and "Our Infirmities" (1883). He died on the 15th of June, 1893.

It is as a hymn-writer and translator that he takes his place in this volume; for as a writer of poetic hymns he stands in the front rank. His original hymns number about fifty, and his translations about ten; and, according to Julian, they are all of them in general use. The best of these are characterised by elevation of tone, dignity of movement, and devoutness of spirit. The solemn side of nature and life seems to have impressed him most; and though he could be bright and joyous at times, as in his translation "Sing Alleluia forth in duteous praise," the hush of the evening hour seems to have inspired him more frequently than the gush of morning song. Mr. Julian, in his "Dictionary of Hymnology," already referred to, says, "His sympathy with nature, especially in her sadder moods, is great; he loves the fading light and the peace of eve, and lingers in the shadows. Unlike many writers who set forth their illustrations in detail, and then tie to them the moral which they wish to teach, he weaves his moral into his metaphor, and pleases the imagination and refreshes the spirit together." "Hymns, Original and Translated" is a volume no hymn-lover should be without.

ALFRED H. MILES.

ORIGINAL HYMNS

JOHN ELLERTON.

I.—GOD OF THE LIVING.

GOD of the living, in Whose eyes
    Unveiled Thy whole creation lies;
All souls are Thine; we must not say,
That those are dead who pass away;
From this our world of flesh set free,
We know them living unto Thee.

Released from earthly toil and strife,
With Thee is hidden still their life;
Thine are their thoughts, their works, their powers,
All Thine, and yet most truly ours;
For well we know, where'er they be,
Our dead are living unto Thee.

Not spilt like water on the ground,
Not wrapped in dreamless sleep profound,
Not wandering in unknown despair
Beyond Thy voice, Thine arm, Thy care;
Not left to lie like fallen tree;
Not dead, but living unto Thee.

Thy word is true, Thy will is just;
To Thee we leave them, Lord, in trust;
And bless Thee for the love which gave
Thy Son to fill a human grave,
That none might fear that world to see
Where all are living unto Thee.

O Breather into man of breath,
O Holder of the keys of death,
O Quickener of the life within,
Save us from death, the death of sin
That body, soul, and spirit, be
For ever living unto Thee.

II.—THRONED UPON THE AWFUL TREE

THRONED upon the awful Tree,
King of grief, I watch with Thee
Darkness veils Thine anguished face,
None its lines of woe can trace,
None can tell what pangs unknown
Hold Thee silent and alone.

Silent through those three dread hours
Wrestling with the evil powers;
Left alone with human sin,
Gloom around Thee and within,
Till the appointed time is nigh,
Till the Lamb of God may die.

Hark that cry that peals aloud
Upward through the whelming cloud
Thou, the Father's only Son,
Thou, His own Anointed One,
Thou dost ask Him—can it be?
Why hast Thou forsaken Me?

Lord, should fear and anguish roll
Darkly o'er my sinful soul,
Thou, who once wast thus bereft
That Thine own might ne'er be left—
Teach me by that bitter cry
In the gloom to know Thee nigh.

III.—THE DAY THOU GAVEST, LORD IS ENDED.

THE day Thou gavest, Lord, is ended;
   The darkness falls at Thy behest;
To Thee our morning hymns ascended,
   Thy praise shall sanctify our rest.

We thank Thee that Thy Church unsleeping,
   While earth rolls onward into light,
Through all the world her watch is keeping,
   And rests not now by day or night.

As o'er each continent and island
   The Dawn leads on another day,
The voice of prayer is never silent,
   Nor dies the strain of praise away.

The sun that bids us rest is waking
   Our brethren 'neath the Western sky,
And hour by hour fresh lips are making
   Thy wondrous doings heard on high.

So be it, Lord; Thy throne shall never,
   Like earth's proud empires, pass away;
Thy kingdom stands, and grows for ever,
   Till all Thy creatures own Thy sway.

IV.—SAVIOUR, AGAIN TO THY DEAR NAME.

(ORIGINAL VERSION.)

SAVIOUR, again to Thy dear name we raise
   With one accord our parting hymn of praise:
We stand to bless Thee ere our worship cease;
Then lowly kneeling wait Thy word of peace.

Grant us Thy peace, Lord, through the coming night,
Turn Thou for us its darkness into light;
From harm and danger keep Thy children free,
For dark and light are both alike to Thee.

Grant us Thy peace upon our homeward way;
With Thee began, with Thee shall end the day;
Guard Thou the lips from sin, the hearts from shame,
That in this house have called upon Thy Name.

Grant us Thy peace—the peace Thou didst bestow
On Thine Apostles in Thine hour of woe;
The peace Thou broughtest when at eventide
They saw Thy piercèd Hands, Thy wounded Side.

Grant us Thy peace throughout our earthly life,
Peace to Thy Church from error and from strife;
Peace to our land, the fruit of truth and love,
Peace in each heart, Thy Spirit from above;

Thy peace in life, the balm of every pain;
Thy peace in death, the hope to rise again;
In that dread hour speak Thou the soul's release;
And call it, Lord, to Thine eternal peace.

TRANSLATED HYMNS.

JOHN ELLERTON.

I.—SING ALLELUIA FORTH.

MOZARABIC BREVIARY.

SING Alleluia forth in duteous praise,
   Ye citizens of heaven; O sweetly raise
      An endless Alleluia.

Ye Powers who stand before the Eternal Light,
In hymning choirs re-echo to the height
      An endless Alleluia.

The Holy City shall take up your strain,
And with glad songs resounding wake again
      An endless Alleluia.

In blissful antiphons ye thus rejoice
To render to the Lord with thankful voice
      An endless Alleluia.

Ye who have gained at length your palms in bliss,
Victorious ones, your chant shall still be this,
      An endless Alleluia.

There, in one grand acclaim, for ever ring
The strains which tell the honour of your King,
      An endless Alleluia.

This is sweet rest for weary ones brought back,
This is glad food and drink which ne'er shall lack,
      An endless Alleluia.

While Thee, by whom were all things made, we praise
For ever, and tell out in sweetest lays
      An endless Alleluia.

Almighty Christ, to Thee our voices sing
Glory for evermore; to Thee we bring
      An endless Alleluia.

II.—WELCOME, HAPPY MORNING! (EASTER.)
Venantius Fortunatus, 530—609.

"Welcome, happy morning!" age to age shall say;
Hell to-day is vanquished; Heaven is won to-day
Lo! the Dead is living, God for evermore!
Him, their true Creator, all His works adore!
"Welcome, happy morning!" age to age shall say.

Earth with joy confesses, clothing her for Spring,
All good gifts returnèd with her returning King:
Bloom in every meadow, leaves on every bough,
Speak His sorrows ended, hail His triumph now.
Hell to-day is vanquished; Heaven is won to-day!

Months in due succession, days of lengthening light,
Hours and passing moments praise Thee in their flight
Brightness of the morning, sky and fields and sea,
Vanquisher of darkness, bring their praise to Thee.
"Welcome, happy morning!" age to age shall say.

Maker and Redeemer, Life and Health of all,
Thou from Heaven beholding human nature's fall,
Of the Father's Godhead true and only Son,
Manhood to deliver, manhood didst put on.
Hell to-day is vanquished; Heaven is won to-day!

Thou of Life the Author, death didst undergo,
Trod the path of darkness, saving strength to show;
Come, then, True and Faithful, now fulfil Thy word;
'Tis Thine own Third Morning! rise, O buried Lord!
"Welcome, happy morning!" age to age shall say.

Loose the souls long prisoned, bound with Satan's chain
All that is now fallen raise to life again;
Show Thy face in brightness, bid the nations see;
Bring again our daylight: day returns with Thee!
Hell to-day is vanquished; Heaven is won to-day!

Richard Wilton.

1827—1903.

RICHARD WILTON, son of the late Mr. Matthew Wilton, was born at Doncaster on Christmas Day, 1827. He was educated at the Doncaster Grammar School, and at St. Catharine's College, Cambridge, of which he was a Scholar and Prizeman in Classics and Divinity, and took his degree of B.A. in 1851, and M.A. in 1861. He was ordained Deacon on the 21st of December, 1851, and Priest in December 1852, both by Dr. Hampden, Bishop of Hereford.

Mr. Wilton became Curate of Broseley in Shropshire on his ordination in 1851, under the Hon. and Rev. Orlando W. W. Forester, to whose son, afterwards Lord Forester, he was tutor. In 1853 he removed to York, as Curate of St. John's in that city. In the following year he was appointed by Dr. Musgrave, Archbishop of York, the first Incumbent of St. Thomas's, York, which he retained until 1857, when he was presented to the Vicarage of Kirkby Wharfe. In 1860 Lord Londesborough appointed him his domestic chaplain, and in 1866 gave him the living of the Rectory of Londesborough, East Yorkshire. In 1890 he was made Canon of Givendale in York Minster.

Mr. Wilton's first volume of poems, "Wood Notes and Church Bells," was published in 1873, but he had previously been a contributor in prose and verse to various periodicals, his first sonnet appearing in *Good Words* in 1864. "Lyrics, Sylvan and Sacred" was issued in 1878, "Sungleams: Rondeaux and Sonnets" in 1881, and "Benedicite and other Poems" in 1889. The late Mr. Ashcroft Noble says: "There are in this [last] volume a rich yet restrained admiration, a fine feeling for the fitting relations of substance and form, and an aptitude of felicitous expression. Mr. Wilton's verse is always achieving a certain freshness altogether different from the spurious originality of strain and spasm. The title poem is a series of rondels, one being allotted to each verse in the Church's great hymn of praise; and the solemn symmetries of the lofty chant are admirably and winningly rendered in the sequence of ordered measures. Mr. Wilton's sonnets are not only excellent, but singularly equal in their excellence. Mr. Wilton's deftness in the use of the ballade as a vehicle for the treatment of familiar domestic themes is manifested in the charming little poem 'My Grandchildren at Church'" (p. 187).

Mr. Wilton assisted Dr. Grosart in translating into English verse the sacred Latin poems of George Herbert and Richard Crashaw for the editions of those old poets in the "Fuller Worthies Library." In 1888 he edited the poems of his friend George Morine.

Canon Wilton married, in 1855, the eldest daughter of the late Robert Storrs, Esq., of Doncaster, and two of his sons took Holy Orders. He died on the 10th of August, 1903.

ALFRED H. MILES.

SELECTED SONNETS.

RICHARD WILTON.

I.—AN INCIDENT.

NOTE.—The east window of Kirkby Wharfe Church is filled with stained glass by Capronnier of Brussels, the subject being the Crucifixion.

AT the Lord's Table waiting, robed and stoled,
   Till all had knelt around, I saw a sign!
   In the full chalice sudden splendours shine,
Azure and crimson, emerald and gold.
I stooped to see the wonder, when, behold!
   Within the cup a Countenance Divine
   Looked upwards at me through the trembling wine,
Suffused with tenderest love and grief untold.
The comfort of that Sacramental token
   From Memory's page Time never can erase;
The glass of that rich window may be broken,
   But not the mirrored image of His grace,
Through which my dying Lord to me has spoken,
   At His own Holy Table, face to face!

II.—THE SPARROW.

A SPARROW lighted chirping on a spray
   Close to my window, as I knelt in prayer,
   Bowed by a heavy load of anxious care.
The morn was bitter, but the bird was gay,
And seemed by cheery look and chirp to say,—
   What though the snow conceals my wonted fare,
   Nor have I barn or storehouse anywhere,
Yet I trust Heaven e'en on a winter's day.
That little bird came like a wingèd text,
   Fluttering from out God's Word to soothe my breast
What though my life with wintry cares be vext,
   On a kind Father's watchful love I rest;
He meets this moment's need, I leave the next,
   And, always trusting, shall be always blest!

III.—THE TIDES.

UP the long slope of this low sandy shore
   Are rolled the tidal waters day by day;
   Traces of wandering feet are washed away,
Relics of busy hands are seen no more.
The soiled and trampled surface is smooth'd o'er
   By punctual waves that high behests obey;
   Once and again the tides assert their sway,
And o'er the sands their cleansing waters pour.
Even so, Lord, daily, hourly, o'er my soul
   Sin-stained and care-worn, let Thy heavenly Grace—
A blest, atoning flood—divinely roll,
   And all the footsteps of the world efface,
That like the wave-washed sand this soul of mine,
Spotless and fair, smooth and serene, may shine!

IV.—THE WELL-HEAD.

I TRACED a little brook to its well-head,
   Where, amid quivering weeds, its waters leap
   From the earth, and hurrying into shadow, creep
Unseen but vocal in their deep-worn bed.
Hawthorns and hazels interlacing wed
   With roses sweet, and overhang the steep
   Moss'd banks, while through the leaves stray sunbeams pe
And on the whispering stream faint glimmerings shed.
Thus let my life flow on, through green fields gliding,
   Unnoticed, not unuseful in its course,
Still fresh and fragrant, though in shadow hiding,
   Holding its destined way with quiet force,
Cheered with the music of a peace abiding,
   Drawn daily from its ever-springing source.

V.—FLAMBOROUGH LIGHTHOUSE.
(From Bridlington.)

AS on the beach, moist with an ebbing tide,
  Pensive I wandered at the close of day,
  I saw a crimson beacon, miles away,
Beam suddenly above the waters wide
Then chancing to look downwards, I espied
  Burning across the sands, a level ray,
  Which, moving as I moved, before me lay,
And the low shore with a red glory dyed
Thus, o'er the rolling ages, lifted high,
  The beacon of the Cross afar I see,
And through the misty centuries strain my eye;
  But bright reflections from that Crimson Tree
Across the sands of Time stretch sweetly nigh,
  Right to my feet, as if for none but me!

VI.—THE HAWTHORN AND THE WILD ROSE.

I LEARNT a lesson from the flowers to-day:—
  As o'er the fading hawthorn-blooms I sighed,
  Whose petals fair lay scattered far and wide,
Lo, suddenly upon a dancing spray
I saw the first wild roses clustered gay.
  What though the smile I loved, so soon had died
  From one sweet flower—there, shining at its side
The blushing Rose surpassed the snowy May.
So, if as life glides on, we miss some flowers
  Which once shed light and fragrance on our way
Yet still the kindly-compensating hours
  Weave us fresh wreaths in beautiful array;
  And long as in the paths of peace we stay,
Successive benedictions shall be ours!

RONDEAUX.

RICHARD WILTON.

.—SWEET, SOFT, AND LOW, OR THE WILLOW WARBLER.

SWEET, soft, and low, in wood and lane
  The Willow Warbler weaves its chain
  Of melody—a plaintive song
  That seems to breathe of ancient wrong
And dimly-recollected pain.

Its melting cadences retain
Your ear again and yet again,
    Through notes more clear and blithe and strong—
        Sweet, soft, and low.

Thus after Life's most happy strain
A minor music will remain,
  Recurring oft and lingering long,
  And heard the gayest scenes among;
Of lost joys hinting not in vain—
        Sweet, soft, and low.

II.—WHEN I AM GONE.

WHEN I am gone from mortal view
  The skies will wear their wonted blue;
  The clouds distil the summer rain
  On leafy wood and grassy plain;
And flowers will smile through morning dew.

The birds I loved will still be true
To their old haunts, and flutter through
  The boughs, nor alter one sweet strain
        When I am gone.

The silent moon will wax and wane
Heedless that I ne'er come again;
  Cold stars roll round in order due;
  But hearts—warm hearts—perchance a few
With loving tears some cheeks will stain
        When I am gone.

BALLADES.

RICHARD WILTON.

I.—MY GRANDCHILDREN AT CHURCH.

BRIGHT Dorothy, with eyes of blue,
   And serious Dickie, brave as fair,
Crossing to Church you oft may view
   When no one but myself is there:
   First to the belfry they repair,
And, while to the long ropes they cling,
   And make believe to call to prayer,
For angels' ears the bells they ring.

Next, seated gravely in a pew
   A pulpit homily they share,
Meet for my little flock of two,
   Pointed and plain, as they can bear:
   Then venture up the pulpit stair,
Pray at the desk or gaily sing:
   O sweet child-life, without a care—
For angels' ears the bells they ring.

Dear little ones, the early dew
   Of holy infancy they wear,
And lift to Heaven a face as true
   As flowers that breathe the morning air
   Whate'er they do, where'er they fare,
They can command an angel's wing:
   Their voices have a music rare,—
For angels' ears the bells they ring.

O parents, of your charge beware;
   Their angels stand before the King;
In work, play, sleep, and everywhere
   For angels' ears the bells they ring

II.—THE SUMMER OF SAINT LUKE.
(October 18th.)

WHEN slowly sinks the fading year,
   And early falls the shortening day,
There comes a season crisp and clear,
   And decked in beautiful array:
   The redbreast sings from the red spray
A song contented and serene;
   And smiling to its artless lay
The Summer of Saint Luke is seen!

A painter was Saint Luke, I hear,
   And I believe 'tis as they say;
Such colours gleam from tree and mere,
   Such rainbow hues around us play:
   They flash on us by wood and way,
Crimson and orange, brown and green;
   O'er hill and dale, where'er we stray,
The Summer of Saint Luke is seen!

Physician, too, devout and dear,
   So holy books our Saint portray:
And such he doth e'en now appear,
   Touching our hearts with healing ray:
   He drives depressing thoughts away,
And where dull mists and rains have been.
   Lo, brightness comes and sunbeams stay—
The Summer of Saint Luke is seen!

Friend, art thou withered, old, and grey?
   Not always shalt thou droop, I ween:
Heaven respite sends thee, if thou pray—
   The Summer of Saint Luke is seen!

LYRICS.

RICHARD WILTON.

I.—AUBURN.
A Seaside Elegy.

"Here Auburn stood which was washed away by the sea.
Map of East Yorkshire.

HERE Auburn stood
   By pleasant fields surrounded,
Where now for centuries the ocean-flood
With melancholy murmur has resounded.

   Here Auburn stood
Where now the sea-bird hovers—
Here stretched the shady lane and sheltering wood,
The twilight haunt of long-forgotten lovers.

   The village spire
Here raised its "silent finger,"
Sweet bells were heard and voice of rustic choir,
Where now the pensive chimes of ocean linger.

   Dear, white-faced homes
Stood round in happy cluster,
Warm and secure, where the rude breaker foams,
And Winter winds with angry billows bluster.

   Here, in still graves,
Reposed the dead of ages:
When lo! with rush of desecrating waves,
Through the green churchyard the loud tempest rages.

   Here Auburn stood
Till washed away by ocean,
Whose waters smile to-day in careless mood
O'er its whelmed site, and dance with merry motion.

   Here now we stand,
'Mid life's dear comforts dwelling:
Soon we shall pass—Oh! for a Saviour's hand
When round our "earthly house" Death's waves are swelli

II.—HYMN TO THE HOLY SPIRIT.

COME, Holy Dove,
    Descend on silent pinion,
Brood o'er my sinful soul with patient love,
Till all my being owns Thy mild dominion.

    Round yon sad Tree
With frequent circles hover,
That in my glorious Surety I may see
Grace to redeem and righteousness to cover.

    On wings of peace
Bring from that precious Altar
The Blood which bids the storms of conscience cease,
And blots out all the debt of the defaulter.

    Spirit of Grace,
Reveal in me my Saviour,
That I may gaze upon His mirrored Face,
Till I reflect it in my whole behaviour.

    Oh, let me hear
Thy soft, low voice controlling
My devious steps with intimations clear,
With comforts manifold my heart consoling.

    Let that sweet sound
To holy deeds allure me,
With heavenly echoes make my spirit bound,
And of my Home in Paradise assure me.

    Come, Holy Dove,
Guide me to yon bright portal,
Where I shall see the Saviour whom I love,
And enter on the joys which are immortal

BENEDICITE.
RICHARD WILTON.
SELECTED RONDELS.
I.—O ALL YE WORKS.
O all ye Works of the Lord; bless ye the Lord, praise Him and magnify Him for ever.

O ALL ye Works of God most High,
  Bless ye the Lord and praise His Name;
  Whose hand has built this goodly frame
Of emerald earth and sapphire sky;
And fashioned man to magnify
  His love, and spread abroad His fame:
O all ye Works of God most High,
  Bless ye the Lord and praise His Name.

Ye mighty suns through space that fly,
  Ye glow-worms with your tiny flame,
  From the same source of light ye came
To shine before your Maker's eye:
O all ye Works of God most High,
  Bless ye the Lord and praise His Name.

II.—YE HEAVENS.
O ye Heavens, bless ye the Lord; praise Him and magnify Him for ever.

YE Heavens, with your encircling blue,
  Prepare a temple for His praise;
  An azure dome of song upraise,
Distilling music like the dew:
Let angels warble out of view,
  And men reply with gladsome lays:
Ye Heavens, with your encircling blue,
  Prepare a temple for His praise.

Ye larks, to rosy dawn be true,
  Ascending your melodious ways;
  Ye linnets, charm the listening days,
And nightingales, the strain renew:
Ye Heavens, with your encircling blue
  Prepare a temple for His praise.

III.—LIGHTNINGS AND CLOUDS.

O ye Lightnings and Clouds, bless ye the Lord; praise Him and magnify Him for ever.

LIGHTNINGS and Clouds, in praise of Him
   Unfurl your banners in the sky:
   Ye Lightnings, let your pennons fly,
Illumining the midnight dim,
Till all the landscape seems to swim
   In fire, before the dazzled eye:
Lightnings and Clouds, in praise of Him,
   Unfurl your banners in the sky.

Ye Clouds, upon the ocean's brim,
   In sunset-hues your streamers dye;
   Your gold and crimson wave on high
And beautify the horizon's rim:
Lightnings and Clouds, in praise of Him,
   Unfurl your banners in the sky.

IV.—O LET THE EARTH

O let the Earth bless the Lord; yea, let it praise Him and magnify Him for ever.

O LET the Earth in fair array
   Breathe to the Lord a gladsome strain;
   Weave round her brow a radiant chain
Of apple-bloom or fragrant may,
And dance along her sunny way
   Through waving grass and springing grain:
O let the Earth in fair array
   Breathe to the Lord a gladsome strain.

In sylvan aisles her worship pay,
   Or praise Him by the azure main:
   When morning smiles without a stain,
Or evening dons her mantle grey—
O let the Earth in fair array
   Breathe to the Lord a gladsome strain.

V.—YE HILLS AND MOUNTAINS.

O ye Mountains and Hills, bless ye the Lord; praise Him and magnify Him for ever.

YE Hills and Mountains, lift His praise,
   To your high calling be ye true:
   Let your pure summits pierce the blue,
And catch His earliest morning rays;
And with a lingering glory blaze
   When earth puts on her twilight hue:
Ye Hills and Mountains, lift His praise,
   To your high calling be ye true.

Along your silent upland ways
   His holy feet have brushed the dew,
   When hiding out of human view
He sought lone nights for busy days:
Ye Hills and Mountains, lift His praise,
   To your high calling be ye true.

VI.—O ALL YE GREEN THINGS.

O all ye Green things upon the Earth, bless ye the Lord; praise Him and magnify Him for ever.

O ALL ye Green Things on the earth,
   Bless ye the Lord in sun and shade;
   To whisper praises ye were made,
Or wave to Him in solemn mirth:
For this the towering pine had birth,
   For this sprang forth each grassy blade:
O all ye Green Things on the Earth,
   Bless ye the Lord in sun and shade.

Ye wayside weeds of little worth,
   Ye ferns that fringe the woodland glade
   Ye dainty flowers that quickly fade,
Ye steadfast yews of mighty girth:
O all ye Green Things on the Earth,
   Bless ye the Lord in sun and shade.

VII.—O WELLS AND SPRINGS.

O ye Wells, bless ye the Lord; praise Him and magnify Him for ever.

O WELLS and Springs, where'er ye flow,
   Bless God with your sweet undersong;
   His ceaseless praises bear along,
Rippling and tinkling as ye go:
What though your voice is soft and low,
   'Tis musical your flowers among:
O Wells and Springs, where'er ye flow,
   Bless God with your sweet undersong.

When fainting with the noonday glow,
   Some traveller quaffs you, and is strong;
   When under midnight's shining throng
A mirror to some star ye show:
O Wells and Springs, where'er ye flow,
   Bless God with your sweet undersong.

VIII.—YE SEAS AND FLOODS.

O ye Seas and Floods, bless ye the Lord; praise Him and magnify Him for ever.

YE Seas and Floods, with voice of might
   Resound His Name for evermore:
   Ye rushing falls, that thunder o'er
The rifted rocks, and daze the sight:
Ye waves that with your crests of white
   Incessant dash upon the shore:
Ye Seas and Floods, with voice of might
   Resound His Name for evermore.

Ye torrents from the mountain height,
   Round your grey boulders dance and roar;
   Ye billows on the ocean floor,
Your hands in jubilation smite:
Ye Seas and Floods, with voice of might
   Resound His Name for evermore.

Joseph John Murphy.

1827—1894.

THE prose of Joseph John Murphy is familiar enough to those who are *en rapport* with present-day philosophic-scientific high thinking. His "Habit and Intelligence in Connection with the Laws of Matter and Force," "The Scientific Bases of Faith," and other masterly works have been accepted as of unique value and as likely to remain classics, but only to a limited circle is he known as a poet. He was born in Belfast on the 13th of January, 1827, both of his parents being Friends or Quakers. It is one of the curiosities of family history that this name Murphy—long so out-and-out Irish—is historically English. The first-comer to Ireland of the name arrived in Strafford's time. He was a liveryman of the city of London, and the first of the name of Murphy that ever was in Ireland. Joseph Murphy was born into exceptional advantages, as his parents were of considerable wealth and of high social standing. The father was a merchant manufacturer—a pioneer of the great Ulster trade that remains distinctive to-day. His education was almost wholly "at home"—*id est*, he had no University training, a loss due to the fact that Nonconformists were then excluded from all the Universities. He was always studious, and an omnivorous reader, but independent and outspoken in his judgments, sentiments, opinions, speculations. Later in life his former large income was much reduced by unfortunate investments, but to his honour be it told he continued to be open-handed and generous up to his full means to every good cause. The sorrow is that no memoir of him has yet appeared. So masculine an intellect, so many-sided a thinker, and so strenuously bold a speculator (but ever on a basis of patiently observed and recorded facts), should certainly not go without adequate record. Toward the evening of his life he held office within the Diocese of Down, of the disestablished Church of Ireland, and rendered it yeoman service. He married happily, but was childless. He died on the 25th of January, 1894, and was interred in the cemetery of Malone, just outside the borough of Belfast.

From his boyhood Joseph Murphy was given to rhyming and love of poetry. He must have written a considerable quantity, but he was exacting in quality. Hence his slender volume entitled "Sonnets and other Poems, chiefly Religious" (1890) is of purged and sifted electness. Pensive reflection, tranquil faith hardly won, heavenly aspiration, and sweet graciousness characterise these poems. The workmanship is excellent; the variety noticeable; the teaching catholic—after Denison Maurice and Robertson of Brighton. Now and again are notes that haunt. Few will gainsay that this poet is worthy of a place in this series.

ALEXANDER B. GROSART.

SONNETS AND OTHER POEMS, CHIEFLY RELIGIOUS.

1890.

JOSEPH JOHN MURPHY.

I.—A THOUGHT OF STOICISM.

I HAVE ere now been half inclined
   To wish the present life were all ;
   That death upon the soul might fall,
And darkness overwhelm the mind.

Not that I envied then the beast
   Which never thinks of good or ill,
   And only cares to eat his fill
At mighty Nature's bounteous feast ;

But that our motives might be pure,
   And free our choice and clear our way,
   The law of conscience to obey,
Whether to act or to endure ;

To fight with sin, without regard
   To conquests in the battle won ;
   To say at last, " My work is done ;
I die, and seek for no reward."

And yet I know, 'tis etter far
   That faith should look beyond the grave
   On Him who died the world to save,
And rose to be the Polar Star,

For ever, of our hope and love ;
   To guide us on through death and night,
   To realms of deathless life and light,
To mansions of the blest above.

I know 'tis well to trust the Power
   Who makes the buried seeds to bloom
   That He will raise me from the tomb
As summer's breath awakes the flower ;

> To take a child upon my knee,
>   Or lay what was my friend in dust,
>   And feel a reverential trust
> That He who made them both to be,—
>
> Who gives us death as well as birth,
>   And maketh children grow to men,—
>   Will give us other life again,
> More blessèd than the life on earth.

II.—FIRST SORROW.

THE days of childhood—were they golden?
  We see them through a golden haze
Of memory; but, when near beholden,
  Were they indeed such golden days?

No, not of gold those early hours,
  Although their passing pleased us well;
They were but lovely vernal flowers,
  Fading and withering ere they fell.

But when our earliest grief was blended
  With trembling faith, our hearts to melt;
When childhood's careless joys were ended,
  And life's reality was felt;

When first we cried to God alone;—
  That was indeed the golden hour!
Then seed of heavenly life was sown
  In weakness, to be raised in power.

The richest store of heavenly gain
  May spring from deepest earthly loss.
The holiest joy has roots in pain—
  Eternal glory in the Cross.

III.—THE POTTER AND THE CLAY.

WHY hast Thou made me so,
My Maker? I would know
Wherefore Thou gav'st me such a mournful dower,—
Toil that is oft in vain,
Knowledge that deepens pain,
And longing to be pure, without the power?

"Shall the thing formed aspire
The purpose to require
Of him who formed it?" Make not answer thus!
Beyond the Potter's wheel
There lieth an appeal
To Him who breathed the breath of life in us.

When the same Power that made
My being has arrayed
Its nature with a dower of sin and woe,
And thoughts that question all;—
Why should the words appal
That ask the Maker why He made me so?

I know we are but clay,
Thus moulded to display
His wisdom and His power who rolls the years;
Whose wheel is Heaven and earth;—
Its motion, death and birth;—
Is Potter, then, the name that most endears?

To Him we bow as King;
As Lord His praise we sing;
To Him we pray as Father and as God;
Saviour in our distress;
Guide through the wilderness;
And Judge that beareth an avenging rod.

        I grudge not, Lord, to be
        Of meanest use to Thee ;—
Make me a trough for swine if so Thou wilt ;—
        But if my vessel's clay
        Be marred and thrown away
Before it takes its form, is mine the guilt?

        I trust Thee to the end,
        Creator, Saviour, Friend,
Whatever name Thou deignest that we call.
        Art Thou not good and just?
        I wait, and watch, and trust
That Love is still the holiest name of all.

        I watch and strive all night ;
        And when the morning's light
Shines on the path I travelled here below ;—
        When day eternal breaks,
        And life immortal wakes,
Then shalt Thou tell me why Thou mad'st me so.

IV.—ETERNITY.

ETERNITY is not, as men believe,
    Before and after us, an endless line.
No; 'tis a circle, infinitely great,
All the circumference with creatures thronged:
God at the centre dwells, beholding all.
And, as we move in this eternal round
The finite portion which alone we see,
Behind us, is the Past ; what lies before
We call the Future. But to Him who dwells
Far in the centre, equally remote
From every point of the circumference,
Both are alike the Future and the Past.

Christina G. Rossetti.

1830—1894.

CHRISTINA GEORGINA ROSSETTI, sister of Dante Gabriel Rossetti and William Michael Rossetti, was born in London on the 5th of December, 1830. When no more than sixteen years of age, her first verse attempts were printed by her grandfather, G. Polidori, at his private press, under the title "Verses by Christina G. Rossetti" (1847); and three years later she contributed verses to *The Germ*, using the *nom de plume* Ellen Alleyn. In 1862 she published "Goblin Market and other Poems," and in 1866 "The Prince's Progress." These were followed by a collection of tales, "Commonplace and other Short Stories" (1870); "Sing-Song, a Nursery Rhyme-book" (1872); "Speaking Likenesses," three short tales (1874); "Annus Domini, a Collect for each Day of the Year" (1874); "Seek and Find: Short Studies of the Benedicite" (1879); "Called to be Saints, the Minor Festivals devotionally Studied" (1881); "A Pageant and other Poems" (1881); "Letter and Spirit: Notes on the Commandments" (1883); "Time Flies, a Reading Diary" (1885); and "Poetical Works" (1890). Miss Rossetti died on the 29th of December, 1894.

Miss Rossetti's general poetry is dealt with in the volume of this series devoted to the Women Poets of the Century, where her verse is introduced by a critical article from the pen of Mr. Arthur Symons. But so much of her later work was of a religious or devotional character, that, even at the cost of repetition, it is not possible to omit a selection from a representative volume of sacred poetry. The following selection is from the small and inexpensive volume "Time Flies," published by the Society for the Promotion of Christian Knowledge, and is included in this work by the courtesy of that society. For a critical and illustrative explanation of Miss Rossetti's method and style the reader is referred to the article by Mr. Symons in the former volume. The following selection may be allowed to speak for itself.

ALFRED H. MILES.

TIME FLIES.

CHRISTINA G. ROSSETTI.

I.—JANUARY 6.

(FEAST OF THE EPIPHANY.)

"Lord Babe, if Thou art He
   We sought for patiently,
Where is Thy court?
Hither may prophecy and star resort;
Men heed not their report."—
     "Bow down and worship, righteous man:
     This Infant of a span
     Is He man sought for since the world began."—
"Then, Lord, accept my gold, too base a thing
For Thee, of all kings King."

"Lord Babe, despite Thy youth
I hold Thee of a truth
Both Good and Great:
But wherefore dost Thou keep so mean a state,
Low lying desolate?"—
     "Bow down and worship, righteous seer:
     The Lord our God is here
     Approachable, Who bids us all draw near."—
"Wherefore to Thee I offer frankincense,
Thou Sole Omnipotence."

"But I have only brought
Myrrh; no wise afterthought
Instructed me

To gather pearls or gems, or choice to see
Coral or ivory."—
 "Not least thine offering proves thee wise:
 For myrrh means sacrifice,
 And He that lives, this same is He that dies."—
"Then here is myrrh: alas! yea, woe is me
That myrrh befitteth Thee."

Myrrh, frankincense and gold:.
And lo! from wintry fold
Good will doth bring
A Lamb, the innocent likeness of this King
Whom stars and seraphs sing:
 And lo! the bird of love, a Dove
 Flutters and cooes above:
 And Dove and Lamb and Babe agree in love:—
Come, all mankind, come, all creation, hither,
Come, worship Christ together.

II.—MARCH 3.

LAUGHING Life cries at the feast,—
 Craving Death cries at the door,—
"Fish, or fowl or fatted beast?"—
"Come with me, thy feast is o'er."—

"Wreathe the violets."—"Watch them fade."—
"I am sunlight."—"I am shade:
I am the sun-burying west."—
"I am pleasure."—"I am rest:
Come with me, for I am best."

III.—MARCH 5.

WHERE shall I find a white rose blowing?—
   Out in the garden where all sweets be.—
But out in my garden the snow was snowing
   And never a white rose opened for me.
Nought but snow and a wind were blowing
And snowing.

Where shall I find a blush rose blushing?—
   On the garden wall or the garden bed.—
But out in my garden the rain was rushing
   And never a blush rose raised its head.
Nothing glowing, flushing or blushing;
Rain rushing.

Where shall I find a red rose budding?—
Out in the garden where all things grow.—
But out in my garden a flood was flooding
   And never a red rose began to blow.
Out in a flooding what should be budding?
All flooding!

Now is winter and now is sorrow,
   No roses but only thorns to-day:
Thorns will put on roses to-morrow,
   Winter and sorrow scudding away.
No more winter and no more sorrow
To-morrow.

IV.—APRIL 6.

WEIGH all my faults and follies righteously,
   Omissions and commissions, sin on sin;
   Make deep the scale, O Lord, to weigh them in;

Yea, set the Accuser vulture-eyed to see
All loads ingathered which belong to me :
    That so in life the judgment may begin,
    And Angels learn how hard it is to win
One solitary sinful soul to Thee.
I have no merits for a counterpoise :
    Oh vanity my work and hastening day,
What can I answer to the accursing voice ?
    Lord, drop Thou in the counterscale alone
One Drop from Thine own Heart, and overweigh
    My guilt, my folly, even my heart of stone.

V.—APRIL 20.

PITEOUS my rhyme is,
    What while I muse of love and pain,
Of love misspent, of love in vain,
Of love that is not loved again :
    And is this all then ?
    As long as time is
Love loveth. Time is but a span,
The dalliance space of dying man :
And is this all immortals can ?
    The gain were small then.

    Love loves for ever,
And finds a sort of joy in pain,
And gives with nought to take again,
And loves too well to end in vain :
    Is the gain small then ?
    Love laughs at "never,"
Outlives our life, exceeds the span
Appointed to mere mortal man :
That which love is and does and can,
    Is all in all then.

VI.—MAY 14.

Young girls wear flowers,
 Young brides a flowery wreath,
But next we plant them
 In garden plots of death.
Whose lot is best:
The maiden's curtained rest,
 Or bride's whose hoped-for sweet
 May yet outstrip her feet?
Ah! what are such as these
To death's sufficing ease?
He sleeps indeed who sleeps in peace
 Where night and morning meet.

Dear are the blossoms
 For bride's or maiden's head,
But dearer planted
 Around our blessed dead.
Those mind us of decay
And joys that fade away,
 These preach to us perfection,
 Long love, and resurrection.
We make our graveyards fair
For spirit-like birds of air,
For Angels may be finding there
 Lost Eden's own delection.

VII.—JUNE 2.

"As cold waters to a thirsty soul, so is good news from a far country."

"Golden haired, lily white,
 Will you pluck me lilies?
Or will you show me where they grow,
 Show where the limpid rill is?

But is your hair of gold or light,
    And is your foot of flake or fire,
And have you wings rolled up from sight,
    And songs to slake desire?"

"I pluck fresh flowers of Paradise,
    Lilies and roses red,
A bending sceptre for my hand,
    A crown to crown my head.
I sing my songs, I pluck my flowers
    Sweet-scented from their fragrant trees:
I sing, we sing amid the bowers,
    And gather palm branches."

"Is there a path to Heaven
    My stumbling foot may tread?
And will you show that way to go,
    That bower and blossom bed?"
"The path to Heaven is steep and straight
    And scorched, but ends in shade of trees,
Where yet awhile we sing and wait,
    And gather palm branches."

VIII.—JULY 5.

INNOCENT eyes not ours,
    Are made to look on flowers,
Eyes of small birds and insects small:
    Morn after summer morn,
    The sweet rose on her thorn
Opens her bosom to them all.
    The least and last of things
    That soar on quivering wings,
Or crawl among the grass-blades out of sight,
Have just as clear a right
To their appointed portion of delight,
    As Queens or Kings.

IX.—JULY 11.

MAN'S life is but a working day
  Whose tasks are set aright:
A time to work, a time to pray,
  And then a quiet night.
And then, please God, a quiet night
Where palms are green and robes are white,
A long-drawn breath, a balm for sorrow,—
And all things lovely on the morrow.

X.—JULY 16.

HAVE I not striven, my God, and watched and prayed?
  Have I not wrestled in mine agony?
  Wherefore dost Thou still turn Thy Face from me?
Is Thine Arm shortened that Thou canst not aid?
Thy silence breaks my heart: speak though to upbraid,
  For Thy rebuke yet bids us follow Thee.
  I grope and grasp not; gaze, but cannot see.
When out of sight and reach, my bed is made,
And piteous men and women cease to blame,
  Whispering and wistful of my gain or loss;
  Thou who for my sake once didst feel the Cross,
  Lord, wilt Thou turn and look upon me then,
And in Thy glory bring to nought my shame,
  Confessing me to angels and to men?

XI.—JULY 29.

THROUGH burden and heat of the day
  How weary the hands and the feet,
That labour with scarcely a stay,
  Through burden and heat!

Tired toiler whose sleep shall be sweet,
  Kneel down, it will rest thee to pray:
Then forward, for daylight is fleet.

Cool shadows show lengthening and grey,
  Cool twilight will soon be complete:—
What matters this wearisome way
  Through burden and heat?

XII.—SEPTEMBER 25.

SORROW hath a double voice,
  Sharp to-day but sweet to-morrow:
Wait in patience, hope, rejoice,
  Tried friends of sorrow.

Pleasure hath a double taste,
  Sweet to-day, but sharp to-morrow:
Friends of pleasure, rise in haste,
  Make friends with sorrow.

Pleasure set aside to-day
  Comes again to rule to-morrow:
Welcomed sorrow will not stay,
  Farewell to sorrow!

XIII.—OCTOBER 30.

WHO is this that cometh up not alone
  From the fiery-flying serpent wilderness
Leaning upon her own Beloved One,
  Who is this?

Lo, the King of King's daughter, a high princess,
Going home as bride to her Husband's Throne,
  Virgin queen in perfected loveliness.

Her eyes a dove's eyes and her voice a dove's moan,
  She shows like a full moon for heavenliness,
Eager saints and angels ask in heaven's zone:
  Who is this?

XIV.—NOVEMBER 16.

THE goal in sight! Look up and sing,
  Set faces full against the light,
Welcome with rapturous welcoming
  The goal in sight.

Let be the left, let be the right:
Straight forward make your footsteps ring
  A loud alarum through the night.

Death hunts you, yea, but reft of sting;
  Your bed is green, your shroud is white:
Hail! Life and Death and all that bring
  The goal in sight.

XV.—DECEMBER 5.

BURY Hope out of sight,
  No book for it and no bell;
It never could bear the light
  Even while growing and well;
Think if now it could bear
The light on its face of care
And grey scattered hair.

No grave for Hope in the earth,
  But deep in that silent soul
Which rang no bell for its birth
  And rings no funeral toll.
Cover its once bright head:
Nor odours nor tears be shed:
It lived once, it is dead.

Brief was the day of its power,
   The day of its grace how brief;
As the fading of a flower,
   As the falling of a leaf,
So brief its day and its hour;
No bud more and no bower
Or hint of a flower.

Shall many wail it? not so:
   Shall one bewail it? not one:
Thus it hath been from long ago,
   Thus it shall be beneath the sun.
O fleet sun, make haste to flee;
O rivers, fill up the sea;
O Death, set the dying free.

The sun nor loiters nor speeds,
   The rivers run as they ran,
Through clouds or through windy reeds
   All run as when all began.
Only Death turns at our cries:—
Lo, the Hope we buried with sighs
Alive in Death's eyes!

XVI.—ADVENT SUNDAY.

BEHOLD, the Bridegroom cometh:—go ye out
   With lighted lamps and garlands round about
To meet Him in a rapture with a shout.

It may be at the midnight black as pitch
Earth shall cast up her poor, cast up her rich.

It may be at the crowing of the cock
Earth shall upheave her depth, uproot her rock.

For lo, the Bridegroom fetcheth home the Bride :
His Hands are Hands she knows, she knows His Side.

Like pure Rebekah at the appointed place,
Veiled she unveils her face to meet His Face.

Like great Queen Esther in her triumphing,
She triumphs in the presence of her King.

His Eyes are as a Dove's, and she's Dove-eyed ;
He knows His lovely mirror, sister, Bride.

He speaks with Dove-voice of exceeding love,
And she with love-voice of an answering Dove.

Behold, the Bridegroom cometh :—go we out
With lamps ablaze and garlands round about
To meet Him in a rapture with a shout.

XVII.—EASTER EVEN.

THE tempest over and gone, the calm begun.
   Lo, "it is finished," and the Strong Man sleeps :
All stars keep vigil watching for the sun,
   The moon her vigil keeps.

A garden full of silence and of dew,
   Beside a virgin cave and entrance stone :
Surely a garden full of Angels too,
   Wondering, on watch, alone.

They who cry "Holy, Holy, Holy," still
   Veiling their faces round God's Throne above,
May well keep vigil on this heavenly hill
   And cry their cry of love.

Adoring God in His new mystery
   Of Love more deep than hell, more strong than death ;
Until the day break and the shadows flee,
   The Shaking and the Breath.

XVIII.—EASTER DAY.

WORDS cannot utter
   Christ His returning:—
Mankind, keep Jubilee,
   Strip off your mourning,
Crown you with garlands,
   Set your lamps burning.

Speech is left speechless;—
   Set you to singing,
Fling your hearts open wide,
   Set your bells ringing:
Christ the Chief Reaper
   Comes, His sheaf bringing.

Earth wakes her song birds,
   Puts on her flowers,
Leads out her lambkins,
   Builds up her bowers:
This is man's sponsal day,
   Christ's day and ours

Alexander B. Grosart.

1835—1899.

ALEXANDER BALLOCH GROSART, D.D., LL.D., was born on the 18th of June, 1835, at Stirling, N.B., and was educated at the Falkirk Parish School, Edinburgh University, and the Theological Hall of the United Presbyterian Church. After completing his college course, he became minister of the First United Presbyterian Church, Kinross (October 29th, 1856), where he found time amid pastoral duties for much literary work. He edited the works and biographies of Dr. Richard Sebbes, Thomas Brookes, and others for "Nichol's Puritan Divines and Puritan Commentaries," and wrote several religious works of exegetical teaching and appeal. Later he became minister of Prince's Park United Presbyterian Church, Liverpool, and in 1868 that of St. George's United Presbyterian Church, Blackburn, Lancashire. He was made LL.D. by Edinburgh University, and D.D. by the University of St. Andrews.

Dr. Grosart's work in literature is unique. His "Lord Bacon not the Altruism of Christian Paradoxes" (1865); his discovery that "Britain's Ida" was written by Phineas Fletcher and not by Edmund Spenser; and his identification of "The Phœnix" and "The Turtle Dove" in Sir Robert Chester's "Love Martyr, or Rosalind's Complaint" as representing Queen Elizabeth and the Earl of

Essex, were triumphs of research and criticism; while his reprints of early English literature have supplied some of the richest and rarest additions to the modern library. His works include "The Fuller Worthies Library," 39 vols.; "The Chertsey Worthies Library," 14 vols.; "The Huth Library," 39 vols.; "Spenser's Works," 10 vols.; "Works of Samuel Daniel," 5 vols.; "Works of George Daniel," 4 vols.; "The Townley MSS.," 2 vols.; "Sir John Eliot MSS.," 6 vols.; "Lismore Papers," 10 vols.; "Prose Works of Wordsworth," 3 vols.; besides occasional issues of unique and rare books, 38 vols. He died in March, 1899.

Among the MSS. published for the first time by Dr. Grosart are a number of poems by George Herbert, to whose verse that of his own muse may be said to approximate. His original verse, published in instalments at different times, was republished in a collected form under the title "Songs of Day and Night" in 1891. This volume, with its curious inversions and quaint experiments in rhythm, is a rich storehouse of Christian experience and spiritual refreshment. Dr. Grosart has founded his style upon that of the old bards among whom he has laboured so much, and drawn his inspiration from the prophets and psalmists whom he has studied to such great advantage.

ALFRED H. MILES.

SONGS OF DAY AND NIGHT.

ALEXANDER B. GROSART.

I.—GOD NEAR AND FAR.

1 KINGS viii. 46.

NO one so far away as God,
   Yet none Who is so near
Eternity is His abode;
   But lo! I find Him here;
Within my heart—that by His grace
He chosen has for dwelling-place.

No one so far away as God,
   Yet none Who is so near;
O how it lighteneth our load,
   And stilleth ev'ry fear!
To look upon the Earth and sky,
Assur'd that God is ever nigh.

No one so far away as God,
   Yet none Who is so near;
For He Who this Earth's acres trod,
   Wipes still the falling tear;
Altho' His Throne is far above,
He liveth yet, Incarnate Love.

No one so far away as God,
   Yet none Who is so near;
The Universe shakes at His nod,
   But guiltiest needs not fear;
"My Lord, my God," doth see the BLOOD,
And His great Covenant stands good.

No one so far away as God,
   Yet none Who is so near;
Far mightier than Moses' rod,
   Is the great rod of prayer;
Upheld within the hand of FAITH,
Sure-fulfill'd is all "He saith."

No one so far away as God,
   Yet none Who is so near;
For lo! 'twixt Heav'n and Earth the ROOD
   Uniteth sphere and sphere;
In light of light the great God dwells,
But visiteth in lowliest cells.

No one so far away as God,
   Yet none Who is so near;
Eternity is His abode;
   But lo! I find Him here;
Within my heart—that by His grace
He chosen has for dwelling-place.

II.—THE EVERLASTING ARMS UNDERNEATH.

DEUT. xxxiii. 27.

THE child, that to his mother clings,
   Lies not all safely on her breast,
Till she her arms around him flings,
   Sweetly caressing and caressed;
Ev'n so, my God, Thy mighty arms,
Not my poor FAITH, shield me from harms.

I bless Thy Name for every grace,
   Wherewith Thou dost enrich Thine own;
Yea, I would seek each day to trace
   Myself more like my Master grown;
Yet, O my God, Thy mighty arms,
Not my faint LOVE, shield me from harms.

I walk along this sin-scarr'd Earth,
  In brightness now and now in dole;
Now all "cast down" and now in mirth;
  Now griefs, now joys, possess my soul;
But, O my God, Thy mighty arms,
Not my dim HOPE, shield me from harms.

Within, amidst the world's unrest,
  Thou, Lord! the calming word hast given;
Thy peace abides, howe'er I'm press'd;
  And yields an antepast of Heaven:
But, O my God, Thy mighty arms,
Not my own PEACE, shield me from harms.

My mouth Thou fillest with "sweet songs";
  Makest my feet run in "the WAY";
Giv'st me the joy to Thine belongs;
  Nor scarcely ever sayest me nay:
But, O my God, Thy mighty arms,
Not my scant JOY, shield me from harms.

The child, that to his mother clings,
  Lies not all safely on her breast,
Till she her arms around him flings,
  Sweetly caressing and caressed:
Ev'n so, my God, Thy mighty arms,
Not aught of mine, shield me from harms.

III.—HE LEADS ROUND.

EXOD. xiii. 18 (cf. DEUT. ii. 7; viii. 2; xxxii. 10).

HE leads round, but He leads right:
  All the way is in His sight;
Be it rough, or be it long;
Void of joy, or set to song;
Bringing much, or mite by mite;
He leads round, but He leads right.

He leads round, but He leads right:
He is with us in the fight;
Sin may lure, or doubts assail,
Clad in Faith's celestial mail,
We are guarded by His might;
He leads round, but He leads right.

He leads round, but He leads right:
Let no danger then affright;
When to Him we lift our eyes,
Help doth like the Morn arise;
Chasing clouds with conquering light;
He leads round, but He leads right.

He leads round, but He leads right:
Giveth songs ev'n in the night;
O to listen to His voice
When in tears He bids rejoice;
He our blackest can make white;
He leads round, but He leads right.

He leads round, but He leads right:
Heaviest burden groweth light;
Marah! Elim! Wilderness!
Each in turn the Lord doth bless;
Canaan shines, far-off but bright;
He leads round, but He leads right.

He leads round, but He leads right:
Cloud by day and fire by night;
Morn by morn "Let God arise,
Scattering all our enemies";
And we'll sing with evening light;
He leads round, but He leads right.

IV.—THE GOOD DIE NOT.
2 Cor. v. 4; St. John v. 24; Col. iii. 3.

THE good die not; they but undress
   And lay them down to sleep;
They wake anon in blessedness,
   Ev'n whilst for them we weep;
Let Faith ascend within the vail,
Nor as disconsolate still wail.

The good die not; He went before,
   A mansion to prepare;
And if we only could thus soar,
   We should not shed a tear;
Laying aside their chrysalis,
Bless'd are they in that Day of His.

The good die not; but disappear
   For the Lord's "little while";
Let us now watch; the day draws near,
   Shall close the brief exile;
In hope and patience let us wait;
Soon will unclose the Golden Gate.

The good die not; an ampler life
   Is theirs where they have gone
No more of sin, or grief, or strife,
   Can vex His haven'd one;
"Life more abundant" their reward;
Not lying dead 'neath daisied sward.

The good die not; they but undress
   And lay them down to sleep;
They wake anon in blessedness,
   Ev'n whilst for them we weep;
Let Faith ascend within the vail,
Nor as disconsolate still wail.

V.—GOD THE HOLY SPIRIT.

Rom. xv. 30.

O HOLY GHOST! come as the DEW,
    All soft and still this quiet eve;
Our first-love's joy do Thou renew,
    As to those who did first believe.

O Holy Ghost! come as the FIRE,
    In our cold hearts light up Thy flame;
That touch'd of Thee, we may aspire,
    And shrink not from His glorious shame.

O Holy Ghost! come as the WIND,
    To shake quick ev'ry barrier down;
That, restfully on Him reclin'd,
    We Him, He us, may gracious own.

O Holy Ghost! come as the RAIN,
    That sweetly heals the new-mown grass;
Refresh and strengthen, that again
    We on our upward way may pass.

O Holy Ghost! come as the LIGHT,
    Pure-breaking as doth break the Day;
Work in us by Thy gentle might,
    Such hopes as shall our fears affray.

O Holy Ghost! be Thou our LIFE,
    Our life that's hid with Christ in God;
Make Thou us strong in the sore strife,
    Guarding us in the paths He trod.

O Dew! O Fire! O Wind! O Rain!
    O Light of Life! O Life of Light!
We would the height of heights attain,—
    We would be strengthen'd by Thy MIGHT.

VI.—THE CROSS.

Col. i. 20; ii. 14.

ONCE a thing of woe and shame,
   Lo! the Cross now towers sublime!
Gath'ring lustre to its name,
   In the onward march of TIME;
Rais'd 'twixt malefactors twain,
   "*In the place call'd Calvary*";
Who may gauge the deep disdain,
   Of men's vengeful mockery?

Thorns—but grapes upon them blush;
   Gall—yet sweeter far than honey,
Thirst—and "living waters" gush;
   Poor—but rich beyond all money;
Helpless all, in hands and feet,
   Yet saves one, the lion's prey;
Terrible—but oh, how sweet!
   Darkness—and yet clearest Day.

Branded—and thrice glorious;
   Naked—yet the "white robe" weaves;
Conquerèd—and victorious;
   Weak—yet the vast world upheaves;
Dead—and yet source of all life;
   Woe—but symbol of all bliss;
Peace—and centre of all strife;
   Was e'er paradox like this?

Sin's last trophy—and defeat;
   Wrath—and heart of Love reveals;
Law upheld—yet pardon meet;
   Justice, mercy, it unseals;
Man condemned—and yet acquitted;
   Fix'd—yet round it all revolves,
"Bitter tree"—where WHITE DOVE flitted;
   Mystery—and all mystery solves.

Cross of Christ! in thee I boast,
   Bearing high THE CRUCIFIED;
And my heart when anguish-tost,
   Finds peace only by Thy side;
Hold it up, ye men of God,
   Earth's heart aches for your good news·
Tell it out at home, abroad,
   Bid, accept it or refuse.

Mighty conquests of the past,
   Shadow mightier to come;
The Lord's promise standeth fast,
   Drawing countless myriads home;
Once a thing of woe and shame,
   Lo! the Cross now stands sublime;
Gath'ring lustre to its name,
   In the onward march of TIME.

VII.—ANGELIC MINISTRY.
HEB. i. 14; ST. LUKE xv. 7.

LET God THE SPIRIT anoint my eyes,
   A-flame are seen the azure skies,
With seraphim and cherubim—
Who noon-day's utmost blaze bedim;
On wings of whiteness, lo! they fly
'Twixt our dark world and fields on high;
Heirs of salvation bringing home,
To gain the joyous welcome "Come."

There is a glory on the grass
As tho' angelic feet did pass;
There is a splendour 'midst the trees,
As he sees who the unseen sees;
Amongst the hollows of the hills,
A hush of awe as all else stills;
O God! Thy Spirit on me lies,
Lifting me up in ecstasies.

Ye holy angels ministrant,
Why is it now ye will not grant
E'en unto FAITH and HOPE and LOVE,
Your seal of silence to remove?
Speaking as once ye used to speak,
To weary hearts and like to break;
Glad tidings of glad souls set free,
That e'en in glory fresh joy see.

Where'er I see a little child,
I know ye there, ye undefil'd;
To guide, to guard, to bless, to keep,
With love that knows not how to sleep;
And wheresoe'er a sinner turns
And for the sinner's Saviour burns;
But O to catch a whisper'd word,
That not in vain I serve the Lord.

O idle yearning thus to grieve!
Our part, as servants to believe;
To labour and still labour on
Until the world for Christ is won;
In faith, that unto us *is* given
Abundantly to people Heav'n;
That souls by day, by night repent,
And angels still their names present.

VIII.—THE RESURRECTION.
ROM. i. 4.

ARISE, my soul, Faith's wings expand,
   Soar upward to the Heav'nly Land;
Behold the great stone roll'd away!
Thy Saviour's Resurrection Day!
    A conqueror forth He came,
    Death and the Grave to shame.

Hark! hark! it is an angel's voice,
Who tidings brings that bid rejoice;
He stands by Death's wide-open'd door,
And cries "Christ lives for evermore!"
    A conqueror forth He came,
    Death and the Grave to shame.

O hallow'd Day! O blessed Day!
That all Death's darkness did affray;
Far-flaming still o'er all the world,
Strong Satan from his vast throne hurl'd:
    A conqueror forth He came,
    Death and the Grave to shame.

Thou Prince of Life! Thou Saviour dear!
For us in Heav'n Thou dost appear;
Nor need most tim'rous tremble now,
Since Faith beholds Thy crown-clasp'd brow;
    A conqueror forth He came,
    Death and the Grave to shame.

O Lord! do Thou help us to watch
That we Thy mighty word may catch,
"Because I live ye too shall live":
What could more strong assurance give?
    A conqueror forth He came,
    Death and the Grave to shame.

Arise, my soul, Faith's wings expand,
Soar upward to the Heav'nly Land;
Behold thy Saviour's grave unbarr'd!
White-wingèd angels for His guard:
    A conqueror forth He came,
    Death and the Grave to shame.

IX.—IF IT BE POSSIBLE.
St. Matt. xxvi. 39.

I MAY not tread Gethsemane,
  I may not share Thy agony,
    O Jesus Christ my Saviour!
Yet hear me, Lord, Thy prayer I pray,
As I am fainting on my way,
    O Jesus Christ my Saviour!

Darkness around me thick enfolds,
A "cup of trembling" my hand holds,
    O Jesus Christ my Saviour!
Forgive me, O forgive my cry,
"*If it be possible*, pass it by,"
    O Jesus Christ my Saviour!

My "little one" Thou lovest is sick,
And hour by hour he grows more weak,
    O Jesus Christ my Saviour!
I mark the thinning of his face,
And awful lines upon him trace,
    O Jesus Christ my Saviour!

This is the cup to me Thou'rt reaching,
Lord, hear me in my poor beseeching,
    O Jesus Christ my Saviour!
"*If it be possible*," spare him, Lord;
Speak Thou ev'n now the healing word,
    O Jesus Christ my Saviour!

We gave him to Thee in our vow,
Thy name was nam'd upon his brow,
    O Jesus Christ my Saviour!
Life is a great gift; I would fain
Have him a MAN for Thee to train,
    O Jesus Christ my Saviour!

"Yet not my will but Thine be done,"-
Alas! alas! my little son,—
  O Jesus Christ my Saviour!
My heart is sore; I can but sigh—
"*If it be possible,*" hear my cry,
  O Jesus Christ my Saviour!

X.—INDWELLING—DWELLING IN.
St. John vi. 56.

O DWELL in me, my Lord,
  That I in Thee may dwell;
Fulfil Thy tender word,
  That Thy evangels tell;
In me Thou, I in Thee
By Thy sweet courtesy.

But wilt Thou my guest be,
  In this poor heart of mine?
Thy guest? Is this for me,
  In that pure heart of Thine?
In me Thou, I in Thee,
By Thy sweet courtesy.

Thy chamber, Lord, prepare,
  Whither Thou deignest come;
I may not seek to share
  The making of Thy home;
In me Thou, I in Thee,
By Thy sweet courtesy.

Thy gracious gifts bestow,
  Humility and love;
O cause my heart to glow
  By fire sent from above;
In me Thou, I in Thee,
By Thy sweet courtesy.

John Owen.

1836—1896.

JOHN OWEN was the eldest son of John Owen, for many years actuary of the Savings Bank, Pembroke. He was born in 1836, in the town of Cardigan in South Wales; and after the local school attended the Grammar School at Haverfordwest. At the end of 1856 he proceeded to St. David's College, Lampeter, where he came under the influence of Dr. Rowland Williams, then Vice-President—a connection continued to the close of Dr. Williams' life. This sums up his academic advantages; but from first to last he was a keen and enriched philologist, hanging language after language as so many golden keys to his girdle. Perhaps his books in certain lines bear out that all along he was mainly self-taught ($αὐτοδίδακτος$), though making it certain that he had extensive scholarly acquirements. On leaving Lampeter he became curate of a Wiltshire parish, joined to and under the charge of Dr. Williams. He was ordained deacon in 1859 by the Bishop of Salisbury, and in the following year became priest. What leisure was left him was occupied with linguistic studies and occasional contributions to leading theological and literary journals —*e.g.*, Beard's *Theological Review* and *Frazer* (under Froude). In 1869 he was appointed to the rectorship of East Anstey in the county of Devon, and in 1870 he preached the funeral sermon of his master and friend Dr. Rowland Williams. He died on the 6th of February, 1896.

This is not the place to do more than name his chief books—viz '(a) "Evenings with the Skeptics," 2 vols., 8vo (1881); (β) a revival of Glanvil's "Scepsis Scientifica" (1885); (γ) "The Skeptics of the Italian Renaissance, and the Skeptics of the French Renaissance," 2 vols., 8vo (1893-4); (δ) "Essay on the Organisations of the Early Church" (1895), prefixed to Harnack's "Sources of the Apostolic Canons."

But it is as a poet that we have to do with John Owen. In 1889 appeared "Verse Musings on Nature, Faith, and Freedom." A revised and enlarged edition of this volume was published in 1894. This volume is more remarkable—and it *is* remarkable—for its weight of thinking ("Musings") than for its technique of rhyme and rhythm. It is marred by faults of measure, uncouth terms, and involute phrasings; nevertheless, when most irate with these, we come on the "higher strain," and jets of melody, and quaint conceits of fancy, and memorabilia of axiomatic truths. A favourite fashion of his is to beat out a couplet, or stanza, and the like, of a prior poet. The result is not always a success, for the tiny nugget becomes extremely thin gold-leaf. And yet some of the finest things in the volume spring out of his texts. None can read a page without having avenues of thought and speculation opened out. Selection, to be just, would need to be fuller than our limits admit. But the poems that we have taken may be left to speak for themselves.

Alexander B. Grosart.

VERSE MUSINGS ON NATURE, FAITH, AND FREEDOM.

1889.

JOHN OWEN.

I.—*FAITH.*

I.—On Defining God.

OBSERVE yon concave blue,
   That seems to close around our human view,
  And ends by sun and star
Our keenest survey of those heavens afar.

  And yet we know full well,
False is the specious tale our senses tell;
  That is no azure sky,
Or solid vault, that meets our lifted eye.

  What curtains round our gaze,
The background of the sun or starry maze,
  Is but blue-tinted light
That veils from us the aërial infinite.

  And so, when we define
Great heaven's immensity by verbal sign,
  We act as though our bent
Were here again to feign a *firmament*.

  Words in array we place,
And deem therewith we see God face to face.
  Poor fools, and blind; not seeing
Our words but mask and hide His unsearched Being.

II.—What is Religion?

(AFTER SCHLEIERMACHER.)

NOT a moral codex taught,
   In legal maxims hard and cold,
By legal minds together brought,
  From ethic teachers new and old.

Nor yet a mode or form of thought
   Of God or man, the world a life;
By various diff'ring systems wrought,
   Inducing hate and wordy strife.

Religion is a secret fire,
   Kindling spontaneous in the breast,
The soul's instinctive blind desire
   To *feel* its God and be at rest.

Religion is a sense Divine,
   Perception of the Infinite,
The pure heart's pulse, the only sign,
   To mark its being or prove its might.

Above, below, and all around,
   In thing without, in thought within,
Is pure Religion's hallowed ground,
   The temple we must worship in.

To lean in trust upon the Power,
   Through all the universe made known,
This is the soul's divinest dower,
   This is Religion—this alone.

III.—WHERE IS RELIGION?

(AFTER SCHLEIERMACHER.)

NOT in the text of Holy Writ,
   Or words or writings elsewhere brought,
With sacred fire, though once uplit,
   But now—the mere dead signs of thought.

Not in a church's rule or plan,
   Its public prayer or sacred rite,
Imperfectly devised by man,
   To body forth the Infinite.

Not in confessions nor in creeds,
  Or lifeless dogmas cut and squared,
Or pious acts or ritual deeds,
  For quickening holy life prepared.

Such formal systems we discard,
  No vital warmth can they inspire,
Like lava streams, now cold and hard,
  Which erst flowed on—a living fire.

Such burnt-out systems have we seen,
  Embers instead of burning glow,
The ashes tell where fire hath been;
  No further use—cold embers know.

But in the heart, experience-taught,
  Of faith and hope and love which tells
In th' infinite of human thought,
  There there alone, Religion dwells.

IV.—WHAT IS FAITH?

FAITH is—not sight,
  It boasts not of the sun at noonday bright,
While groping in the starlit haze of night.

  —Nor Dogma proud,
Fierce vaunting of all Truth in accents loud,
Beguiling with bold words th' unthinking crowd.

  —Nor Science known,
Seated in queenly robes upon her throne,
Meting the boundless with her claspèd zone.

  —Nor Certainty,
The overweening claim that Truth must be
What we forecast from what we hear and see.

*   *   *   *   *   *

8*

  Faith does but muse
With heed upon the data she *must* use,
Nor Likelihood's fair claim durst she refuse.
  Faith does but think
That walking on the Infinite's dread brink,
She dare not mete its chain by one small link.
  Faith does but feel
That which she deems all dimly, may be real,
On her blind guess she will not set Truth's seal.
  Faith doth but hope
She shall see clear—whereas she doth but grope—
When earth's dark vistas widen to heaven's scope.
  She doth but will
The healthful impulses she would instil
May, by heaven's prospering, all good fulfil.
  She can but trust
Her wistful craving for the True and Just,
Not only *may* be realised but *must*.

V.—Life and Thought.

UNSOUGHT came Life to me,
 And with it brought
A precious, perilous gift—
 The gift of Thought.

Life grew, and with its growth
 Grew also Thought,
Like twin-born beings, from birth
 To rivalry wrought.

First, Life claimed precedence,
 In that it sought
To merge in its own being,
 The being of Thought.

Said Life, "No useful end
  Is gained by Thought,
And all its doubts and quests
  Come but to nought."

But Thought in turn replied,
  "Life cannot choose
But live; nor yet can Thought
  Its subtler being refuse.

"By direful stress ondriven,
  I still must quest,
Though answer full and true
  Ne'er bring me rest.

"Thou, Life, mayst easy live,
  Deprived of Thought,
Nay, myriads pass through life
  To think untaught.

"Yet to man's life doth Thought,
  Though vain its quest,
Lend all the power that makes
  It nobly blest."

Then, sighing, Life replied,
  "Too-bounded scope,
Poor foolish thought, gives Life
  For thy great hope.

"And space and time, and all
  That men call being,
Are objects much too small
  For thy far-seeing."

To which Thought once more said,
  "Thus it must be,
That Thought can more than Life,
  And further see.

"Wherefore thou seest, Life,
  Howe'er distraught,
By her great quest—far higher
  Than Life is Thought."

*   *   *   *   *

Then I at last, well-learned
  In power of Thought,
And worth of Life—to soothe
  Their rivalry sought.

Thus to the twain said I,
  " What needs this strife?
Twin mysteries are ye,
  Both Thought and Life."

II—FREEDOM.
I.—FATE AND MAN.

MEANING well, men compass ill,
  Scheming ill, they good fulfil;
Such is Fate's ironic will,
Such her metamorphic skill,
From one substance to distil,
Balm to quicken—bane to kill.

Children-like, our laps we load
With flowers culled upon life's road;
These we bear to Fate's abode,
Nothing witting, but her mode
To distil, from gifts bestowed,
Drugs that solace or corrode.

Fate is sightless, Fate is free,
Yet her limits knoweth she;
Thus, though purblind mortals, we
All her methods cannot see,
Yet we know supreme is He
Who hath made Fate blind and free

II.—THE DEVOUT SKEPTIC'S DYING PRAYER.

Apropos of the Creed: "I believe in God. . . . Amen."

AT last I come, O God of Truth, to Thee,
   From human error longing to be free;
  Earth's dubious dogmas I have long since scorned,
And, tired of blindly groping, hope to see.

Men call me skeptic—this at least is truth,
Their skeptic I—distrustful of their sooth,
  Their clamorous certainties, convictions rash,
Unfounded as the baseless dreams of youth.

I own it, God, my creed I have postponed,
From earth to heaven, with weakness unbemoaned;
  I dare not formulate, assert, pronounce,
Until I see Thee, who art Truth enthroned.

My mental tablet I have hence kept *razed*,
Whereat, with angry wonderment amazed,
  Men with their tablets trebly written on,
And crossed and blotted, cry, "The man is crazed."

No! mine shall be the heaven-inscribèd roll,
Truth's clear and golden impress on my soul;
  No palimpsest, with earth-born error blurr'd
And surface scratched; but new and clean and whole.

Thus then, my doubt to Thee I humbly bring,
A sacrifice to truth—far hence I fling,
  With dying breath, beliefs, convictions, creeds,
Mere human baggage—to Thyself I cling.

III.—To the Future World.

Dark World! I ask not if thou be,
  Thy Being or non-Being frets not me;
I would not lift—if so I might,
The curtain that enshrouds thy night.

For grant *thou art*—that could not change
Stern duty's sphere—in Earth-life's range;
Still must I work, learn, think, and say,
As now I do, from day to day.

Grant *thou art not*; yet must I still
One round with Man, Life, Thought fulfil;
With these, their Life-course done—I must
In death commingle—dust to dust.

The flower that grows, matures, and dies,
One moment brightening living eyes,
Demands no more of Life, Tune, Bloom,
And space, than Earth allots it room.

Goodness is great, Truth still bides true,
Though Earth-things 'scape man's Earth-born view,
Eternal Time claims this one day,
Though Heaven and Earth both pass away.

Content am I—my Here-life be
Worthy of Immortality;
Yet, careless somewhat—if its lot
Be *that*, or death-still'd and forgot.

Content—as by high wisdom plann'd,
This Earth- to Heaven-life to expand,
Or else this Life itself to guard
As its sole duty, worth, reward.

Frances Ridley Havergal.
1836—1879.

FRANCES RIDLEY HAVERGAL was born at Astley, n Worcestershire, on the 14th of December, 1836. Her father, the Rev. W. H. Havergal, himself a writer of hymns as well as a distinguished Church musician, was at this time rector of Astley, and afterwards successively rector of St Nicholas', Worcester (1842), and Shareshill, near Wolverhampton (1860). In 1850 Frances entered a school kept by Mrs. Teed, and under the favourable influences of her surroundings consecrated her life and talents to religious exercise and work. On the removal of her father from Worcester she resided at different periods at Leamington and Caswell Bay, Swansea, at which latter place she died on the 3rd of June, 1879.

Much of Miss Havergal's verse was first published in leaflet form; but from time to time her poems were collected and published with others in volumes bearing titles as follows: "Ministry of Song" (1869); "Twelve Sacred Songs for Little Singers" (1870); "Under the Surface" (1874), "Loyal Responses" (1878); "Life Mosaic" (1879); "Life Chords" (1880); "Life Echoes" (1883). Miss Havergal's verse owes its popularity more to its religious teaching than to its poetic merit—teaching which has been aptly described as "mildly Calvinistic without the severe dogmatic tenet of reprobation." Without making any pretensions to the *rôle* of a poet, she gave lyrical expression to her own spiritual experiences and aspirations, and in doing so voiced the feelings and desires of others less able to express themselves. In this, though it cannot be said that she showed any marked originality of thought or felicity of expression, she at least fulfilled one of the offices of poetry. Many of her hymns have become widely popular, and have been included in various hymn-books in England and America. Her "Consecration Hymn," beginning

> Take my life, and let it be
> Consecrated, Lord, to Thee,

has been, as we imagine she would have desired it to be, one of the most popular. Whatever qualities her verse may lack, there can be no doubt as to its sincerity; and this is a quality not always found in religious verse. The entire consecration she sought to make included her powers of versification; and had they been much greater than they were, they would doubtless have been devoted as unreservedly to Christian service.

ALFRED H. MILES.

POEMS.

FRANCES RIDLEY HAVERGAL.

I.—CONSECRATION HYMN.

"Truly I am Thy servant."—PSALM CXVI. 16.

TAKE my life, and let it be
Consecrated, Lord, to Thee;
Take my moments and my days,
Let them flow in ceaseless praise.

Take my hands, and let them move
At the impulse of Thy love;
Take my feet, and let them be
Swift and beautiful for Thee.

Take my voice, and let me sing,
Always, only, for my King;
Take my lips, and let them be
Filled with messages from Thee.

Take my silver and my gold,
Not a mite would I withhold;
Take my intellect, and use
Every power as Thou shalt choose.

Take my will, and make it Thine;
It shall be no longer mine:
Take my heart, it is Thine own;
It shall be Thy royal throne.

Take my love, my Lord, I pour
At Thy feet its treasure-store
Take myself, and I will be
Ever, *only*, ALL for Thee.

II.—A WORKER'S PRAYER.

LORD, speak to me, that I may speak
   In living echoes of Thy tone;
As Thou hast sought, so let me seek
   Thy erring children, lost and lone.

O lead me, Lord, that I may lead
   The wandering and the wavering feet;
O feed me, Lord, that I may feed
   Thy hungering ones with manna sweet.

O strengthen me, that while I stand
   Firm on the Rock and strong in Thee,
I may stretch out a loving hand
   To wrestlers with the troubled sea.

O teach me, Lord, that I may teach
   The precious things Thou dost impart;
And wing my words, that they may reach
   The hidden depths of many a heart.

O give Thine own sweet rest to me,
   That I may speak with soothing power
A word in season, as from Thee,
   To weary ones in needful hour.

O fill me with Thy fulness, Lord,
   Until my very heart o'erflow
In kindling thought and glowing word,
   Thy love to tell, Thy praise to show.

O use me, Lord, use even me,
   Just *as* Thou wilt, and *when*, and *where*;
Until Thy blessèd Face I see,
   Thy rest, Thy joy, Thy glory share.

III.—NOW AND AFTERWARD.

NOW, the sowing and the weeping,
   Working hard and waiting long;
Afterward, the golden reaping,
   Harvest home and grateful song.

Now, the pruning, sharp, unsparing;
   Scattered blossom, bleeding shoot!
Afterward, the plenteous bearing
   Of the Master's pleasant fruit.

Now, the plunge, the briny burden,
   Blind, faint gropings in the sea;
Afterward, the pearly guerdon
   That shall make the diver free.

Now, the long and toilsome duty
   Stone by stone to carve and bring;
Afterward, the perfect beauty
   Of the palace of the King.

Now, the tuning and the tension,
   Wailing minors, discord strong;
Afterward, the grand ascension
   Of the Alleluia song.

Now, the spirit conflict-riven,
   Wounded heart, unequal strife;
Afterward, the triumph given,
   And the victor's crown of life.

Now, the training, strange and lowly,
   Unexplained and tedious now;
Afterward, the service holy,
   And the Master's "Enter thou!"

IV.—ADORATION.

O MASTER, at Thy feet
    I bow in rapture sweet!
Before me, as in darkening glass,
    Some glorious outlines pass,
Of love, and truth, and holiness, and power·
I own them Thine, O Christ, and bless Thee for this ho

    O full of truth and grace,
    Smile of Jehovah's face,
O tenderest heart of love untold!
    Who may Thy praise unfold?
Thee, Saviour, Lord of lords and King of kings,
Well may adoring seraphs hymn with veiling wings.

    I have no words to bring
    Worthy of Thee, my King,
And yet one anthem in Thy praise
    I long, I long to raise;
The heart is full, the eye entranced above,
But words all melt away in silent awe and love.

    How can the lip be dumb,
    The hand all still and numb,
When Thee the heart doth see and own
    Her Lord and God alone?
Tune for Thyself the music of my days,
And open Thou my lips that I may show Thy praise.

    Yea, let my whole life be
    One anthem unto Thee,
And let the praise of lip and life
    Outring all sin and strife.
O Jesus, Master! be Thy name supreme,
For heaven and earth the one, the grand, the eternal th

William Hall.
1838.

THE solace of song is responsible for much verse, spiritually if not technically "made perfect through suffering." Especially is this true of religious verse. It is the spirit of the fruit crushed in the press that gives fire and verve to the wine. When not simply didactic, religious poetry is largely religious experience in verse form, and it affects the reader in proportion as it gives definition to his own feelings with a clearness of insight and a felicity of expression he cannot himself command. On the other hand, there are poets, debarred by physical disabilities from other service, like the Rev. William Hall, whose ministry was interrupted by weakness and failure of voice, "who, passing through the valley of Baca, make it a well," and who, turning their obstacles into means, devote their enforced leisure seriously to the composition of religious verse as a vocation, working to loosen "well springs in dry places," that "the desert may blossom as the rose."

Mr. Hall was born near Cork in the year 1838, and was educated at the university of his native land. Compelled to abandon public ministry in the Church, and living largely the life of a student and recluse, he adopted the ministry of verse to give expression to the thoughts, experiences, and lessons of his life. He published "The Victory of Defeat, and Other Poems" (1896); "The Way of the Kingdom, and Other Poems"

(1899); "Renunciation, and Other Poems" (1902); and "Via Crucis," a volume of selections from his former volumes, with additions (1906). "The Victory of Defeat" is based upon the story of Jacob and the Angel, and the other poems of the volume are chiefly upon Hebrew themes. "The Way of the Kingdom" volume is also largely inspired by the Hebrew poets. "Renunciation, and Other Poems" shows a freer hand, and if it does not touch a deeper note, breathes a warmer atmosphere. "Via Crucis," which forms one of Messrs Routledge's Devotional Library, is a series impressed with the stamp of the Cross. This includes many of the best of the poems from former volumes, but there are other longer and more important poems which should not be over-looked. Of these, "The Victory of Defeat," "The Redeemed City," and "Epictetus" in the first volume, and "Forget not yet," and "A Hymn from the Depths" in the second, may be mentioned.

It is in his longer poems that Mr. Hall's best work is found; a fact which makes it very difficult to represent it within present limits. The selected stanzas given in the following pages may induce the further study of these. "A Bruised Reed," and "Good Night" favourably represent the lyrics.

ALFRED H. MILES.

VIA CRUCIS.
1906.
WILLIAM HALL.

I.—*RENUNCIATION: SELECTED STANZAS.*

(SECTION II.)

THE breaking dawn the darkness puts to flight,
   Kindling to flame each cold, bleak, naked height;
Its splendours strike thy sleep-locked, shrouded sight.

Part with the visionary for the real,—
Phantoms of night when dreams the eyelids seal;
Let not the illusive show the substance steal:
              Shake off thy sleep, let go!

(SECTION XV.)

Wrapt in her cerements, prisoned in the tomb
Of flesh, thy spirit sighs for ampler room,
Buried in night-shades and sepulchral gloom.

This is the note of each progressive thing—
Reluctance to its cruder stage to cling,
Fain the growth-hindering husk away to fling.

Who shun the birth-pangs ushering from the womb
Abortions of the universe become,
Cast on the void—their spirit-sense all numb.

Develop thou the nobler life within,
Fling off the veil—the envelope of sin,
Die to the death of life, to live begin!
              Divest thy sheath; let go!

(SECTION XVI.)

Let the gay gauze-winged fly apt lesson teach,—
Matured she mounts some reed at easy reach,
Leaves low companionship of eft and leech·

Hangs for a tremulous moment while she dries
Her veined diaphanous fans,—then venturous tries
A region strange, while functions new she plies.

Above her stretch the fields of azure air;
Beneath—the foul depths of her stagnant mere,
Of loathsome creeping things the horrid lair.

Of her stupendous change now on the eve,
Prepared new large endowments to receive,
Such uncongenial scenes she joys to leave.

Thy wings for heavenly flight all plumed and drest,
Why lingerest still in this thy sorry nest?
In prison-cage fledged spirits find scant rest:
                    Poor straitened soul, let go!

(SECTION XVIII.)

Learn in self-sacrifice to find thy joy,
The only bliss unmingled with alloy;
All lesser pleasures soon must pall and cloy.

Better it is to give than to receive,
All to forsake than unto aught to cleave;—
'Tis in the act of giving that we live.

All spiritual Being lives by this—
The ground and basis of the Godhood's bliss;
Who turn therefrom the Life Eternal miss.

For though discharged in full strict duty's round,
If in the chains of self-hood thou art bound—
Lifeless and void of worth thy works are found.

Throughout the extent of Nature's wide domain
See this great law of sacrifice obtain,
The creature's loss conditioning its gain.

The very elements this law obey,—
The beams that from the solar source outray,
The springing fount's perpetual sparkling play.

All living things are constituted so,
All organisms from out earth's womb that grow;
As is the outward, so the to-ward flow:

So that whate'er impedes or hindereth
The pores' free play, the issue of the breath,
Is the concomitant or cause of death:
      Would'st truly live ?—let go !

(SECTION XIX.)

E'en when thou hast parted with these meaner things,
Christ's law of sacrifice fresh claims still brings;
To life's last close the imperious summons rings.

Driv'n from each hold—self builds thereof in lieu
Some later refuge with materials new,
For life at any cost content to sue.

To virtue's supreme summits would'st thou press,—
Thy righteousness must be renounced no less
Than erst thine evil and unrighteousness.

To the whole human family akin—
Accept as thine the common guilt and sin,
Whose undeveloped germs thou bear'st within.

Howsoe'er pure and blameless in men's eyes
Thy life and deeds—beneath a thin disguise
An unknown world of foul corruption lies.

Shun not the Spirit's probing of thine heart,
The full disclosure of the thing thou art,
However keen and painful be the smart.

Yea, welcome all that weakens self-esteem
Awakes thee from each vain, self-flattering dream;
Meanest of all men learn thyself to deem.

Abase thee in thine own and others' sight,
A just and lowly estimate invite,
Take the last place—in thy false pride's despite;
All vain pretence let go!

(SECTION XX)

Whate'er thou'st won, remaineth still much more;
Heaven hath abundance yet for thee in store;
Still glows the grand Ideal on before!—

Which all thy best achievements doth degrade,
Thy boasted virtues dwarfs, and makes to fade,
Yea pass into complete eclipse and shade.

Ev'n he who such high eminence had gained
Yet counted not that aught was yet attained,
But onward to the goal with ardour strained,—

Reckoning his reach but as the starting-place,
Whence to pursue the spirit's boundless race;
Of life's grand edifice but laid the base.

E'en saints on high with heavenly honours crowned
Their crowns of glory cast upon the ground,
Not otherwise loyal and faultless found.

Great is the goal, the guerdon 'fore thee set,
No self-complacence must thy progress let,
Press boldly on, the things behind forget;
Part with thy past, let go!

(SECTION XXI.)

This moment's thine, thou never more may'st hear
The clarion-summons-call thus loud and clear;
What now thou buyest cheap may yet prove dear.

Part with thine all, spare not the needed cost;
That which thou partest with were better lost,
Thy selfish worldly schemes more wisely crossed.

Thy loss infinitesimal, thy gain
Endless, immense; thy momentary pain
The single step the boundless bliss to attain!

These idol loves that gender loveless lust—
Weighed in the balances, whose scales are just,
With the bright hopes thou spurn'st—are breath-borne
    dust!

Eye hath not seen, man's ear hath never heard,
Nor heart conceived—save some faint image blurred—
The bliss of those who keep the Christly word—
              Let go; my soul, let go!

II.—SELF-COMMUNION: SELECTED STANZAS.

COMMUNE with thine own heart!—no need
    To wander the wide earth around;
If but in thine own breast thou read
    Aright—thy God thou wilt have found;
Who habiteth Eternity
There condescends to dwell with thee.

(SECTION V.)

Commune with thine own heart! for there
   The Heaven-ascending ladder lies,
A pathway into purer air,
   A window giving on the skies;
Through which thou mayest wing thy flight,
And mingle with the Infinite.

There-through thy thoughts may pass at large
   When ill with thee it here doth fare,
Procuring thee a full discharge
   From harassing and carking care:
From Earth's enthralling fetters free
There thou may'st range at liberty.

Yea there thou may'st shut-to the door
   Against all envy, strife, and hate;
Though outwardly they rave and roar,
   Within they may not penetrate:
Safe-guarded in that still recess
Thou shalt defy the angry press.

(SECTION VI.

Commune with thine own heart!—for there
   The better, nobler self resides,
That in the life divine doth share,
   And ever in the Presence bides;
The self with Deity at one,
As with its beam the central sun.

There—from the world of sense aloof—
   Such insight shall be granted thee
As shall afford thee ample proof
   Of thine august paternity;
The Spirit witnessing with thine
That thou art sprung from seed divine.

III.—A BRUISED REED.

A REED, torn rudely from its native bed,
  Where murmuring streams its living verdure fed,
Bruised, broken, marred, upon the miry bank
Lies—'mid the rotting herbage, fetid, dank—

Neglect and useless, till some master hand
Repair, touch, tune it for high service grand;
Breathe through the tremulous stem some plaintive air,
And wake the memories long dormant there.

Once more it whispers of the winds, the waves,
The purling brook—its sister reeds that laves;
Drinks the clear shine, the cool refreshing shower;
For nesting warblers furnishes a bower.

The impressions from its life-experience brought
Into its fibrous texture are inwrought
So deep, the smooth cylindric walls vibrate
With tender memories dear and delicate

But still the sweetest, most entrancing notes
On eve's calm air it rapturously floats,
Potent to assuage and soothe pain, grief, and care,
Were learned in the dark hour of its supreme despair.

IV.—WHO WILL SHOW US ANY GOOD:

SECTION II.

SELECTED STANZAS.

WHENAS the skilful hand dissects
  The slumbering pupa of the worm,
The keen and cunning eye detects
  The winged imago's embryo form:

Look but attentively beneath
   Integument and covering,—
Thou'lt see, close folded in their sheath,
   The rudiments of foot and wing.

The soul of man, laid bare to view,
   Supplies like singular augury;
Therein we find the guiding clue
   To all he's fore-ordained to be:
It needs no cunning eye therein
   To read presumptively his fate,
Some forecast of his future win,
   His goal and scope anticipate.

Not surer does the nascent fin
   Or wing some special use foretell;
The embryo members, shut within
   The safe enclosure of the shell,
Predict the noble life and free
   The full-developed bird awaits,
The blissful, rapturous ecstacy
   It yet shall share in with its mates.

Each organ immature shows forth
   Its true connatural element,
Whether of ocean, air, or earth,
   Towards which, its vesicle but rent,
Forthwith precipitate it speeds,
   Nor will by ought be turned aside,
For thence alone the pressing needs
   Wherewith it wakes can be supplied.

GOOD-NIGHT.

I.

GOOD-NIGHT! Good-night!—no long farewell,
   A brief adieu we wave to thee;
Toll o'er thee no wild funeral knell,
   Wail out no threnody;
                Good-night! Good-night!

Where evil none molests or harms,
   Nor racking cares disturb the breast,
—Into the Everlasting Arms
   We give thee—take thy rest!

While we through lone night-watches toil,
   'Mid howling blast, and drenching spray,
Attempting tasks our efforts foil,
   Waiting the lingering day,

—Thou, upon some empyrean height,
   Stand'st girt with spirits of the Blest,
To help us in the weary fight,
   Whisper of welcome rest;

And as fair morn uplifts the veil
   From off night's sombre, stormy brow,
Thine it may be the first to hail
   Our homeward-veering prow;
                Good-night! Good-night!

II.

Good-night! Good-night!—this is but sleep
   That gently creepeth o'er thy brain,—
Drink the bland potion, large and deep,
   Cure for life's long sore pain;
                Good-night! Good-night!

Sleep!—nay, but rather thou dost wake
   From life's wild feverish fretful dream;
From off thee the illusions shake
   Wherewith the night-hours teem:

—'Tis *we* who sleep, we, we alone!
   Prey of vain visionary fears;—
For thee the phantom mists are flown,
   The splendent dawn appears,

—Driving to dark Oblivion's caves
   The spectral forms wherewith we fight,
The airy dreams fond hope still waves
   Before the baffled sight;
               Good-night! Good-night!

III.

Good-night!—some blest celestial band
   Ev'n now may greet thee with good-morn.
And welcome to the Heavenly strand
   A spirit newly born.

As insect waked from wintry trance
   By the mild breath of quickening Spring,
To join its fellows' blithesome dance
   On light-plumed feathery wing:

So thou, thy proper peers among,
   A wingèd thing of light and fire,
Art one with the Throne-circling throng,
   The fair seraphic choir;
               Good-night! Good-night!

Samuel John Stone.

1839—1900.

SAMUEL JOHN STONE, son of the Rev. William Stone, was born at Whitmore, Staffordshire, on the 25th of April, 1839. He was educated at the Charterhouse School, and at Pembroke College, Oxford, where he graduated B.A. in 1862. On taking Holy Orders, he became Curate of Windsor in 1862, and of St Paul's, Haggerston, in 1870, succeeding his father as vicar of the same parish in 1874. His principal works are "Lyra Fidelium" (1866); "The Knight of Intercession and other Poems" (1872); "Sonnets of the Christian Year," first published in the *Leisure Hour* and afterwards in volume form (1875); "Order of the Consecutive Church Service for Children, with Original Hymns" (1883); and "Hymns Original and Translated" (1886). "The Knight of Intercession," Mr. Stone's first volume of general poetry, has run through a number of editions, and many of his hymns have become popular, nearly fifty of them having come into general use.

The Rev. John Julian says: "Mr. Stone's hymns vary considerably in metre and subject, and thus present a pleasing variety, not always found in the compositions of popular hymn-writers. His best hymns are well designed and clearly expressed. The tone is essentially dogmatic and hopeful. The absence of rich poetic thought and graceful fancy is more than atoned for by a masterly condensation of Scripture facts and of Church teaching, given tersely and with great vigour. His changes and antitheses are frequently abrupt, in many instances too much so for congregational purposes, and his vocabulary is somewhat limited. His rhythm, except where broken either by long or by compound words, is rarely at fault, and his rhyme is usually perfect. A few of his hymns are plaintive and pathetic, as the tender 'Weary of earth and laden with my sin'; others are richly musical, as 'Lord of the harvest! it is right and meet'; but the greater part are strongly outspoken utterances of a manly faith, where dogma, prayer, and praise are interwoven with much skill. Usually the key-note of his song is Hope."

But Mr. Stone's muse was not wholly occupied with devotional verse; indeed, his hymns comprise but a small portion of his volume, in which nature, legendary, pastoral, idyllic, and descriptive poems, memorial verses, songs and sonnets, form the largest portion, though it must be admitted that the religious spirit is ever present, be the mood whatever it may. Humour, moreover, has its part, as the following will show:—

THE SOLILOQUY OF A RATIONALISTIC CHICKEN.

On the Picture of a Newly Hatched Chicken Contemplating the Fragments of its Native Shell.

Most strange!
Most queer,—although most excellent a change!
Shades of the prison-house, ye disappear!
My fettered thoughts have won a wider range,
And, like my legs, are free;

No longer huddled up so pitiably:
Free now to pry and probe, and peep and peer,
  And make these mysteries out
Shall a free-thinking chicken live in doubt?
For now in doubt undoubtedly I am :
 This problem's very heavy on my mind,
And I'm not one to either shirk or sham :
 I won't be blinded, and I won't be blind!

   Now, let me see ;
First, I would know how did I get in *there* ?
   Then, where was I of yore ?
Besides, why didn't I get out before ?

   Bless me !
Here are three puzzles (out of plenty more)
Enough to give me pip upon the brain !
   But let me think again.
How do I know I ever *was* inside?
Now I reflect, it is, I do maintain,
Less than my reason, and beneath my pride
   To think that I could dwell
In such a paltry miserable cell
   As that old shell
Of course I couldn't ! How could *I* have lain,
Body and beak and feathers, legs and wings,
And my deep heart's sublime imaginings,
   In there ?

I meet the notion with profound disdain;
It's quite incredible ; since I declare
(And I'm a chicken that you can't deceive)
What I can't understand I won't believe.
Where *did* I come from, then ? Ah! where, indeed ?
This is a riddle monstrous hard to read.
   I have it ! Why, of course,
All things are moulded by some plastic force
Out of some atoms somewhere up in space,
Fortuitously concurrent anyhow .—
   There, now !
That's plain as is the beak upon my face.

>   What's that I hear?
> My mother cackling at me! Just her way,
> So prejudiced and ignorant *I* say;
> So far behind the wisdom of the day!
>
>   What's old I *can't* revere.
> Hark at her. "You're a little fool, my dear,
>   That's quite as plain, alack!
> As is the piece of shell upon your back!"
> How bigoted! upon my back, indeed!
>   I don't believe it's there;
> For I can't *see* it; and I do declare,
>   For all her fond deceivin',
> *What I can't see I never will believe in!*

The hymn "Lord of our souls' salvation," p. 649, written for the occasion of the National Thanksgiving on the recovery of the Prince of Wales (February 27th, 1872), was abbreviated to four verses by the author for use at the service at St. Paul's Cathedral, but was used generally throughout the country in its complete form.

ALFRED H. MILES.

HYMNS.

SAMUEL JOHN STONE.

I.—THE CHURCH'S ONE FOUNDATION.

"I Believe in the Holy Catholic Church, the Communion of Saints."

THE Church's one Foundation
   Is Jesus Christ her Lord:
She is His new creation
   By water and the Word;
From heaven He came and sought her
   To be His holy Bride,
With His own Blood He bought her,
   And for her life He died.

Elect from every nation,
   Yet one o'er all the earth,
Her charter of salvation
   One Lord, one Faith, one Birth;
One Holy Name she blesses,
   Partakes one Holy Food,
And to one Hope she presses,
   With every grace endued.

The Church shall never perish!
   Her dear Lord to defend,
To guide, sustain, and cherish,
   Is with her to the end:
Though there be those who hate her,
   And false sons in her pale,
Against or foe or traitor
   She ever shall prevail.

Though with a scornful wonder
  Men see her sore opprest,
By schisms rent asunder,
  By heresies distrest;
Yet saints their watch are keeping,
  Their cry goes up "How long?"
And soon the night of weeping
  Shall be the morn of song.

'Mid toil and tribulation,
  And tumult of her war,
She waits the consummation
  Of peace for evermore;
Till with the vision glorious
  Her longing eyes are blest,
And the great Church victorious
  Shall be the Church at rest.

Yet she on earth hath union
  With FATHER, SPIRIT, SON,
And mystic sweet communion
  With those whose rest is won;
With all her sons and daughters,
  Who, by the Master's Hand
Led through the deathly waters,
  Repose in Eden-Land.

Oh, happy ones and holy!
  LORD, give us grace that we
Like them, the meek and lowly,
  On high may dwell with Thee!
There past the border mountains,
  Where in sweet vales the Bride
With Thee by living fountains
  For ever shall abide.

II.—ROUND THE SACRED CITY GATHER.

BATTLE HYMN OF CHURCH DEFENCE.

ROUND the Sacred City gather
   Egypt, Edom, Babylon;
All the warring hosts of error,
   Sworn against her, are as one:
Vain the leaguer! her foundations
   Are upon the holy hills,
And the love of the ETERNAL
   All her stately temple fills.

Get thee, watchman, to the rampart!
   Gird thee, warrior, with thy sword!
And be strong as ye remember
   In your midst is GOD the LORD:
Like the night-mists from the valley,
   These shall vanish, one by one,
Egypt's malice, Edom's envy,
   And the hate of Babylon.

But be true, ye sons and daughters,
   Lest the peril be within;
Watch to prayer, lest in your slumber
   Stealthy foemen enter in;
Safe the mother and the children
   If their will and love be strong,
While their loyal hearts go singing
   Prayer and praise for battle-song.

Church of GOD! if we forget thee,
   Let His blessing fail our hand;
When our love shall not prefer thee,
   Let His love forget our land—
Nay! our memory shall be steadfast
   Though in storm the mountains shake,
And our love is love for ever,
   For it is for JESUS' sake.

Church of JESUS! His thy Banner
   And thy Banner's awful Sign:
By His passion and His glory
   Thou art His and He is thine:
From the Hill of His Redemption
   Flows thy sacramental tide:
From the Hill of His Ascension
   Flows the grace of God thy Guide.

Yea: thou Church of GOD the SPIRIT!
   His Society Divine,
His the living Word thou keepest,
   His thy Apostolic line,
Ancient prayer and song liturgic,
   Creeds that change not to the end,
As His gift we have received them,
   As His charge we will defend.

Alleluia, Alleluia,
   To the FATHER, SPIRIT, SON,
In Whose will the Church at warfare
   With the Church at rest is one:
So to THEE we sing in union,
   GOD in earth and Heav'n adored,
Alleluia, Alleluia,
   Holy, Holy, Holy LORD.

III.—LORD OF OUR SOULS' SALVATION.

Hymn of Thanksgiving for the Recovery of H.R.H. The Prince of Wales.

Sung in St. Paul's Cathedral on February 27, 1872.

LORD of our souls' salvation!
   Lord of our earthly weal!
We who in tribulation
   Did for Thy mercy kneel,
Lift up glad hearts before Thee,
   And eyes no longer dim,
And for Thy grace adore Thee
   In eucharistic hymn.

When vine and fig-tree languish,
   And every fount is dry,
When hearts in supreme anguish
   To Thee lift up their cry:
Then doth Thy love deliver!
   From Thine unshortened hand
Joy, like the southern river,
   O'erflows the weary land.

Lay dark o'er field and city
   Death's shadow, and in fear
To Thee, O LORD of Pity,
   GOD of the hearing ear!
By the dear Grace that bought us
   We cried as in the night,
And lo! the morning brought us
   From Thee the living light.

Went forth the nation weeping,
   With precious seed of prayer,
Hope's awful vigil keeping
   'Mid rumours of despair,

Now, to Thy glory bringing
   Its sheaves of praise along,
Again it cometh singing
   A happy harvest song.

O sweet and divine fashion
   Of Grace sublime in power!
That meteth out compassion
   By sorrow's direst hour:
O Love, most high, most holy!
   The merciful in might,
That unto hearts most lowly
   Is ever Depth and Height.

Bless Thou our adoration!
   Our gladness sanctify!
Be this rejoicing nation
   To Thee by joy more nigh:
Oh be this great Thanksgiving,
   That with one voice we raise,
Wrought into holier living
   Through all our after days.

Bless, FATHER, him Thou gavest
   Back to the loyal land;
O SAVIOUR, him Thou savest
   Still cover with Thine Hand;
O SPIRIT, the Defender,
   Be his to guard and guide,
Now in life's mid-day splendour,
   On to the eventide!

IV.—WEARY OF EARTH.
"I BELIEVE IN THE FORGIVENESS OF SINS."

WEARY of earth and laden with my sin,
   I look at heaven and long to enter in,

But there no evil thing may find a home—
And yet I hear a Voice that bids me "Come."

So vile I am, how dare I hope to stand
In the pure glory of that holy land?
Before the whiteness of that Throne appear?—
Yet there are Hands stretched out to draw me near.

The while I fain would tread the heavenly way,
Evil is ever with me day by day—
Yet on mine ears the gracious tidings fall,
"Repent, confess, thou shalt be loosed from all."

It is the voice of JESUS that I hear,
His are the Hands stretched out to draw me near,
And His the Blood that can for all atone,
And set me faultless there before the Throne.

'Twas He Who found me on the deathly wild,
And made me heir of heaven, the FATHER's child,
And day by day, whereby my soul may live,
Gives me His grace of pardon, and will give.

O great Absolver, grant my soul may wear
The lowliest garb of penitence and prayer,
That in the FATHER's courts my glorious dress
May be the garment of Thy righteousness.

Yea, Thou wilt answer for me, Righteous LORD:
Thine all the merits, mine the great reward;
Thine the sharp thorns, so mine the golden crown,
Mine the life won, through Thine the life laid down.

Naught can I bring, dear LORD, for all I owe,
Yet let my full heart what it can bestow;
Like Mary's gift let my devotion prove,
Forgiven greatly, how I greatly love.

V.—THEIR NAMES ARE NAMES OF KINGS.
The "Athletes of the Universe."
(An expression used by S. Chrysostom.)

THEIR names are names of kings
  Of heavenly line,
The bliss of earthly things
  Who did resign.

Chieftains they were, who warr'd
  With sword and shield;
Victors for God the Lord
  On foughten field.

Sad were their days on earth,
  'Mid hate and scorn;
A life of pleasures dearth,
  A death forlorn.

Yet blest that end in woe,
  And those sad days;
Only man's blame below—
  Above, God's praise!

A city of great name
  Was built for them,
Of glorious golden fame—
  Jerusalem.

Redeemed with precious Blood
  From death and sin,
Sons of the Triune God,
  They entered in.

So did the life of pain
  In glory close;
Lord God, may we attain
  Their grand repose!

Frederick William Orde Ward.
1843.

THERE have probably been few more prolific writers of verse than the Rev. F. W. Orde Ward. Under the *nom-de-plume*, F. Harald Williams, he published, in 1890, "'Twixt Kiss and Lip" (800 large pages of closely printed verse); in 1894, "Confessions of a Poet" (492 pages); in 1897, "Matin Bells" (550 pages), in 1899, "English Roses" (600 pages); and in 1904, "The Prisoner of Love" (400 pages), besides other volumes which need not be enumerated.

The writer has a theory that there are only three or, at most, four reasons which can justify a writer in publishing a book. The first, is that he is prepared to say something that has not been said before. The second, is that he is prepared to say something that has been said before better than it has been previously said. The third, is that some good purpose may be served by repeating something previously said, even though the saying cannot be improved upon, in which case, it should be quoted; and the fourth, is that it may be urgent that something should be repeated which cannot be improved upon, but which, from failure of memory or inaccessibility of reference, it is impossible to quote, in which case, the circumstances should be stated and the obligation indicated. If these rules were observed far fewer books would be published, but the literature which would remain would be a never-failing source of refreshment and inspiration.

Of course, the adoption of such a standard would be fatal to much that is published by most men, and all that is published by some. Had the author of these many volumes followed it, he would have found that one of his closely-printed volumes,—which would accommodate all the verse that Keats ever wrote, twice over—would have been more than sufficient for all the poetry he has produced. Absence of restraint always means redundance, and incontinence inevitably carries with it the seeds of disintegration. They do so here. "I never saw," said a critic, in a letter written to the present writer in this connection, "a case of one of so much ability, apparently so eager to bury himself in a wilderness of his own creation." He who may desire with loving hand to raise an enduring monument to the memory of this poet, will have to clear the ground of a mass of wordy exuberance before he can hope to find sufficient materials for his purpose.

Born on the 9th of April, 1843, Orde Ward was educated at Tonbridge School, Wadham College and Charsley Hall, Oxford. He was successively curate of St Giles', Oxford; Rockingham, Northants; Vicar of Pishill, and Rector of Nuffield, Henley-on-Thames.

In the preface of "The Prisoner of Love," the poet says—"I have endeavoured to articulate in verse the most advanced religious and other truths of our time. . . . Whether I have succeeded or not . . . in supplying fresh reconciliations or suggesting other avenues of faith and feeling, I am convinced that the message of the cross remains as new as ever still, and is all the music of our lives."

ALFRED H. MILES.

THE PRISONER OF LOVE.

1904.

F. W. ORDE WARD.

I.—CHRIST THE OUTCAST.

"He came unto His own, and His own received Him not."—
St. John i. 11.

WHEN Jesus came to earth below
To make men Godlike too and free,
And gave what Heaven could but bestow
On those blue hills of Galilee,
They thrust Him from them unto death,
Even in His own dear Nazareth.

Foxes had holes, the bird its nest,
The leper knew a corner dim
For weary brow and wounded breast—
His earth had nowhere room for Him;
Against Him strove the wind and wave,
He found no shelter but the grave.

Yea, though He simply sought men's good
And lavished on them Living Bread,
Who as our High Priest loved and stood
Betwixt the dying and the dead,
Yet they that felt His mercies most,
Drave Him an exile from their coast.

O shall He homeless walk the lands
Which reap the blessings He hath sown,
And plead in vain with piercèd hands
For that which always was His own?
Shall He, our Fountain from the first,
Be yet the only one athirst?

II.—THE CUP.

"O my Father, if this cup may not pass away from Me, except I drink it, Thy will be done."—St. Matt. xxvi. 42.

There is a Cup, the Saviour drank,
Who drained it to the very lees,
We take from God and humbly thank
When shadow falls and sunshine flees;
The sorrow which doth make the king
Who would be crowned by suffering
And knowledge which alone is rank.

We all must deeply drink the cup
Of grief, if we would enter in
Christ's fellowship which raiseth up
The souls redeemèd from their sin;
And then, when we have tasted death
In Him and trodden it beneath,
With God Himself at last we sup.

If it be possible, we say,
Let this affliction from me fly,
And bid me walk some softer way
Than that of Christ's own Agony!
But there is Grace sufficient then,
For God is merciful to men—
And Heaven is opened as we pray.

Himself in trial by us stands
And strengthens us to bear it all,
The Cup He holdeth in His Hands
And on His Bosom breaks our fall;
He drinketh too the bitter first,
And leaves the sweetness for our thirst—
Who gives the powers with the commands.

III.—THE RESURRECTION OF THE FLOWERS.

"He feedeth among the lilies."—Sol. Song ii. 16.

THE seed was sown, perhaps in tears,
 And then the miracle appears
Where once was only desert dearth;
And from a hidden realm and root
Leaps into life the tender shoot,
Out of its chambers in the earth;
It gathers grace of light and air,
And laughs to find itself so fair.

Ah, it may have a vision sweet,
Unmarked by us, of Holy Feet
Which are for ever passing by;
And washing these in dainty dew,
With kisses, it may thus renew
Its glories at eternity;
For when they break the scentless sod,
The flowers reflect the Face of God.

Each is a little word or line
Of the great Mystery Divine,
Each has a lesson in its look:
The varying hue, the virgin green,
To humble hearts that spell between
Are Revelation's open book;
And still the Spirit moves in might,
For those that have the secret sight.

IV.—SUMMER'S PARABLE.

"The Lord is good to all: and his tender mercies are over all His works."—Ps. cxlv. 9.

I SEE the ripple on the corn
 Which runneth gaily to and fro,
And watch the rising of the morn
Or hear the noon-tide breezes blow;

The shadow rests on belfry walls,
I mark the nodding grasses raise
Their pennons when the wild wind calls,
And song-birds join the general praise.

The blossom blushes as it bows
Its head more humbly, and the dew
In pearls and diamonds decks those brows
It washes every night anew;
The keel grates on the golden beach,
The blue smoke riseth as a prayer,
And far off on the upland reach
Through red earth gleams the silver share.

I hear the pulsing of the wheels
And mighty springs that work Thy Law,
Father, and all my spirit kneels
To Thine in knowledge that is awe;
O Thou art beautiful and blest
In every flower and every tree,
For what is nature but Thy Breast
Which draws Thy children close to Thee?

V.—GOD AND THE HARVEST.

"I have planted, Apollos watered; but God gave the increase."—1 Cor. iii. 6.

HAST thou, dear brother, toiled through many years
  And seen no fruits, though thou hast freely sown
Thy life in labour and with watchful tears
Watered the soil yet none the richer grown?
Remember that the reaping is God's own,
And He can gather even of doubts and fears;
We only plough and plant our little field—
He is our Harvest, and His Love the yield.

Be sure, no kindly word or work may fail
To leave a blessing, if we know it not
And our poor efforts often err and ail,
While nothing that we do is without spot;
Christ stands Yoke-fellow, in the lowliest lot;
He is the light, and prayers at last prevail;
And, should thy service seem a wasted part,
It still shall blossom in some happier heart.

Not ours to finish tasks or seek the sight
Of precious increase and the praise of man,
But just to scatter seed in nature's night
And leave with God the issue of His plan;
He will complete what He in Grace began,
And order even thine errors all aright.
Thou wert well paid, whatever clouds do come,
If thou hast helped one wandering sinner Home.

VI.—OUR OPEN CAGE.

"All the paths of the Lord are mercy and truth."—Ps. xxv. 10.

BY different paths, O Lord, from many lands
   We come, we come unconscious of Thy will,
And the eternal Patience of those Hands
   Guiding us still;
For all the roads of knowledge and of faith,
   Descents of man, ascents Divine and free,
Through joy or sorrow and by life or death
   Lead unto Thee.

There is one Goal to these our many cares,
   While blindly we pursue mere selfish ends,
And but one way at last if unawares
   It upward tends.
We think the track is moulded by our pains,
   We hew us idols, raise the temple dome,
To reach by altars dead and broken chains
   Somehow our Home.

We choose or seem to choose the daily deed,
    The apportioned task and triumph for an hour,
But Thine was ever the immortal seed
    And Thine the flower;
We strive against Thee with our idle strength.
    As in an open cage a foolish dove,
Until we find our liberty at length
    Within Thy Love

VII.—LOSING AND SAVING.

"Fear not: for they that be with us are more than they that be with them."—2 KINGS vi 16.

O IF we always love the good,
    Yet stand upon the losing side
Where martyrs have before us stood,
And scorn the vulgar baits of pride,
Then shall we never know retreat,
Though suffering wrong and sore defeat.

If we still walk the narrow way
And stumble on the cruel stone,
Which telleth us to pause and pray,
While pilgrims are we left alone;
When we seem vanquished in the fight,
We must be victors for the right.

If we have not a helper near
And danger daily hems us round,
While everywhere some foe or fear
Encroacheth on our holiest ground;
Ah, though we suffer grimly thus,
The awful odds are yet with us.

If Heaven looks veiled and shadows fall
Upon the heart and cloud the sight,
Or weakness garrisons our wall
And darkness is the only light;
Though drifting hopeless with the tide,
We must be winners on God's side.

VIII.—SPRING.

"I see a rod of an almond (wakeful) tree. . . . Then said the Lord, . . . I will hasten (am wakeful over) my word to perform it."—JER i. 11, 12.

THE almond tree breaks into flower,
It feels the springtide's pulse and power
Through all its quickening frame;
Along each branch its blossoms run
And catch the kisses of the sun,
Bodied in bliss and flame.
And once more Aaron's prophet rod,
Blooms at the bidding of its God.

Lo, every bird is now a song
The fresher for its silence long,
And every leaf a lay;
The tiniest blade of trembling grass
Laughs as it feels the Spirit pass,
A green and living ray.
Up in its heaven of blue, the lark
Rains music from the dazzling dark.

Dear Father, may I feel Thy Spring
At heart, and in each upward wing
Of happy prayer and praise;
O make my soul burst into love
Rising to Thee my Home above,
And others with it raise.
Yea, let new shoots of stronger trust
Leap up, like altar fires, from dust.

IX.—WHO GOES HOME?

"Here have we no continuing city, but we seek one to come."
—Heb. xiii. 14.

TRAVELLER, traveller, whither bound
On the journey thou dost tread?
Every clod is heavenly ground,
Or a graveyard of the dead;
As thou makest it by deed
Charnal roof or church's dome,
Bleaching bones or blessèd seed—
Who goes Home?

Traveller, traveller, each new stage
Takes thee nearer to the close
Of thy mortal pilgrimage—
Dust of doom or Sharon's Rose;
Each new step is something lost,
Something gained, whate'er may come—
Soon thy Jordan must be crost—
Who goes Home?

Traveller, traveller, at thy side
Walketh Enemy or Friend,
But alone the crucified
Find the way is also end;
Hours and moments lightly flit,
God will shut thy earthly time
When the final page is writ—
Who goes Home?

Selwyn Image.

A DAINTY little volume of dainty verse, issued by Mr. Elkin Mathews in 1894, introduced Mr. Selwyn Image's name to those unfamiliar with it through serial literature. The book contains thirty-three poems, of which sixteen are, to use conventional terms, secular, and seventeen sacred. The secular songs are love lyrics, chaste in form and style as in thought and feeling. The sacred numbers are a series of carols for Christmas, Holy Week, and Easter Day. Of the former, the lyrics entitled "Her Confirmation" (quoted below), "A Summer Day," and "La Rose Du Bal," are among the best. Of the latter, the three carols which follow are good examples:—

HER CONFIRMATION.

When my Clorinda walks in white
Unto her Confirmation Rite,
   What sinless dove can show to heaven
A purer sight?

Beneath a lawn, translucent, crown
Her lovely curls conceal their brown;
   Her wanton eyes are fastened, even,
Demurely down.

And that delicious mouth of rose
No words, no smile, may discompose;
   All of her feels the approaching awe,
And silent grows.

> Come, then, Thou noiseless Spirit, and rest
> Here, where she waits Thee for her Guest;
> Pass not, but sweetly onward draw,
> Till heaven's possessed!

Mr. Selwyn Image, who is by profession an artist, was educated at Brighton College, Marlborough, and New College, Oxford, at which latter he held an exhibition, and took his degree in 1872.

ALFRED H. MILES.

POEMS AND CAROLS.

1894.

SELWYN IMAGE.

I.—A MEDITATION FOR CHRISTMAS.

CONSIDER, O my soul, what morn is this!
  Whereon the eternal Lord of all things made,
For us, poor mortals, and our endless bliss,
    Came down from heaven; and in a manger laid,
    The first, rich, offerings of our ransom paid;
Consider, O my soul, what morn is this!

Consider what estate of fearful woe
Had then been ours, had He refused this birth;
From sin to sin tossed vainly to and fro,
    Hell's playthings, o'er a doomed and helpless earth!
    Had He from us withheld His priceless worth,
Consider man's estate of fearful woe!

Consider to what joys He bids thee rise,
  Who comes, Himself, life's bitter cup to drain!
Ah! look on this sweet Child, Whose innocent eyes,
    Ere all be done, shall close in mortal pain,
    That thou at last Love's Kingdom may'st attain;
Consider to what joys He bids thee rise!

Consider all this wonder, O my soul:
  And in thine inmost shrine make music sweet!
Yea, let the world, from furthest pole to pole,
    Join in Thy praises this dread birth to greet;
    Kneeling to kiss Thy Saviour's infant feet!
Consider all this wonder, O my Soul!

II.—GABRIEL AND MARY.

"Hail! Lady Mary!" said Gabriel:
   Sing all the world, and all the world:
"God sends me now good news to tell."
"And what is the news, O Gabriel?"

"Lady Mary, God gives you grace";
   Sing all the world, and all the world:
"For a Child you shall bear within a space,
And look on God to His very face."

"Nay, Gabriel, how may this thing be?"
   Sing all the world, and all the world:
"Since there's never a man that knoweth me."
Said Gabriel, "Sooth, and you shall see."

The Lady Mary, she bowed her head;
   Sing all the world, and all the world:
Nor ever an answer more she said,
Till all things were accomplishèd.

For the Lady Mary, she bare her Son:
   Sing all the world, and all the world:
When the day's full course at length was run,
God's Self was born for her Little One.

Then the Lady Mary, she wept and spake;
   Sing all the world, and all the world:
"I have borne my Child for the world's sake,
And the cruel world His life will take!"

But the Lady Mary, she laughed and said,
   Sing all the world, and all the world:
"My Child shall rise again from the dead,
Lord of all by His great Godhead!"

Now, Lady Mary, we pray you say,
   Sing all the world, and all the world:
Some gracious thing to your Son that day,
When we, poor creatures, pass away.

Yea, Lady Mary, Mother of God,
Save us from sin's rod!
Lady Mary, Mother of Grace,
Bend on us your sweet face!
O Lady Mary, bring us at length
By strength of Jesus to Jesus' strength!
                          Amen.

III.—THE HEAVENLY HOST.

DEEP and hard the snow lay,
  Deep was the ice on the water-way;
       Deus misericordiae!
On their frozen fingers the shepherds blew,
And the wolf-skins round them tighter drew.
God, how the wind cut! huddled low,
Herdsmen and herds lay shelt'ring so.
       Deus misericordiae!
       Venti furorem reprime,
       Ne pereamus frigore,

Suddenly, hark! what sound breaks?
And the heaven's aglow with golden flakes,
       Archangelorum Domine!
As the quiv'ring tongues of a mighty fire;
From the midst whereof, in choir on choir,
What Sons of the Lord of heaven and earth
Are these, that herald a God's birth?
       Archangelorum Domine!
       Mortalium quis intime
       Spectabit, Lux tremenda, te?

The wild wind's stayed, the earth's warm;
O herdsmen and herds, what thought of harm?
   Omnipotenti gloria!
On their knees they're fallen: an angel cries,
"The winter's over, O shepherds, rise!
Be not afraid; to Bethlehem Town
This night is the very God come down!"
   Omnipotenti gloria!
   Qui natus nobis omnia
   Vertisti in pacifera.

What the sight they find there?
A Child new-born, in a stable bare:
   Jesu, Deus demississime!
A Child in a manger, a Mother-Maid,
By whom shall the terrors of hell be laid;
The proud fly scattered, the weak prevail!
Sweet Child and Mother, we cry you, Hail!
   Jesu, Deus demississime!
   Finito mundi tempore
   In coeli domum accipe
   Humiles nos, Rex altissime!
      Amen.

AC ETIAM.

Besides the religious and didactic poets represented in the foregoing pages, there are many whose verse—often of rare beauty and wide acceptance—calls for less extended representation, and who can therefore be more conveniently dealt with under a general heading than in individual notices separated and signed upon the plan adopted for the body of this work. These have been reserved for treatment in the following pages, not because they mark a different standard of excellence or selection, but simply for typographical and economic reasons—the preservation of a certain uniformity of appearance and the saving of space.

The religious revivals of the century have all found some expression in original song, while they have stimulated the labours of many scholars who have enriched English hymnody from the wide field of translation. Some of these writers are already represented in the preceding pages; others are treated in the pages which follow. The arrangement, as throughout this work, is chronological.

Anna Lætitia Barbauld was born at Kibworth-Harcourt, Leicestershire, on the 20th of June, 1743. Her father, Dr. Aiken, kept a private school for boys, and under his instruction she acquired a knowledge of both Greek and Latin. At her father's house, too, she met Dr. Priestley, Dr. Taylor, Roscoe, Pennant the naturalist, and other men of culture, who influenced her thought and stimulated the development of her mind. In 1773 she published a volume of poems, and, encouraged by its success, in conjunction with her brother, a volume of "Miscellaneous Pieces in Prose." In the following year she married the Rev R Barbauld, a Nonconformist minister, who shortly after opened a school for boys at Palgrave, Suffolk. While here Mrs. Barbauld published "Hymns in Prose for Children" (1781), a work that had a large sale both in England and America, and which was translated into several languages. In 1787 the Barbaulds gave up their school and removed to Hampstead, where Mr. Barbauld became minister of a Nonconformist Church. Here they formed the acquaintance of Agnes and Joanna Baillie, and Mrs Barbauld wrote a number of pieces for her brother's "Evenings at Home." In 1802 Mr. Barbauld accepted the charge of a Church at Newington Green, where his wife had the great advantage of living near to her brother, who had become a physician. Here Mr. Barbauld developed symptoms of mental derangement, and, after attempting the life of his wife—who escaped him by leaping from a window—was placed under restraint, from which, however, he managed to escape in November 1808, when he committed suicide by throwing himself into the New River. Mrs. Barbauld, engaged frequently in literary work, edited a selection for the "British Essayists"; an edition of "Richardson's Letters"; a collection of the "British Novelists," with biographical notices, which latter work was published in 1810. In 1811 she edited "The Female Speaker," and wrote a long poem on the current year. For some years she enjoyed the friendship of Wordsworth, Lamb, Rogers, Crabb Robinson, and others, who visited her and felt the charm of her manners and conversation. She died at the age of eighty-two, on the 9th of March, 1825. Her poems were published in two volumes in 1826.

Much of Mrs. Barbauld's poetry is commonplace to our eyes, but some of it justifies the judgment of her contemporaries, and seems likely to hold its place in hymn-books and anthologies for many years to come.

Wordsworth committed the following lines, from a poem entitled "Life," to memory, and said of them, "I am not in the habit of grudging other people their good things, but I wish I had written these lines."

> Life! we've been long together,
> Through pleasant and through cloudy weather
> 'Tis hard to part when friends are dear;
> Perhaps 'twill cost a sigh, a tear;
> Then steal away, give little warning,
> Choose thine own time;
> Say not Good-Night, but in some brighter clime
> Bid me Good-Morning.

As Mr. Eric Robinson says, "Few will deny the lyric charm of the concluding lines."

Walter Savage Landor, who was an admirer of Mrs. Barbauld's verse, quoted the following lines from "A Summer Evening's Meditation" with high praise:—

> But are they silent all? or is there not
> A tongue in every star that talks with man,
> And woos him to be wise? nor woos in vain?
> This dead of midnight is the noon of thought,

And wisdom mounts her zenith with the stars.
At this still hour the self-collected soul
Turns inward, and beholds a stranger there
Of high descent, and more than mortal rank;
An embryo God, a spark of fire divine,
Which must burn on for ages, when the sun
(Fair transitory creature of a day)
Has closed his golden eye, and, wrapt in shades,
Forgets his wonted journey through the east.

Of her devotional verse the two following hymns are fine examples, and it would not be difficult to add to the number.—

I.

Praise to God, immortal praise,
For the love that crowns our days!
Bounteous source of every joy,
Let Thy praise our tongues employ;

For the blessings of the field,
For the stores the gardens yield;
For the vine's exalted juice,
For the generous olive's use:

Flocks that whiten all the plain;
Yellow sheaves of ripen'd grain;
Clouds that drop their fattening dews,
Suns that temperate warmth diffuse:

All that Spring with bounteous hand
Scatters o'er the smiling land;
All that liberal Autumn pours
From her rich o'er-flowing stores:

These to Thee, my God, we owe,—
Source whence all our blessings flow;
And for these my soul shall raise
Grateful vows and solemn praise.

Yet, should rising whirlwinds tear
From its stem the ripening ear;
Should the fig-tree's blasted shoot
Drop her green untimely fruit,

Should the vine put forth no more,
Nor the olive yield her store
Though the sickening flocks should fall,
And the herds desert the stall;

Should Thine alter'd hand restrain
The early and the latter rain;
Blast each opening bud of joy,
And the rising year destroy;

Yet to Thee my soul should raise
Grateful vows and solemn praise;
And, when every blessing's flown,
Love Thee—for Thyself alone.

II.

Awake, my soul, lift up thine eyes,
See where thy foes against thee rise,
In long array, a numerous host;
Awake, my soul, or thou art lost!

Here giant Danger threatening stands,
Mustering his pale terrific bands;
There Pleasure's silken banners spread,
And willing souls are captive led.

See where rebellious passions rage,
And fierce desires and lusts engage;
The meanest foe of all the train
Has thousands and ten thousands slain!

Thou tread'st upon enchanted ground,
Perils and snares beset thee round;
Beware of all, guard every part,
But most, the traitor in thy heart.

Come then, my soul, now learn to wield
The weight of thine immortal shield;
Put on the armour from above
Of heavenly Truth and heavenly Love.

The terror and the charm repel,
And powers of earth, and powers of hell;
The Man of Calvary triumph'd here:
Why should His faithful followers fear!

One of the most prolific as well as one of the most successful of the early hymn-writers of the century was THOMAS KELLY (1769-1854). The son of an Irish judge of Common Pleas, he was born in Dublin on the 13th of July, 1769, and was educated at Trinity College, Dublin, after which he studied for the Bar, but ultimately turned his back upon the Law, and took Holy Orders in 1792. He was an earnest preacher of the Evangelical school, and a friend of the Rev. Rowland Hill. Archbishop Fowler interdicted his preaching in Dublin, and finally he seceded from the Church of England and erected places of worship at Athy, Portarlington, Wexford, and other places, where he preached from time to time. In 1802 he published "A Collection of Psalms and Hymns from various Authors," in which he included thirty-three original hymns; in 1804 "Hymns on Various Passages of Scripture"; and in 1815 "Hymns by Thomas Kelly, not before Published." According to Julian, Kelly wrote seven hundred and sixty-five hymns, during a period of fifty-one years. All of these hymns are included in the edition of his hymns published in 1853.

I.

The head that once was crowned with thorns,
   Is crowned with glory now:
A royal diadem adorns
   The mighty Victor's brow.

The highest place that heaven affords
   Is His, is His by right
The King of kings, and Lord of lords,
   And heaven's eternal Light.

The joy of all who dwell above,
    The joy of all below,
To whom He manifests His love,
    And grants His name to know:

To them the cross with all its shame
    With all its grace, is given:
Their name an everlasting name,
    Their joy the joy of heaven.

They suffer with their Lord below,
    They reign with Him above;
Their profit and their joy to know
    The mystery of His love.

The cross He bore is life and health,
    Though shame and death to Him,
His people's hope, His people's wealth,
    Their everlasting theme.

II.

Look, ye saints, the sight is glorious:
    See the Man of Sorrows now,
From the fight returned victorious:
    Every knee to Him shall bow.
        Crown Him, crown Him:
    Crowns become the Victor's brow.

Crown the Saviour, angels crown Him:
    Rich the trophies Jesus brings;
In the seat of power enthrone Him,
    While the vault of heaven rings.
        Crown Him, crown Him:
    Crown the Saviour, King of kings!

Sinners in derision crowned Him,
    Mocking thus the Saviour's claim;
Saints and angels crowd around Him,
    Own His title, praise His name.
        Crown Him, crown Him:
    Spread abroad the Victor's fame.

> Hark, those bursts of acclamation!
> > Hark, those loud triumphant chords!
> Jesus takes the highest station:
> > O what joy the sight affords!
> > > Crown Him, crown Him,
> > > King of kings, and Lord of lords!

Deservedly remembered chiefly for one sweet lyric which has become universally popular, HARRIET AUBER was born in London on the 4th of October, 1773, and died at Hoddesdon, Herts, on the 20th of January, 1862, at the great age of eighty-eight. In 1829 she published her "Spirit of the Psalms," which contained a number of metrical versions of the Psalms from her pen. Twenty-five of these, according to Julian, are in common use, more particularly in America; but the hymn already referred to, and quoted in full below, is her most widely accepted contribution to hymnody, and seems likely to survive long in the service of the Christian Church

> Our blest Redeemer, ere He breathed
> > His tender last farewell,
> A Guide, a Comforter bequeathed,
> > With us to dwell.
>
> He came in semblance of a dove,
> > With sheltering wings outspread,
> The holy balm of peace and love
> > On earth to shed.
>
> He came in tongues of living flame,
> > To teach, convince, subdue;
> All-powerful as the wind He came—
> > As viewless too.
>
> He came sweet influence to impart,
> > A gracious, willing guest,
> While He can find one humble heart
> > Wherein to rest.

And His that gentle voice we hear,
　　Soft as the breath of even,
That checks each fault, that calms each fear,
　　And speaks of Heaven.

And every virtue we possess,
　　And every victory won,
And every thought of holiness,
　　Are His alone.

Spirit of purity and grace,
　　Our weakness pitying see;
O make our hearts Thy dwelling-place,
　　And worthier Thee.

Eccentricities of inspiration, which sometimes result in productions that may almost be called fortuitous, occur in poetry as in other departments of art; and single poems, like single speeches and single pictures, sometimes baffle all accounting for. Of such the famous sonnet "To Night," by JOSEPH BLANCO WHITE, is perhaps the most striking example.

Joseph Blanco White (1775-1839) was born at Seville, in the year 1775, of Irish parents. He published "Letters from Spain" (1822), "Practical and Internal Evidence against Catholicism" (1825), and other works of theological polemics. He also translated into Spanish the "Evidences" of Porteus and Paley, "The Book of Common Prayer," and some of the "Homilies," and at one time edited the *London Review*. He wrote little verse, and, with the exception of the sonnet on Night and Death, none that calls for remark. This sonnet Coleridge characterised as "the finest and most greatly conceived sonnet in our language"; and Leigh Hunt declared that for thought it "stands supreme perhaps above all in any language, nor can we ponder it too deeply or with too hopeful a reverence." As Mr.

Sharp pointed out in his "Sonnets of the Century," quite a Blanco-White literature has grown up round this sonnet, further particulars concerning which may be found in Main's "Treasury of English Sonnets."

TO NIGHT.

Mysterious Night! when our first parent knew
  Thee from report divine, and heard thy name,
  Did he not tremble for this lovely frame,
This glorious canopy of light and blue?
Yet 'neath a curtain of translucent dew,
  Bathed in the rays of the great setting flame,
  Hesperus with the host of heaven came,
And lo! Creation widened in man's view.
Who could have thought such darkness lay concealed
Within thy beams, O Sun! or who could find,
  Whilst fly and leaf and insect stood revealed,
That to such countless orbs thou mad'st us blind!
  Why do we then shun Death with anxious strife?
  If Light can thus deceive, wherefore not Life?

Among the successful translations from the Latin which have taken their place in the common use of the Church is the fine, picturesque hymn by PHILIP PUSEY (1779-1855) given below. Philip Pusey was the eldest son of Philip Pusey, son of the first Viscount Folkestone, and brother of Dr. Pusey.

Lord of our life, and God of our salvation,
Star of our night, and Hope of every nation,
Hear and receive Thy Church's supplication,
  Lord God Almighty.

See round Thine ark the hungry billows curling;
See how Thy foes their banners are unfurling;
Lord, while their darts envenomed they are hurling,
  Thou canst preserve us.

Lord, Thou canst help when earthly armour faileth,
Lord, Thou canst save when deadly sin assaileth,
Lord, o'er Thy Rock nor death nor hell prevaileth,
  Grant us Thy peace, Lord

Grant us Thy help till foes are backward driven,
Grant them Thy truth that they may be forgiven,
Grant peace on earth, and, after we have striven,
    Peace in Thy heaven.

THOMAS MOORE (1779-1852), best known as the author of "Lalla Rookh" and of the "Irish Melodies" represented among the general poets of this series, published a small number of sacred songs in 1816, of which several have been widely used in Christian worship. Of these, "O Thou who dry'st the mourner's tear," in a modified form, has been one of the most popular; and "Thou art, O God, the life and light," and "Sound the loud timbrel," the latter wedded to the music of Avison, and made noteworthy by Browning in "Parleyings with Certain People," have been among the most widely used.

1.

Thou art, O God, the life and light
Of all this wondrous world we see:
Its glow by day, its smile by night,
Are but reflections caught from Thee:
Where'er we turn, Thy glories shine,
And all things fair and bright are Thine.

When day with farewell beam delays
Among the opening clouds of even,
And we can almost think we gaze
Through golden vistas into heaven,—
Those hues, that make the sun's decline
So soft, so radiant, Lord! are Thine.

When night, with wings of starry gloom,
O'ershadows all the earth and skies,
Like some dark, beauteous bird whose plume
Is sparkling with unnumbered eyes,—
That sacred gloom, those fires divine,
So grand, so countless, Lord! are Thine.

When youthful Spring around us breathes,
Thy Spirit warms her fragrant sigh,
And every flower the Summer wreathes
Is born beneath that kindling eye,—
Where'er we turn, Thy glories shine,
And all things fair and bright are Thine.

II.

Sound the loud timbrel o'er Egypt's dark sea!
Jehovah has triumph'd—His people are free.
Sing—for the pride of the tyrant is broken;
  His chariots, his horsemen, all splendid and brave,
How vain was their boasting!—the Lord hath but spoken,
  And chariots and horsemen are sunk in the wave.
Sound the loud timbrel o'er Egypt's dark sea!
Jehovah has triumph'd—His people are free.

Praise to the Conqueror, praise to the Lord;
His word was our arrow, his breath was our sword!—
Who shall return to tell Egypt the story
  Of those she sent forth in the hour of her pride?
For the Lord hath look'd out from His pillar of glory,
  And all her brave thousands are dash'd in the tide.
Sound the loud timbrel o'er Egypt's dark sea!
Jehovah has triumph'd—His people are free.

"Hymns for the Nursery" (1806) and "Hymns for Infant Minds" (1809), both by ANN and JANE TAYLOR, deserve mention, as early attempts to reach the child-level in simple verse. Besides these works the sisters collaborated in "Original Poems" (1805), and Ann, afterwards Mrs. Gilbert (1782-1866), published separately "Hymns for Sunday-School Anniversaries" (1827) and "Hymns for Infant Schools" (1827), Jane (1783-1824) publishing separately "Display: a Tale" (1815) and "Essays in Rhyme" (1816). Jane also contributed to the annuals and to the *Youth's Magazine*, from which a number of her essays were reprinted as the posthumous contributions of "Q. Q." in 1824. An authorised edition of the "Hymns" was published by Mrs. Gilbert's son, Josiah Gilbert, the artist, in 1886. Of these, those of Mrs. Gilbert are the stronger, the best being "Great God, and wilt Thou condescend," "Jesus, who lived above the sky," and "Lo, at noon 'tis sudden night." Of Jane's hymns, "There is a path that leads to God" and "When daily I kneel down to pray" are perhaps the best. Her "Essays in Rhyme" are interesting and well written, her poem "The Squire's Pew" having a pathos in it which has not altogether evaporated with the years. The following is from the pen of Mrs. Gilbert:—

> Great God, and wilt Thou condescend
> To be my Father and my Friend?
> I, a poor child, and Thou so high,
> The Lord of earth, and air, and sky?
>
> Art Thou my Father? Canst Thou bear
> To hear my poor imperfect prayer?
> Or wilt Thou listen to the praise
> That such a little one can raise?
>
> Art Thou my Father? Let me be
> A meek, obedient child to Thee;
> And try, in word and deed and thought,
> To serve and please Thee as I ought.
>
> Art Thou my Father? I'll depend
> Upon the care of such a Friend;
> And only wish to do and be
> Whatever seemeth good to Thee.
>
> Art Thou my Father? Then at last,
> When all my days on earth are past
> Send down and take me in Thy love
> To be Thy better child above.

The following hymn is from the pen of Jane Taylor:—

> When daily I kneel down to pray,
>   As I am taught to do,
> God does not care for what I say
>   Unless I feel it too.
>
> Yet foolish thoughts my heart beguile;
>   And when I pray or sing,
> I'm often thinking all the while
>   About some other thing
>
> Some idle play, or childish toy,
>   Can send my thoughts abroad;
> Though this should be my greatest joy—
>   To love and seek the Lord.
>
> Oh! let me never, never dare
>   To act the trifler's part;
> Or think that God will hear a prayer
>   That comes not from my heart.
>
> But if I make His ways my choice,
>   As holy children do,
> Then, while I seek Him with my voice,
>   My heart will love Him too.

In strong contrast to the sentimental school of religious poetry come the hymns of WILLIAM JOHNSON FOX, who was born at Wrentham on the 1st of March, 1786 Educated at a chapel school in Norwich, he worked his way from the position of an errand boy to that of a clerk in a bank, employing all his leisure in self-culture and studying mathematics, Latin, and Greek. In 1806 he entered the Independent College at Homerton under Dr. Pye Smith, and in 1810 became pastor of a Church at Fareham. Two years later, having declared' for Unitarianism, he became pastor of the Unitarian Church, Chichester, whence he removed to Parliament Court Chapel, London, in 1817. In 1824 he migrated with his Church to a new building erected for him at South Place, Finsbury, with which his name became permanently associated. Here he gave much time to literature and politics; became editor, and afterwards proprietor, of the *Monthly Repository*, in connection with which he gathered round him a staff of writers, which included John Stuart Mill, Harriet Martineau, Crabb Robinson, Robert Browning, Sarah Flower Adams, and others. For the details of his literary and political career the reader is referred to an article by Dr. Garnett in "The Dictionary of National Biography," from which these facts are taken. Suffice it to say here that he became a regular contributor to the *Morning Chronicle* and later to the *Daily News*, a leader of the anti-Corn-Law movement 1840, and Member of Parliament for Oldham 1847. He died on the 3rd of June, 1864.

For the use of his congregation at South Place, he prepared and published a book of hymns and anthems, which contained a number of original hymns, of which the following are examples :—

L

A little child, in bulrush ark,
  Came floating on the Nile's broad water;
That child made Egypt's glory dark,
  And freed his tribe from bonds and slaughter.

A little child enquiring stood
  In Israel's temple of its sages;
That child, by lessons wise and good,
  Made pure the temples of past ages

'Mid worst oppressions, if remain
   Young hearts to Freedom still aspiring;
Though nursed in Superstitious chain,
   If human minds be still enquiring,—

Then, let not priest or tyrant dote
   On dreams of long the world commanding;
The ark of Moses is afloat,
   And Christ is in the temple standing.

II.

"Make us a god," said man;
   Power first the voice obeyed;
And soon a monstrous form
   Its worshippers dismayed;
Uncouth and huge, by nations rude adored,
With savage rites and sacrifice abhorred

"Make us a god," said man,
   Art next the voice obeyed;
Lovely, serene, and grand,
   Uprose the Athenian maid;
The perfect statue, Greece with wreathèd brows,
Adores in festal rites and lyric vows.

"Make us a god," said man:
   Religion followed Art,
And answered, "Look within;
   God is in thine own heart—
His noblest image there, and holiest shrine,
Silent revere—and be thyself divine."

III.

The sage his cup of hemlock quaffed,
And calmly drained the fatal draught:
Such pledge did Grecian justice give
To one who taught them how to live.

The Christ, in piety assured,
The anguish of His cross endured:
Such pangs did Jewish bigots try
On Him who taught us how to die.

'Mid prison-walls, the sage could trust
That men would grow more wise and just;
From Calvary's mount the Christ could see
The dawn of immortality.

Who know to live, and know to die,
Their souls are safe, their triumph nigh:
Power may oppress and priestcraft ban;
Justice and faith are God in man.

For the use of his own congregation ANDREW REED (1787-1862), philanthropist and preacher, prepared a hymn-book, which, subject to modifications, passed through many editions from its first publication as a supplement to that of Dr. Watts in 1817. To this work he contributed anonymously original hymns from time to time to the number of twenty-one, of which the following seems likely to survive the longest:—

Spirit Divine, attend our prayers,
 And make this house Thy home;
Descend with all Thy gracious powers,—
 O come, Great Spirit, come!

Come as the *light*—to us reveal
 Our emptiness and woe;
And lead us in those paths of life
 Where all the righteous go.

Come as the *fire*—and purge our hearts
 Like sacrificial flame;
Let our whole soul an offering be
 To our Redeemer's name.

Come as the *dew*—and sweetly bless
 This consecrated hour;
May barrenness rejoice to own
 Thy fertilising power.

Come as the *dove*—and spread Thy wings,
  The wings of peaceful love;
And let Thy Church on earth become
  Blest as the Church above.

Come as the *wind*—with rushing sound,
  And pentecostal grace;
That all of woman born may see
  The glory of Thy face.

Spirit Divine, attend our prayers,
  Make a lost world Thy home;
Descend with all Thy gracious powers,—
  O come, Great Spirit, come!

As a philanthropist Andrew Reed left behind him unique memorials of practical religion in the numerous institutions which he founded for the help of the poor and needy and the amelioration of the sufferings of the afflicted, any one of which would have been a noble legacy. These include the London Orphan Asylum, the Asylum for Fatherless Children, the Asylum for Idiots, the Infant Orphan Asylum, and the Hospital for Incurables. He was a minister of the Congregational body.

CHARLOTTE ELIZABETH TONNA, *née* BROWNE, better known as "Charlotte Elizabeth," author of "Derry: a Tale of the Revolution," "Personal Recollections," "Chapters on Flowers," etc., etc., was the daughter of the Rev. Michael Browne, Rector of St. Giles', Norwich, and was born on the 1st of October, 1790. She wrote several hymns, of which the following is the most striking. She died on the 12th of July, 1849.

THE MARINER'S MIDNIGHT HYMN.

O Thou who didst prepare
　　The ocean's caverned cell,
And lead the gathering waters there
　　To meet and dwell:
　　Tossed in our reeling bark
　　On this tumultuous sea,
Thy wondrous ways, O Lord, we mark,
　　And sing to Thee.

How terrible art Thou,
　　In all Thy wonders shown;
Though veiled is that eternal brow,
　　Thy steps unknown!
　　Invisible to sight—
　　But oh! to faith how near—
Beneath the gloomiest cloud of night
　　Thou beamest here.

Borne on the darkening wave
　　In measured sweep we go,
Nor dread th' unfathomable grave
　　That yawns below;
　　For He is nigh who trod
　　Amid that foaming spray,
Whose billows owned th' incarnate God
　　And died away.

Let slumber's balmy seal
　　Imprint our tranquil eyes;
Though deep beneath the waters steal,
　　And circling rise;
　　Though swells the confluent tide,
　　And beetles far above,—
We know in whom our souls confide
　　With fearless love.

Snatched from a darker deep
　　And waves of wilder foam,
Thou, Lord, those trusting souls wilt keep,
　　And waft them home;

> Home, where no tempests sound,
> Nor angry waters roar,
> Nor troublous billows heave around
> The peaceful shore.

JAMES EDMESTON (1791-1867), the author of the popular hymns "Lead us, heavenly Father, lead us" (written for the children of the London Orphan Asylum) and "Saviour, breathe an evening blessing," is said to have written no less than two thousand hymns, of which many have come into general use. An architect by profession, he had Sir Gilbert Scott for a pupil, and published a number of volumes of verse. The principal of these are "The Search and other Poems" (1817); "Sacred Lyrics" (first series, 1820; second series, 1821; third series, 1822); "Patmos, a Fragment, and other Poems" (1824); "The Woman of Shunem and other Poems" (1829); "Fifty Original Hymns" (1833); "Church Hymns and Poems" (1844); "Infant Breathings" (1846); "Sacred Poetry" (1847). He died on the 7th of January, 1867.

I.

> Lead us, heavenly Father, lead us
>   O'er the world's tempestuous sea;
> Guard us, guide us, keep us, feed us,
>   For we have no help but Thee;
>   Yet possessing
>   Every blessing,
>   If our God our Father be!

> Saviour! breathe forgiveness o'er us;
>   All our weakness Thou dost know;
> Thou didst tread this earth before us,
>   Thou didst feel its keenest woe;
>   Lone and dreary,
>   Faint and weary,
>   Through the desert Thou didst go!

Spirit of our God, descending,
  Fill our hearts with heavenly joy;
Love, with every passion blending,
  Pleasure, that can never cloy:
    Thus provided,
    Pardoned, guided,
Nothing can our peace destroy!

II.

Saviour, breathe an evening blessing,
  Ere repose our spirits seal;
Sin and want we come confessing,
  Thou canst save, and Thou canst heal;
Though destruction walk around us,
  Though the arrow past us fly,
Angel-guards from Thee surround us;
  We are safe, if Thou art nigh.

Though the night be dark and dreary,
  Darkness cannot hide from Thee;
Thou art HE, who, never weary,
  Watchest where Thy people be:
Should swift death this night o'ertake us,
  And our couch become our tomb,
May the morn in heaven awake us,
  Clad in light and deathless bloom.

"Hymns for Private Devotion for the Sundays and Saints' Days throughout the Year," by Samuel Rickards (1825), has supplied one or two hymns to subsequent collections, among which the Christmas hymn here quoted is the most notable. The author, SAMUEL RICKARDS, was born in 1796, and educated at Oriel College, Oxford, where he was Newdigate Prizeman in 1815, B.A. 1817, M.A. 1820. He was a Fellow of his college 1819 to 1823, and was contemporary with Newman, Keble, and other famous Churchmen. He was Curate of Ulcombe

1825, and Rector of Stowlangtoft, Ely, 1832. He published, besides the "Hymns," "The Christian Householder; or, Book of Family Prayers," "A Parish Prayer Book," "Short Sermons," etc., and died on the 24th of August, 1865.

CHRISTMAS DAY.

Though rude winds usher thee, sweet day,
    Though clouds thy face deform,
Though nature's grace is swept away
    Before the sleety storm;
Ev'n in thy sombrest wintry vest,
Of blessed days thou art most blest.

Nor frigid air nor gloomy morn
    Shall check our jubilee;
Bright is the day when Christ was born,
    No sun need shine but He;
Let roughest storms their coldest blow,
With love of Him our hearts shall glow.

Inspired with high and holy thought,
    Fancy is on the wing;
It seems as to mine ear it brought
    Those voices carolling,
Voices through heaven and earth that ran,
Glory to God, goodwill to man.

I see the shepherds gazing wild
    At those fair spirits of light;
I see them bending o'er the Child
    With that untold delight
Which marks the face of those who view
Things but too happy to be true.

There, in the lowly manger laid,
    Incarnate God they see;
He stoops to take, through spotless maid,
    Our frail humanity:
Son of high God, Creation's Heir,
He leaves His Heaven to raise us there.

Through Him, Lord, we are born anew,
   Thy children once again;
Oh! day by day our hearts renew,
   That Thine we may remain.
And, angel-like, may all agree,
One sweet and holy family.

Oft, as this joyous morn doth come
   To speak our Saviour's love,
Oh, may it bear our spirits home
   Where He now reigns above;
That day which brought Him from the skies,
So man restores to Paradise!

Then let winds usher thee, sweet day,
   Let clouds thy face deform;
Though nature's grace is swept away
   Before thy sleety storm;
Ev'n in thy sombrest wintry vest,
Of blessed days thou art most blest.

Many modern hymns have been written with a direct view to inculcating religious doctrine, and some have admirably succeeded in their didactic aim without losing altogether poetic character. Of these the following hymn by DR. BINNEY is an example.

Thomas Binney was born at Newcastle-upon-Tyne in the year 1798, and was apprenticed to a bookseller, but made use of what little leisure he had for self-culture by studying the classics with a Presbyterian clergyman. He ultimately entered the Theological Seminary at Wymondley, Hertfordshire, where he remained three years, after which he held pastorates successively at "New Meeting," Bedford, and "St. James's Street," Newport, Isle of Wight, removing in 1829 to the Weigh House Church, Fish Street Hill, London.

He was an eloquent preacher, an earnest controversialist, and a successful author, his most popular books being "Is it Possible to Make the Best of Both Worlds?" (1853) and "Micah the Priest-Maker" (1867). He was a D.D. of Aberdeen. He died on the 23rd of February, 1874, and was buried at Abney Park Cemetery, Dean Stanley taking part in the service. He wrote several hymns, of which the following is the best:—

>Eternal Light! Eternal Light!
> How pure the soul must be,
>When, placed within Thy searching sight,
>It shrinks not, but, with calm delight,
> Can live, and look on Thee!
>
>The spirits that surround Thy throne
> May bear the burning bliss;
>But that is surely theirs alone,
>Since they have never, never known
> A fallen world like this.
>
>O! how shall I, whose native sphere
> Is dark, whose mind is dim,
>Before the Ineffable appear,
>And on my naked spirit bear
> That uncreated beam?
>
>There is a way for man to rise
> To that sublime abode:—
>An offering and a sacrifice,
>A Holy Spirit's energies,
> An Advocate with God:—
>
>These, these prepare us for the sight
> Of Holiness above:
>The sons of ignorance and night
>May dwell in the Eternal Light,
> Through the Eternal Love!

Of "single" poems, the following, written in Richmond Churchyard, Yorkshire, has been one of the most popular. HERBERT KNOWLES, the author, was born at Canterbury in 1798, and died in 1817. Southey, always ready to recognise struggling talent, published these "Lines" in the *Quarterly Review*, vol. xxi., pp. 397, 398, from which it has been reprinted in countless anthologies.

LINES WRITTEN IN THE CHURCHYARD OF RICHMOND, YORKSHIRE.

"It is good for us to be here: if Thou wilt, let us make here three tabernacles, one for Thee, and one for Moses, and one for Elias."—MATT. xvii. 4.

  Methinks it is good to be here;
If Thou wilt, let us build—but for whom?
  Nor Elias nor Moses appear,
But the shadows of eve that encompass the gloom,
The abode of the dead and the place of the tomb.

  Shall we build to Ambition? Oh, no!
Affrighted, he shrinketh away;
  For see! they would pin him below,
In a small narrow cave, and, begirt with cold clay,
To the meanest of reptiles a peer and a prey.

  To Beauty? Ah, no!—she forgets
The charms which she wielded before—
  Nor knows the foul worm that he frets
The skin which but yesterday fools could adore,
For the smoothness it held, or the tint which it wore.

  Shall we build to the purple of Pride—
The trappings which dizen the proud?
  Alas! they are all laid aside;
And here's neither dress nor adornment allowed,
But the long winding-sheet, and the fringe of the shroud.

  To Riches? Alas! 'tis in vain;
Who hid, in their turn have been hid:
  The treasures are squander'd again;
And here in the grave are all metals forbid,
But the tinsel that shone on the dark coffin-lid.

  To the pleasures which Mirth can afford—
The revel, the laugh, and the jeer?
  Ah! here is a plentiful board!
But the guests are all mute as their pitiful cheer,
And none but the worm is a reveller here.

  Shall we build to Affection and Love?
Ah, no! they have wither'd and died,
  Or fled with the spirit above;
Friends, brothers, and sisters, are laid side by side,
Yet none have saluted, and none have replied.

  Unto Sorrow?—The dead cannot grieve:
Not a sob, not a sigh meets mine ear,
  Which compassion itself could relieve!
Ah! sweetly they slumber, nor hope, love, nor fear—
Peace, peace is the watchword, the only one here!

  Unto Death, to whom Monarchs must bow?
Ah, no! for his empire is known,
  And here there are trophies enow!
Beneath—the cold dead, and around—the dark stone,
Are the signs of a Sceptre that none may disown!

  The first tabernacle to Hope we will build,
And look for the sleepers around us to rise!
  The second to Faith, which ensures it fulfill'd;
And the third to the Lamb of the great sacrifice,
Who bequeath'd us them both when He rose to the skies.

MATTHEW BRIDGES, author of "Babbicombe; or, Visions of Memory, and other Poems" (1842), "Hymns of the Heart" (1848), "The Passion of Jesus" (1852), has often been quoted in the hymnals of England and America. The hymn "Crown Him with many crowns," in various modified forms, has been a great favourite, and his version of the hymn "Lo! He comes with clouds descending" is also in use. Mr. Bridges was born at Maldon, Essex, on the 14th of July, 1800, and educated in the

Church of England, but subsequently entered the Church of Rome.

"IN CAPITE EJUS, DIADEMATA MULTA."
Apoc., xix. 12.

 Crown Him with many crowns,
  The Lamb upon His throne ;
Hark! how the heavenly anthem drowns
  All music but its own !
  Awake, my soul, and sing
  Of Him who died for thee ;
And hail Him as thy matchless King,
  Through all eternity.

 Crown Him the Virgin's Son !
  The God Incarnate born,—
Whose Arm those crimson trophies won
  Which now His Brow adorn !
  Fruit of the Mystic Rose,
  As of that Rose the Stem
The Root, whence Mercy ever flows,—
  The Babe of Bethlehem !

 Crown Him the Lord of Love !
  Behold His Hands and Side,—
Rich wounds, yet visible above,
  In beauty glorified :
  No angel in the sky
  Can fully bear that sight,
But downward bends his burning eye
  At mysteries so bright !

 Crown Him the Lord of Peace !
  Whose power a sceptre sways,
From pole to pole,—that wars may cease,
  Absorbed in prayer and praise :
  His reign shall know no end,
  And round His piercèd Feet
Fair flowers of Paradise extend
  Their fragrance ever sweet.

> Crown Him the Lord of Years!
>   The Potentate of Time,—
> Creator of the rolling spheres,
>   Ineffably sublime!
> Glass'd in a sea of light,
>   Where everlasting waves
> Reflect His Throne,—the Infinite!
>   Who lives,—and loves,—and saves.
>
> Crown Him the Lord of Heaven!
>   One with the Father known,—
> And the blest Spirit, through Him given,
>   From yonder triune throne!
>   All hail! Redeemer,—hail!
>   For Thou hast died for me;
> Thy praise shall never, never fail,
>   Throughout eternity!

RICHARD MASSIE (1800) did good service to English hymnody by translating hymns from the German. He published translations of Martin Luther's "Spiritual Songs" (1854); "Lyra Domestica" (first series, 1860), in which he included translations of the first series of Spitta's "Psalter and Harfe"; and vol. ii. (1864), containing translations of Spitta's second series, with an appendix of translations from other German authors; besides which he contributed translations to various hymnals. Of his original hymns, one of the most popular is the one commencing,—

> O Lord, who taught to us on earth
>   This lesson from above,
> That all our works are nothing worth,
>   Unless they spring from love.

The following is a favourable specimen of his translations:—

EVENING.

(C. J. P. Spitta.)

O Lord, who by Thy presence hast made light
    The heat and burden of the toilsome day,
Be with me also in the silent night,
    Be with me when the daylight fades away.
As Thou hast given me strength upon the way,
    So deign at evening to become my guest ;
As Thou hast shared the labours of the day,
    So also deign to share and bless my rest.

No step disturbs me, not a sound is heard,
    I commune in my chamber and am still,
And muse with deep attention on Thy word,
    The faithful record of Thy mind and will.
O speak a word of blessing, gracious Lord,
    Thy blessing is endued with soothing power,
On the poor heart, worn out with toil, Thy word
    Falls soft and gentle as an evening shower.

How sad and cold, if Thou be absent, Lord,
    The evening leaves me, and my heart how dead!
But, if Thy presence grace my humble board,
    I seem with heavenly manna to be fed ;
Fraught with rich blessing, breathing sweet repose,
    The calm of evening settles on my breast ;
If Thou be with me when my labours close,
    No more is needed to complete my rest.

Come then, O Lord, and deign to be my guest
    After the day's confusion, toil, and din ;
O come to bring me peace, and joy, and rest,
    To give salvation, and to pardon sin
Bind up the wounds, assuage the aching smart
    Left in my bosom from the day just past,
And let me, on a Father's loving heart,
    Forget my griefs, and find sweet rest at last.

The following popular national hymn was written by the Rev. JOHN REYNELL WREFORD, D.D. (1800-

1881). He was educated at Manchester College, York, and became co-pastor with the Rev. John Kentish at New Meeting, Birmingham, until failure of voice compelled him to resign. He then started a school at Edgbaston in conjunction with the Rev. Hugh Hutton. His hymns, fifty-five in number, were contributed to the Rev. J. R. Beard's collection of "Hymns for Public and Private Worship" (1837), from which several have been reprinted in other hymnals. Of these one of the best is "Lord, I believe, Thy power I own," and certainly the most widely used is the following:—

> Lord, while for all mankind we pray,
>   Of every clime and coast;
> O hear us for our native land,—
>   The land we love the most!
>
> Our fathers' sepulchres are here,
>   And here our kindred dwell;
> Our children, too:—how should we love
>   Another land so well!
>
> O guard our shores from every foe,
>   With peace our borders bless;
> With prosperous times our cities crown,
>   Our fields with plenteousness.
>
> Unite us in the sacred love
>   Of knowledge, truth, and Thee;
> And let our hills and valleys shout
>   The songs of liberty.
>
> Here may religion, pure and mild,
>   Upon our Sabbaths smile;
> And piety and virtue reign,
>   And bless our native isle.
>
> Lord of the nations thus to Thee
>   Our country we commend;
> Be Thou her Refuge and her Trust
>   Her everlasting Friend!

HARRIET MARTINEAU, who was born in 1802, was one of the band of writers who gathered round William Johnson Fox, editor of the *Monthly Repository*, sending contributions to that journal when not more than nineteen years of age. She was much interested in the movements with which Fox was associated, and with her pen contributed much to the furtherance of social and political reform. In 1831 she began the series of "Illustrations of Political Economy," with which she did so much to popularise the principles laid down by Adam Smith. In 1852 she became a contributor to the *Daily News*, for which she continued to write for many years. She died on the 27th of June, 1876. Harriet Martineau wrote some verse for children in a small volume of "Addresses with Prayers and Original Hymns for the Use of Families and Schools," published in 1826, and contributed two hymns to the "Hymns and Anthems" prepared by W. J. Fox in 1845 for the use of his congregation at South Place. The hymn "Arise, my soul" is from the earlier book; the other examples are from the latter.

I.

Arise, my soul! and urge thy flight,
 And fix thy view on God alone,
As eagles spring to meet the light,
 And gaze upon the radiant sun.

As planets on and onward roll,
 As streams pour forth their swelling tide,
Press on thy steady course, my soul,
 Nor pause, nor stop, nor turn aside.

Planets and suns shall dim their fire;
 Earth, air, and sea, shall melt away;
But though each star of heaven expire,
 Thou may'st survive that awful day.

In life, in death, thy course hold on:
Though nature's self in ruins lie,
Pause not till heaven-gate be won;
Then rest; for there thou canst not die.

II.

Beneath this starry arch
  Nought resteth or is still;
But all things hold their march,
  As if by one great will:
    Moves one, move all:
    Hark to the footfall!
    On, on, for ever!

Yon sheaves were once but seed:
Will ripens into deed.
As cave-drops swell the streams,
Day-thoughts feed nightly dreams;
And sorrow tracketh wrong,
As echo follows song.
    On, on, for ever!

By night, like stars on high,
  The hours reveal their train;
They whisper, and go by;
  I never watch in vain:
    Moves one, move all:
    Hark to the footfall!
    On, on, for ever!

They pass the cradle-head,
And there a promise shed;
They pass the moist new grave,
And bid rank verdure wave;
They bear through every clime
The harvests of all time,
    On, on, for ever!

III.

All men are equal in their birth,
  Heirs of the earth and skies;
All men are equal when that earth
  Fades from their dying eyes.

All wait alike on Him whose power
  Upholds the life He gave;
The sage within his star-lit tower,
  The savage in his cave.

God meets the throngs that pay their vows
  In courts their hands have made;
And hears the worshipper who bows
  Beneath the plantain shade.

'Tis man alone who difference sees,
  And speaks of high and low,
And worships those and tramples these,
  While the same path they go.

Oh, let man hasten to restore
  To all their rights of love;
In power and wealth exult no more;
  In wisdom lowly move.

Ye great! renounce your earth-born pride;
  Ye low, your shame and fear:
Live as ye worship side by side;
  Your brotherhood revere

ISAAC WILLIAMS, son of a Chancery barrister, was born at the house of his grandfather, Cwmeynfelin, Cardiganshire, on the 12th of December, 1802. He was educated privately and at Harrow School and Trinity College, Oxford, where he won the prize for Latin verse in 1823 with a poem entitled "Ars Geologica," a circumstance which gained for him the friendship of Keble. After holding a curacy at Windrush for a short time, he was elected Fellow of Trinity, and, returning to Oxford, was introduced by Hurrell Froude to John Henry Newman, whose curate he afterwards became at St. Mary's, Oxford. On the resignation of the Professorship of Poetry at Oxford by Keble, Williams became a candidate for the office, but met with great opposition, on account of his association with the Tractarian movement, and was defeated, after which he retired from public life. He died on the 1st of May, 1865. He published numerous works, including the following in verse: "The Cathedral" (1838), "Thoughts in Past Years" (1838), "Hymns Translated from the Parisian Breviary" (1839); "Hymns on the Catechism" (1842); "The Baptistry" (1842); "Ancient Hymns for Children" (1842); "The Altar" (1849); and "The Christian Scholar" (1849). Some of these works are ambitious, but cannot be regarded as successes from the poetic point of view. The set purpose of the design of such a work as "The Cathedral" is incompatible with the freedom which favours inspiration, and the result is a work which is far more ecclesiastical than poetical. The following are favourable examples of his lyrics. The first is given as quoted by Lord Selborne in "The Book of Praise"; the second is from the "Translations from the Parisian Breviary."

1.

 The child leans on its parent's breast,
 Leaves there its cares, and is at rest;
 The bird sits singing by his nest,
  And tells aloud
 His trust in God, and so is blest
  'Neath every cloud.

 He has no store, he sows no seed,
 Yet sings aloud, and doth not heed;
 By flowing stream or grassy mead
  He sings to shame
 Men, who forget, in fear of need,
  A Father's name.

The heart that trusts for ever sings,
And feels as light as it had wings;
A well of peace within it springs;
  Come good or ill,
Whate'er to-day, to-morrow brings,
  It is His will!

II.

AT MIDNIGHT.

"Jam desinant suspiria.

Away with sorrow's sigh,
Our prayers are heard on high;
And through Heaven's crystal door,
On this our earthly floor
Comes meek-eyed Peace to walk with poor mortality.

In dead of night profound,
There breaks a seraph sound
Of never-ending morn;
The Lord of glory born
Within a holy grot on this our sullen ground.

Now with that shepherd crowd
If it might be allowed,
We fain would enter there
With awful hastening fear,
And kiss that cradle chaste in reverend worship bowed.

O sight of strange surprise
That fills our gazing eyes:
A manger coldly strew'd,
And swaddling-bands so rude,
A leaning mother poor, and child that helpless lies.

Art Thou, O wondrous sight,
Of lights the very Light,
Who holdest in Thy hand
The sky and sea and land;
Who than the glorious Heavens art more exceeding bright?

'Tis so;—faith darts before,
And, through the cloud drawn o'er,
She sees the God of all,
Where Angels prostrate fall,
Adoring tremble still, and trembling still adore.

No thunders round Thee break,
Yet doth Thy silence speak
From that, Thy Teacher's seat,
To us around Thy feet,
To shun what flesh desires, what flesh abhors to seek.

Within us, Babe divine,
Be born, and make us Thine;
Within our souls reveal
Thy love and power to heal;
Be born, and make our hearts Thy cradle and Thy shrine.

JOHN HAMPDEN GURNEY (1802-1862) was educated at Trinity College, Cambridge, where he graduated 1824. Taking Holy Orders, he became Curate of Lutterworth (1827-1844), and subsequently Rector of St. Mary's, Marylebone, and Prebendary of St. Paul's Cathedral. He died on the 8th of March, 1862. He published "A Collection of Hymns for Public Worship" (1838); "Psalms and Hymns for Public Worship" (1851); and "Church Psalmody," hints for the improvement of a collection of hymns published by the Christian Knowledge Society 1853. To these books he contributed a number of original hymns, which have since been often reprinted, of which the following is one of the most popular:—

Lord of the harvest! Thee we hail!
Thine ancient promise doth not fail;
The varying seasons haste their round,
With goodness all our years are crowned:
  Our thanks we pay
  This holy day;
O let our hearts in tune be found!

If Spring doth wake the song of mirth
If Summer warms the fruitful earth;

When Winter sweeps the naked plain,
Or Autumn yields its ripened grain;
  Still do we sing
  To Thee, our King;
Through all the changes Thou dost reign.

But chiefly when Thy liberal hand
Scatters new plenty o'er the land,
When sounds of music fill the air,
As homeward all their treasures bear;
  We too will raise
  Our hymn of praise,
For we Thy common bounties share.

Lord of the harvest, all is Thine!
The rains that fall, the suns that shine,
The seed once hidden in the ground,
The skill that makes our fruits abound!
  New, every year,
  Thy gifts appear;
New praises from our lips shall sound!

HENRY JAMES BUCKOLL (1803-1871) was educated at Rugby and Queen's College, Oxford. Graduating in 1826, he became Assistant Master at Rugby. In 1839 he edited "A Collection of Hymns for the Rugby Parish Church," and in 1850, with Dr. Goulburn, a new edition of the collection for the Rugby School Chapel, to which he contributed fourteen hymns. He also published "Hymns Translated from the German" (1842). This contained translations, sixty-seven in number, from Bunsen's "Versuch."

(VON CANITZ.)

Come, my soul, thou must be waking—
  Now is breaking
O'er the earth another day;
Come, to Him who made this splendour,
  See thou render
All thy feeble strength can pay.

From the stars thy course be learning;
    Dimly burning
'Neath the sun their light grows pale;
So let all that sense delighted,
    While benighted,
From God's presence fade and fail.

Lo! how all of breath partaking,
    Gladly waking,
Hail the sun's enlivening light!
Plants, whose life mere sap doth nourish,
    Rise and flourish
When he breaks the shades of night.

Thou too hail the light returning;
    Ready burning
Be the incense of thy powers;—
For the night is safely ended;
    God hath tended
With His care thy helpless hours.

Pray that He may prosper ever
    Each endeavour,
When thine aim is good and true;
But that He may ever thwart thee,
    And convert thee,
When thou evil wouldst pursue.

Think that He thy ways beholdeth—
    He unfoldeth
Every fault that lurks within;
Every stain of shame gloss'd over
    Can discover,
And discern each deed of sin.

Fetter'd to the fleeting hours
    All our powers
Vain and brief, are borne away:
Time, my soul, thy ship is steering,
    Onward veering,
To the gulf of death a prey.

May'st thou then on life's last morrow,
    Free from sorrow,
Pass away in slumber sweet:

> And, releas'd from death's dark sadness,
>   Rise in gladness,
>   That far brighter sun to greet.
>
> Only God's free gifts abuse not,
>   His light refuse not,
>   But still His Spirit's voice obey;
> Soon shall joy thy brow be wreathing,
>   Splendour breathing
>   Fairer than the fairest day.
>
> If aught of care this morn oppress thee,
>   To Him address thee,
>   Who, like the sun, is good to all:
> He gilds the mountain tops, the while
>   His gracious smile
>   Will on the humblest valley fall.
>
> Round the gifts His bounty showers,
>   Walls and towers
>   Girt with flames thy God shall rear:
> Angel legions to defend thee
>   Shall attend thee,
>   Hosts whom Satan's self shall fear.

The foregoing text is taken from "The Christian Life: its Course, Hindrances, and its Helps" (1841), a volume of sermons preached in Rugby School Chapel by Dr. Arnold.

SAMUEL GREG (1804-1877) was born at Manchester, and was educated under Dr. Lant Carpenter at Bristol and at Edinburgh University. He was a mill-owner at Bollington, Macclesfield, where he held services for his work-people. He published "Scenes from the Life of Jesus" (1854), a prose work, and wrote a few hymns, of which the following are the best. After his death a volume of his addresses was published (1877), for which Dean Stanley wrote a preface.

I.

DEATH.

Slowly, slowly darkening
   The evening hours roll on,
And soon behind the cloud-land
   Will sink my setting sun.

Around my path life's mysteries
   Their deepening shadows throw
And as I gaze and ponder,
   They dark and darker grow.

But there's a voice above me
   Which says, "Wait, trust, and pray;
The night will soon be over,
   And light will come with day."

Father! the light and darkness
   Are both alike to Thee;
Then to Thy waiting servant,
   Alike they both shall be.

The great unending future,
   I cannot pierce its shroud;
Yet nothing doubt, nor tremble,
   God's bow is on the cloud.

To Him I yield my spirit;
   On Him I lay my load:
Fear ends with death, beyond it
   I nothing see but GOD.

Thus moving towards the darkness
   I calmly wait His call,
Now seeing,—fearing nothing,
   But hoping, trusting—all!

II.

THE TRANSFIGURATION.

Stay, Master, stay upon this heavenly hill
A little longer, let us linger still;

With these two mighty ones of old beside,
Near to the Awful Presence still abide;
Before the throne of light we trembling stand,
And catch a glimpse into the spirit-land.

Stay, Master, stay! we breathe a purer air;
This life is not the life that waits us there:
Thoughts, feelings, flashes, glimpses come and go;
We cannot speak them—nay, we do not know;
Wrapt in this cloud of light we seem to be
The thing we fain would grow—eternally.

"No!" saith the Lord, "the hour is past,—we go;
Our home, our life, our duties lie below.
While here we kneel upon the mount of prayer,
The plough lies waiting in the furrow there;
Here we sought God that we might know His will;
There we must do it,—serve Him,—seek Him still."

If man aspires to reach the throne of God,
O'er the dull plains of earth must lie the road.
He who best does his lowly duty here,
Shall mount the highest in a nobler sphere.
At God's own feet our spirits seek their rest,
And he is nearest Him who serves Him best.

JAMES MARTINEAU was born at Norwich on the 21st of April, 1805; and after passing through the Norwich Grammar School, spent two years under Dr. Lant Carpenter at Bristol, after which he entered Manchester College, York, as a divinity student. From 1828 to 1832 he was minister of Eustace Street Chapel, Dublin; from 1832 to 1857 of Paradise Street (afterwards Hope Street) Church, Liverpool. In 1840 he became Professor of Mental and Moral Philosophy and Political Economy at Manchester New College, removing with the college to London, and becoming President in 1869. In London he ministered to the congregation of

Little Portland Street Chapel until 1873. He was made D.C.L. of Oxford 1888. He edited "A Collection of Hymns for Christian Worship" (1831); "Hymns for the Christian Church and Home" (1840); and "Hymns of Praise and Prayer" (1873). He died on the 11th of January, 1900. He wrote several hymns, which appeared anonymously at first, but which were afterwards acknowledged. The following are the most noteworthy:—

I
"THY WAY IS IN THE DEEP."
1840.

Thy way is in the deep, O Lord!
    E'en there we'll go with Thee:
We'll meet the tempest at Thy word,
    And walk upon the sea!

Poor tremblers at His rougher wind,
    Why do we doubt Him so?
Who gives the storm a path, will find
    The way our feet shall go.

A moment may His hand be lost,—
    Drear moment of delay!—
We cry, "Lord! keep the tempest-tost,"—
    And safe we're borne away.

The Lord yields nothing to our fears,
    And flies from selfish care;
But comes Himself, where'er He hears
    The voice of loving prayer.

O happy soul of faith divine!
    Thy victory how sure!
The love that kindles joy is thine,—
    The patience to endure.

Come, Lord of peace! our griefs dispel,
    And wipe our tears away·
'Tis Thine, to order all things well,
    And ours to bless the sway.

II.

THE INWARD WITNESS OF GOD.

1873.

"Where is your God?" they say;—
Answer them, Lord most Holy!
  Reveal Thy secret way
  Of visiting the lowly:
Not wrapped in moving cloud,
Or nightly-resting fire;
  But veiled within the shroud
  Of silent high desire.

Come not in flashing storm,
Or bursting frown of thunder
  Come in the viewless form
  Of wakening love and wonder;—
Of duty grown divine,
The restless spirit, still;
  Of sorrows taught to shine
  As shadows of Thy will.

O God! the pure alone,—
E'en in their deep confessing,—
  Can see Thee as their own,
  And find the perfect blessing:
Yet to each waiting soul
Speak in Thy still small voice,
  Till broken love's made whole,
  And saddened hearts rejoice.

JOHN F. CHANDLER (1806-1876), Vicar of Witley (1837), was one of the earliest as well as one of the most successful of the translators from the Latin who have done so much to enrich modern hymnody. He was first led to undertake this work by seeing some translations from the Parisian Breviary by Isaac

Williams in the *British Magazine*. He published " The Hymns of the Primitive Church, now first collected, translated, and arranged" (1837), and "The Hymns of the Church, mostly Primitive, collected, translated, and arranged for Public Use" (1841); from which, according to Julian, some thirty or forty hymns have come into general use. The following are examples.—

I.

VICTIS SIBI COGNOMINA.

PARIS BREVIARY.

'Tis for conquering kings to gain
Glory o'er their myriads slain;
Jesu, Thy more glorious strife
Hath restored a world to life.

So no other Name is given
Unto mortals under heaven,
Which can make the dead to rise,
And exalt them to the skies.

That which Christ so hardly wrought,
That which He so dearly bought,
That salvation, mortals, say,
Will you madly cast away?

Rather gladly for that Name,
Bear the cross, endure the shame;
Joyfully for Him to die
Is not death, but victory.

Dost Thou, Jesu, condescend
To be called the sinner's Friend?
Ours then it shall always be
Thus to make our boast of Thee.

II.

SPLENDOR PATERNÆ GLORIÆ.
Ambrose.

O Jesu, Lord of heavenly grace,
Thou Brightness of Thy Father's face;
Thou Fountain of eternal light,
Whose beams disperse the shades of night;

Come, Holy Sun of heavenly love,
Shower down Thy radiance from above;
And to our inward hearts convey
The Holy Spirit's cloudless ray.

And we the Father's help will claim,
And sing the Father's glorious Name;
His powerful succour we implore,
That we may stand, to fall no more.

May He our actions deign to bless,
And loose the bonds of wickedness;
From sudden falls our feet defend,
And bring us to a prosperous end.

May faith, deep-rooted in the soul,
Subdue our flesh, our minds control;
May guile depart, and discord cease,
And all within be joy and peace.

And Christ shall be our daily food,
Our daily drink His precious blood;
And thus the Spirit's calm excess
Shall fill our souls with holiness.

Oh, hallowed be the approaching day!
Let meekness be our morning ray,
And faithful love our noonday light,
And hope our sunset, calm and bright.

O Christ, with each returning morn
Thine image to our hearts is borne;
Oh! may we ever clearly see
Our Saviour and our God in Thee!

GEORGE RAWSON (1807-1889) was a solicitor, practising at Leeds, in which town he was born on the 5th of June, 1807. He took part in the compilation of several hymn-books, to which he contributed many original hymns. He published " Hymns, Verses, and Chants" in 1876, and "Songs of Spiritual Thought" in 1885. He died on the 25th of March, 1889. According to Julian, about fifty of his hymns are in general use in England and America. Among the more popular of these are "By Christ redeemed, in Christ restored," "Come to our poor nature's night," and "Father, in high heaven dwelling." The two examples given represent the writer in contrast of prayer and praise.

I.

TRUST.

My Father, it is good for me
  To trust and not to trace,
And wait with deep humility
  For Thy revealing grace.

Lord, when Thy way is in the sea,
  And strange to mortal sense,
I love Thee in the mystery,
  I trust Thy providence.

I cannot see the secret things
  In this my dark abode;
I may not reach with earthly wings
  The heights and depths of God.

So, faith and patience, wait awhile!—
  Not doubting, not in fear;
For soon in heaven my Father's smile
  Shall render all things clear.

Then Thou shalt end time's short eclipse,
   Its dim, uncertain night;
Bring in the grand apocalypse,
   Reveal the perfect Light.

II.

Psalm cxlviii.

Praise ye the Lord, immortal quire,
   In heavenly heights above,
With harp and voice and souls of fire,
   Burning with perfect love.

Shine to His glory, worlds of light!
   Ye million suns of space,
Fair moons and glittering stars of night,
   Running your mystic race!

Ye gorgeous clouds, that deck the sky
   With crystal, crimson, gold,
And rainbow arches raised on high,
   The Light of Light unfold!

Lift to Jehovah, wintry main,
   Your grand white hands in prayer!
Still summer seas, in dulcet strain
   Murmur hosannas there!

Do homage, breezy ocean floor,
   With many-twinkling sign;
Majestic calms, be hushed before
   The Holiness Divine!

Storm, lightning, thunder, hail and snow,
   Wild winds that keep His word,
With the old mountains far below
   Unite to bless the Lord.

His name, ye forests, wave along!
   Whisper it, every flower!
Birds, beasts, and insects, swell the song
   That tells His love and power!

And round the wide world let it roll,
   Whilst man shall lead it on;
Join every ransomed human soul,
   In glorious unison!

Come, aged man! Come, little child!
   Youth, maiden, peasant, king,—
To God, in Jesus reconciled,
   Your hallelujahs bring!

The all-creating Deity!
   Maker of earth and heaven!
The great redeeming Majesty,
   To Him the praise be given!

The following hymn, used on many State occasions, was written by EDWARD ARTHUR DAYMAN, B.D., who was born at Padstow, Cornwall, on the 11th of July, 1807, and educated at Tiverton and Exeter College, Oxford. A Fellow and Tutor of his College, he became Proproctor in 1835, and, taking Holy Orders, successively Examiner for University Scholarships for Latin 1838, and in Lit. Hum. 1838-9. In 1840 he became Senior Proctor of the University; in 1842, Rector of Shilling-Okeford, Dorset; in 1849, Rural Dean; in 1852, Proctor in Convocation; and in 1862, Honorary Canon of Bitton in Sarum Cathedral. He died on the 30th of October, 1890. He was co-editor, with Canon Woodford and Lord Nelson, of the "Sarum Hymnal" (1868), to which he contributed translations from the Latin, as well as original hymns, including "Sleep thy last sleep," which bears date 1868.

Sleep thy last sleep,
Free from care and sorrow,
   Rest, where none weep,
Till the eternal morrow;

Though dark waves roll
O'er the silent river,
  Thy fainting soul
Jesus can deliver.

  Life's dream is past,
All its sin, its sadness,
  Brightly at last
Dawns a day of gladness;
  Under thy sod,
Earth, receive our treasure,
  To rest in God,
Waiting all His pleasure.

  Though we may mourn
Those in life the dearest,
  They shall return,
Christ, when Thou appearest!
  Soon shall Thy voice
Comfort those now weeping,
  Bidding rejoice
All in Jesus sleeping.

In 1836 a small volume, containing fifty-two hymns, was printed for private circulation at Bridgewater, bearing the following title: "Hymns by the late Joseph Anstice, M.A., formerly Student of Christ Church, Oxford, and Professor of Classical Literature at King's College, London." This little sheaf of Christian verse was the harvest of a period of pain and suffering which ended in early death. As the hymns were dictated to his wife during intervals of teaching, which he continued until the very day of his death, they did not have the advantage of final revision for the press, and for this reason were withheld on their first publication from the general public. Many of them, however, were included in Mrs. Young's "Child's Christian Year," published in 1841, and from this source have found their way into general use. Perhaps the most popular of these hymns is the five-stanza hymn (reduced to four stanzas in some collections) beginning,—

> O Lord! how happy should we be
> If we could cast our care on Thee;
>   If we from self could rest;
> And feel at heart that One above,
> In perfect wisdom, perfect love,
>   Is working for the best.

Others of these hymns show greater finish, of which the evening hymn "Father, by Thy love and power," too long for quotation, and the two examples which follow, may be mentioned. JOSEPH ANSTICE was born at Madeley, Shropshire, in 1808, and was educated at Westminster and Christ Church, Oxford, where he had a distinguished career, gaining two English prizes and graduating a double first. He published "Richard Cœur de Lion," his prize poem, 1828; "The Influence of the Roman Conquest upon Literature and the Arts in Rome," his prize essay; and "Selections from the Choice Poetry of the Greek Dramatic Writers, translated into English Verse" (1832). He died at Torquay on the 29th of February, 1836, at the early age of twenty-eight years.

I.

> "Come to a desert place apart,
>   And rest a little while;"
> So spake the Christ, when limbs and heart
>   Wax'd faint and sick through toil
>
> High communings with God He sought:
>   But, where He sought them, found
> The restless crowd together brought,
>   And labour's weary round.

Then not a thought to self was given,
 Nor breath'd a word of blame;
He fed their souls with bread from Heaven,
 Then stay'd their sinking frame.

Turn'd He, when that long task is done,
 To sleep fatigue away?
When on the desert sank the sun,
 The Saviour waked to pray.

O perfect Pattern from above,
 So strengthen us, that ne'er
Prayer keep us back from works of love,
 Nor works of love from prayer.

II.

Lord of the harvest! once again
We thank Thee for the ripen'd grain;
For crops safe carried, sent to cheer
Thy servants through another year;
For all sweet holy thoughts, supplied
By seed-time and by harvest-tide.

The bare dead grain, in autumn sown,
Its robe of vernal green puts on;
Glad from its wintry grave it springs,
Fresh garnish'd by the King of Kings;
So, Lord, to those who sleep in Thee
Shall new and glorious bodies be.

Nor vainly of Thy Word we ask
A lesson from the reaper's task;
So shall Thine angels issue forth;—
The tares be burnt;—the just of earth,
Playthings of sun and storm no more,
Be gather'd to their Father's store.

Daily, O Lord, our prayer is said
As Thou hast taught, for daily bread;
But not alone our bodies feed;
Supply our fainting spirits' need;
O Bread of Life! from day to day,
Be Thou their Comfort, Food, and Stay!

JOHN SAMUEL BEWLEY MONSELL (1811-1875) was born at Londonderry, and was educated at Trinity

College, Dublin, and became Chaplain to Bishop Mant; Rector of Ramoan; Vicar of Egham, Surrey; and Rector of St. Nicholas', Guildford. He published a number of books, including "Hymns and Miscellaneous Poems" (1837); "His Presence, not His Memory" (1855); "Spiritual Songs" (1857); "Hymns of Love and Praise for the Church's Year" (1863); "The Passing Bell"; "Ode to the Nightingale and other Poems" (1867); "Litany Hymns" (1869); "The Parish Hymnal" (1873); "Watches by the Cross" (1874); also "Simon the Cyrenian and other Poems," "Nursery Carols," etc., etc. To these or other volumes he contributed some three hundred hymns, many of which are widely used. He died on the 9th of April, 1875. The following examples are given as finally revised by the author during his last illness:—

I.

Birds have their quiet nest,
Foxes their holes, and man his peaceful bed;
All creatures have their rest,
But Jesus had not where to lay His head.

And yet He came to give
The weary and the heavy-laden rest;
To bid the sinner live,
And soothe our griefs to slumber on His breast

I who once made Him grieve,
I who once bid His gentle spirit mourn;
Whose hand essay'd to weave
For His meek brow the cruel crown of thorn:—

O why should I have peace?
Why—but for that unchanged, undying love,
Which would not, could not cease,
Until it made me heir of joys above?

  Yes, but for pardoning grace,
I feel I never should in glory see
  The brightness of that face,
Which once was pale and agonized for me!

  Let the birds seek their nest,
Foxes their holes, and man his peaceful bed;
  Come, Saviour, in my breast
Deign to repose Thine oft-rejected head!

  Come! give me rest, and take
The only rest on earth Thou lov'st,—within
  A heart, that for Thy sake
Lies bleeding, broken, penitent for sin.

II.

God is Love, by Him upholden
 Hang the glorious orbs of light,
In their language, glad and golden,
 Speaking to us day and night
  Their great story,
 God is Love, and God is Might.

And the teeming earth rejoices
 In that message from above,
With ten thousand thousand voices
 Telling back, from hill and grove,
  Her glad story,
 God is Might, and God is Love.

With these anthems of creation,
 Mingling in harmonious strife,
Christian songs of Christ's salvation,
 To the world with blessings rife,
  Tell their story,
 God is Love, and God is Life.

Through that precious Love He sought us,
 Wand'ring from His holy ways,
With that precious Life He bought us;
 Then let all our future days
  Tell this story:
 Love is Life—our lives be Praise.

> Gladsome is the theme, and glorious,
>   Praise to Christ our gracious Head,
> Christ, the risen Christ, victorious
>   Death and hell hath captive led.
>   Welcome story!
>   Love lives on, and Death is dead.
>
> Up to Him let each affection
>   Daily rise, and round Him move
> Our whole lives, one Resurrection
>   To the Life of life above;
>   Their glad story,
>   God is Life, and God is Love.

NORMAN MACLEOD was born at Campbeltown, Argyllshire, on the 3rd of June, 1812. He studied at the Universities of Glasgow and Edinburgh, and became parish minister at Loudoun, in Ayrshire, in 1838, and at Dalbeattie in 1843. In 1846 he visited Canada on a mission for the General Assembly of the Church, and in 1851 was inducted into the Barony parish, Glasgow. He was made a D.D. of Glasgow in 1858, and became Editor of *Good Words* on its foundation in 1860. In 1867 he visited the mission field of India on behalf of the General Assembly, and in 1869 was elected Moderator. He died at Glasgow on the 16th of June, 1872.

Norman Macleod wrote little verse, and except for one stirring song would have had no title to recognition here. This song, "Trust in God," first appeared in the *Edinburgh Christian Magazine* for January 1857 (a magazine edited by its author), and has since found its way into countless collections of verse. The justification of the use of verse as a means of expression must be that it is able to express the thought of the writer more effectively than it could be expressed within the same limits in prose. This, if its only justification, must be taken as sufficient, and it justifies the existence of much more or less didactic verse, which, if not poetry, fulfils at least some of the offices of poetry in elevating thought, stimulating action, and quickening love.

TRUST IN GOD.

Courage, brother! do not stumble,
  Though thy path is dark as night;
There's a star to guide the humble:
  "Trust in God, and do the right."

Let the road be long and dreary,
  And its ending out of sight;
Foot it bravely, strong or weary,
  "Trust in God, and do the right."

Perish "policy" and cunning,
  Perish all that fears the light!
Whether losing, whether winning,
  "Trust in God, and do the right."

Trust no forms of guilty passion,
  Fiends can look like angels bright;
Trust no custom, school, or fashion,
  "Trust in God, and do the right."

Trust no party, Church, or faction;
  Trust no leaders in the fight;
But, in every word and action,
  "Trust in God, and do the right."

Some will hate thee, some will love thee,
  Some will flatter, some will slight;
Cease from man, and look above thee;
  "Trust in God, and do the right."

Simple rule, and safest guiding;
  Inward peace, and inward light;
Star upon our path abiding:
  "Trust in God, and do the right."

These verses are full of moral stimulus, much of which would evaporate in the process of reducing them to prose. Hence the justification of their poetic form.

"Hymns from the Land of Luther" (first series, 1854; second series, 1855; third series, 1858; fourth series, 1862), by JANE BORTHWICK (1813) and her sister Sarah (Mrs. FINDLATER, 1823-1886), was one of the earliest systematic attempts to enrich English hymnody from German sources, and was made, singularly enough, practically simultaneously with the efforts of Catherine Winkworth in the same direction. The first series of "Hymns from the Land of Luther" was published by the Borthwicks in 1854; the first edition of "Lyra Germanica" by Catherine Winkworth in 1855. Miss Borthwick contributed a number of translations and original poems to the *Family Treasury*, which were afterwards collected and published under the title "Thoughts for Thoughtful Hours" in 1857. Her most popular original hymn is "Come, labour on," her best-known translation "Jesus, still lead on."

I.

Come, labour on!
Who dares stand idle on the harvest-plain,
While all around him waves the golden grain?
And to each servant does the Master say,
"Go work to-day."

Come, labour on!
Claim the high calling angels cannot share,
To young and old the Gospel gladness bear;
Redeem the time, its hours too swiftly fly,
The night draws nigh.

Come, labour on!
The enemy is watching night and day,
To sow the tares, to snatch the seed away;
While we in sleep our duty have forgot,
    He slumbered not.

Come, labour on!
Away with gloomy doubts and faithless fear!
No arm so weak but may do service here;
By hands the feeblest can our God fulfil
    His righteous will.

Come, labour on!
No time for rest, till glows the western sky,
While the long shadows o'er our pathway lie,
And a glad sound comes with the setting sun—
    "Servants, well done!"

Come, labour on!
The toil is pleasant, and the harvest sure,
Blessèd are those who to the end endure;—
How full their joy, how deep their rest shall be,
    O Lord, with Thee!

II.

(Zinzendorf.)

Jesus, still lead on,
Till our rest be won!
And although the way be cheerless,
We will follow, calm and fearless:
    Guide us by Thy hand
    To our Fatherland

If the way be drear,
If the foe be near,
Let not faithless fears o'ertake us,
Let not faith and hope forsake us;
    For, through many a foe,
    To our home we go.

> When we seek relief
> From a long-felt grief;
> When oppressed by new temptations,
> Lord, increase and perfect patience;
> Show us that bright shore
> Where we weep no more.
>
> Jesus, still lead on
> Till our rest be won;
> Heavenly Leader, still direct us,
> Still support, console, protect us,
> Till we safely stand
> In our Fatherland.

EDWARD CASWELL (1814-1878) was born at Yateley, in Hampshire, on the 15th of July, 1814, and was educated at Brasenose College, Oxford, where he graduated with honours in 1836. In 1838 he took Holy Orders, and in 1840 became Incumbent of Stratford-sub-Castle, near Salisbury, where he remained until 1847, when he resigned his incumbency, and three years later entered the Church of Rome, joining Dr. Newman at the Oratory, Edgbaston, Birmingham, where he died on the 2nd of January, 1878. Caswell's publications include "Lyra Catholica" (1849), a work containing one hundred and ninety-seven translations from the Roman Breviary, Missal, and other sources; "The Masque of Mary and other Poems" (1858), a book containing numerous translations and original hymns; "A May Pageant and other Poems" (1865), including a few more original hymns; and "Hymns and Poems" (1873), a work embodying the three earlier publications, many of the poems of which were revised for republication.

Caswell's original hymns have not been largely used outside the Roman communion, but some of his translations have attained a popularity second only to that of Dr. Neale's translations of hymns from Eastern sources. The best known of his original hymns is the following, from "The Masque of Mary" volume:—

I.

SWIFTNESS OF TIME.

Days and moments quickly flying,
  Blend the living with the dead;
Soon will you and I be lying
  Each within our narrow bed

Soon our souls, to God who gave them,
  Will have sped their rapid flight,—
Able now by grace to save them,
  O, that while we can we might!

Jesu, infinite Redeemer,
  Maker of this mighty frame!
Teach, O teach us to remember
  What we are, and whence we came;

Whence we came, and whither wending,
  Soon we must through darkness go,
To inherit bliss unending,
  Or eternity of woe.

Among the more popular of Caswell's translations are the hymns, "Jesu, the very thought of Thee," "O Jesu, King most wonderful," "When morning gilds the skies," and "The sun is sinking fast," all of which are variously modified from the originals given in "The Masque of Mary and other Poems"

II.

ST. BERNARD'S HYMN; OR, THE LOVING SOUL'S JUBILATION.

Jesu dulcis memoria.

I.

Jesu, the very thought of Thee
    With sweetness fills my breast
But sweeter far Thy face to see,
    And in Thy presence rest.

Nor voice can sing, nor heart can frame,
    Nor can the memory find,
A sweeter sound than Thy blest name,
    O Saviour of mankind!

O hope of every contrite heart!
    O joy of all the meek!
To those who fall, how kind Thou art!
    How good to those who seek!

But what to those who find? ah, this
    Nor tongue nor pen can show:
The love of Jesus, what it is,
    None but His loved ones know.

O Jesu, light of all below!
    Thou Fount of life and fire!
Surpassing all the joys we know,
    And all we can desire,—

Thee will I seek, at home, abroad,
    Who everywhere art nigh;
Thee in my bosom's cell, O Lord,
    As on my bed I lie.

With Mary to Thy tomb I'll haste,
    Before the dawning skies,
And all around with longing cast
    My soul's enquiring eyes.

Beside Thy grave will make my moan,
    And sob my heart away;
Then at Thy feet sink trembling down,
    And there adoring stay;

Nor from my tears and sighs refrain,
    Nor Thy dear knees release,
My Jesu, till from Thee I gain
    Some blessed word of peace!

II.

O Jesu, King most wonderful!
    Thou Conqueror renown'd;
Thou sweetness most ineffable!
    In whom all joys are found!

Stay with us, Lord; and with Thy light
    Illume the soul's abyss;
Scatter the darkness of our night,
    And fill the world with bliss!

When once Thou visitest the heart,
    Then truth begins to shine;
Then earthly vanities depart;
    Then kindles love divine.

Jesu! Thy mercies are untold,
    Through each returning day;
Thy love exceeds a thousandfold
    Whatever we can say;

That love which in Thy Passion drain'd
    For us Thy precious Blood;
Whence with Redemption we have gain'd
    The Vision of our God!

May every heart confess Thy name,
    And ever Thee adore;
And, seeking Thee, itself inflame
    To seek Thee more and more.

Jesu, our only joy be Thou,
    As Thou our prize wilt be;
Jesu, be Thou our glory now,
    And through eternity.

III.

AN EVENING HYMN.

The sun is sinking fast;
    The daylight dies;
Let love awake and pay
    Her evening sacrifice.

As Christ upon the Cross
    In death reclin'd,
Into His Father's hands
    His parting soul resign'd;

So now herself my soul
    Would wholly give,
Into His sacred charge,
    In whom all spirits live;

So now beneath His eye
    Would calmly rest,
Without a wish or thought
    Abiding in the breast,

Save that His will be done,
    Whate'er betide;
Dead to herself; and dead,
    In Him, to all beside.

Thus would I live;—yet now
    Not I, but He;
In all His power and love
    Henceforth alive in me!

One sacred Trinity!
    One Lord divine!
Myself for ever His,
    And He for ever mine!

ARTHUR PENRHYN STANLEY (1815-1881) was born at Alderley, Cheshire, on the 13th of December, 1815. He was educated at Rugby under Dr. Arnold, and at Oxford, where he had a brilliant career,—gaining the Newdigate prize for English verse with a poem on "The Gypsies"; the Ireland scholarship; a first class in Classical honours, 1837; the prize for the Latin essay, 1839; and the English and the Theological essays, 1840. He was a Fellow of University College, and a Tutor for twelve years; Select Preacher, 1845-46; Canon of Canterbury, 1851-55; Regius Professor of Ecclesiastical History, Oxford, 1855; Examining Chaplain to the Bishop of London, 1858; Dean of Westminster, 1863; Lord Rector of St. Andrews, 1875. He died on the 18th of July, 1881. He published "Life and Correspondence of Dr. Arnold" (1844); "Memoirs of Richard Stanley, Bishop of Norwich, and Catherine Stanley" (1850); "Historical Memorials of Canterbury" (1854); "Sinai and Palestine" (1856); "Lectures on the History of the Eastern Church" (1861); "Lectures on the History of the Jewish Church" (1863-65); "Historical Memorials of Westminster Abbey" (1867); and various other works.

Dean Stanley wrote very little verse, and that little does not display high poetic merit. Prose was clearly his natural form of expression, and in the freedom of prose he was much more poetic than when hampered by the fetters of rhyme. Dr. Overton, writing in Julian's "Dictionary of Hymnology," says: "That exquisite taste and felicity of diction which distinguish more or less all his prose writings, seem to desert him when he is writing verse. Like another great writer, Jeremy Taylor, his prose is poetical, but his poetry is prosaic. The divine afflatus is wanting." The following examples are at once the best and most popular of his poems:—

I.

HYMN ON THE TRANSFIGURATION.

"Master, it is good to be
High on the mountain here with Thee."
Here, in an ampler, purer air,
Above the stir of toil and care,
Of hearts distraught with doubt and grief,
Believing in their unbelief,
Calling Thy servants, all in vain,
To ease them of their bitter pain.

"Master, it is good to be
Where rest the souls that talk with Thee:"
Where stand revealed to mortal gaze
The great old saints of other days;
Who once received on Horeb's height,
The eternal laws of truth and right;
Or caught the still small whisper, higher
Than storm, than earthquake, or than fire.

"Master, it is good to be
With Thee, and with Thy faithful Three:"
Here, where the Apostle's heart of rock
Is nerved against temptation's shock;
Here, where the Son of Thunder learns
" The thought that breathes, the word that burns;"
Here, where on eagle's wings we move
With Him Whose last, best creed is Love.

"Master, it is good to be
Entranced, enwrapt, alone with Thee;"
Watching the glistening raiment glow
Whiter than Hermon's whitest snow,
The human lineaments that shine
Irradiant with a light Divine,
Still we, too, change from grace to grace,
Gazing on that transfigured Face.

"Master, it is good to be
In life's worst anguish close to Thee:"
Within the overshadowing cloud
Which wraps us in its awful shroud,
We wist not what to think or say,
Our spirits sink in sore dismay;
They tell us of the dread "Decease":
But yet to linger here is peace.

"Master, it is good to be
Here on the Holy Mount with Thee;"
When darkling in the depths of night,
When dazzled with excess of light,
We bow before the heavenly Voice
That bids bewildered souls rejoice:
Though love wax cold, and faith be dim,
"This is My Son; O hear ye Him!"

II.

HE IS GONE—BEYOND THE SKIES.

He is gone—beyond the skies,
A cloud receives Him from our eyes;
Gone beyond the highest height
Of mortal gaze or angel's flight;
Through the veils of Time and Space,
Pass'd into the Holiest Place;
All the toil, the sorrow done,
All the battle fought and won.

He is gone—and we return,
And our hearts within us burn;
Olivet no more shall greet
With welcome shout His coming feet;
Never shall we track Him more
On Gennesareth's glistening shore;
Never in that look or voice
Shall Zion's hill again rejoice

He is gone—and we remain
In this world of sin and pain;
In the void which He has left,
On this earth of Him bereft,
We have still His work to do,
We can still His path pursue;
Seek Him both in friend and foe,
In ourselves His image show.

He is gone—we heard Him say,
"Good that I should go away."
Gone is that dear Form and Face,
But not gone His present grace;
Though Himself no more we see,
Comfortless we cannot be:
No, His Spirit still is ours,
Quickening, freshening all our powers.

He is gone—towards their goal,
World and Church must onwards roll:
Far behind we leave the past;
Forwards are our glances cast:
Still His words before us range
Through the ages as they change:
Wheresoe'er the Truth shall lead,
He will give whate'er we need.

He is gone—but we once more
Shall behold Him as before;
In the Heaven of Heavens the same,
As on earth He went and came.
In the many mansions there,
Place for us will He prepare:
In that world, unseen, unknown,
He and we may yet be one.

He is gone,—but not in vain;
Wait, until He comes again;
He is risen, He is not here,
Far above this earthly sphere,
Evermore in heart and mind,
Where our peace in Him we find:
To our own Eternal Friend,
Thitherward let us ascend.

Jane Montgomery Campbell (1817-1878) contributed translations from the German to "The Garland of Song; or, an English Liederkranz" (Rev. C. S. Brere, 1862), as well as to "The Children's Choral Book" (same editor, 1869). She also published "A Handbook for Singers." The following, which is a portion of "Im Anfang war's auf Erden," is the most popular of her hymns:—

(M. Claudius.)

We plough the fields, and scatter
  The good seed on the land,
But it is fed and watered
  By God's almighty hand;
He sends the snow in winter,
  The warmth to swell the grain,
The breezes, and the sunshine,
  And soft refreshing rain.
    All good gifts around us
      Are sent from heaven above,
    Then thank the Lord, O thank the Lord,
      For all His love!

He only is the Maker
  Of all things near and far;
He paints the wayside flower,
  He lights the evening star;
The winds and waves obey Him,
  By Him the birds are fed;
Much more to us, His children,
  He gives our daily bread.
    All good gifts around us
      Are sent from heaven above,
    Then thank the Lord, O thank the Lord,
      For all His love!

We thank Thee then, O Father,
  For all things bright and good,
The seed-time and the harvest,
  Our life, our health, our food.

No gifts have we to offer
For all Thy love imparts,
But that which Thou desirest,
Our humble, thankful hearts.
All good gifts around us
Are sent from heaven above,
Then thank the Lord, O thank the Lord,
For all His love!

ANNE BRONTË (1819-1849) was born at Thornton, West Bradford, and was joint author, with her sisters EMILY BRONTË (1818-1848) and CHARLOTTE BRONTË (1816-1849), of a small volume of verse published in 1846. Under the *nom de plume* Acton Bell she published "Agnes Grey" (1847) and "The Tenant of Wildfell Hall" (1847). In 1851 an edition of "Wuthering Heights" by Ellis Bell (Emily Brontë) and "Agnes Grey" by Acton Bell (Anne Brontë), with selections from the verse of both sisters, was published by Charlotte Brontë, whose *nom de plume* was Currer Bell. All these gifted sisters wrote verse, that of Emily being the most successful. Selections from the poetry of Emily Brontë are given in the volume devoted to the Women Poets of the Century, where they are prefaced by an article from the pen of Dr. Garnett; but, even at the cost of repetition, we cannot omit her noble "Last Lines" from this connection.

LAST LINES.

No coward soul is mine,
No trembler in the world's storm-troubled sphere:
I see Heaven's glories shine,
And faith shines equal, arming me from fear.

O God within my breast,
Almighty, ever-present Deity!
　Life—that in me has rest,
As I—undying Life—have power in Thee!

　Vain are the thousand creeds
That move men's hearts: unutterably vain;
　Worthless as withered weeds,
Or idlest froth amid the boundless main,

　To waken doubt in one
Holding so fast by Thine infinity;
　So surely anchored on
The steadfast rock of immortality.

　With wide-embracing love
Thy Spirit animates eternal years,
　Pervades and broods above,
Changes, sustains, dissolves, creates, and rears

　Though earth and man were gone,
And suns and universes ceased to be,
　And Thou were left alone,
Every existence would exist in Thee.

　There is not room for Death,
Nor atom that his might could render void:
　Thou—Thou art Being and Breath,
And what Thou art may never be destroyed.

The distinctive features of the work of the three sisters are sufficiently indicated by Dr. Garnett in the article referred to above, and it will suffice to say here that the verse of Charlotte Brontë does not lend itself to quotation in this connection, while that of Anne will be sufficiently represented by the verses which follow. The last lines of Anne Brontë cannot compare with those of her sister for strength and finish, but they have a pathetic interest of their own.

LAST LINES.

I hoped that with the brave and strong,
   My portioned task might lie;
To toil amid the busy throng,
   With purpose pure and high;

But God has fixed another part,
   And He has fixed it well;
I said so with my bleeding heart,
   When first the anguish fell.

Thou, God, hast taken our delight,
   Our treasured hope away:
Thou bidst us now weep through the night
   And sorrow through the day.

These weary hours will not be lost,
   These days of misery,
These nights of darkness, anguish-tossed,—
   Can I but turn to Thee:

With secret labour to sustain
   In humble patience every blow,
To gather fortitude from pain,
   And hope and holiness from woe.

Thus let me serve Thee from my heart,
   Whate'er may be my written fate:
Whether thus early to depart,
   Or yet a while to wait.

If Thou shouldst bring me back to life,
   More humbled I should be,
More wise,—more strengthened for the strife,—
   More apt to lean on Thee:

Should death be standing at the gate,
   Thus should I keep my vow:
But, Lord! whatever be my fate,
   O let me serve Thee now!

"These lines written," says Charlotte Brontë, the desk was closed, the pen laid aside—for ever."

Sir HENRY WILLIAMS BAKER (1821-1877) was the son of Admiral Sir Henry Lorine Baker, and succeeded to the baronetcy in 1851. He was born in London, and educated at Trinity College, Cambridge, where he graduated B.A. 1844, and M.A. 1847. From 1851 until his death in 1877 he was Vicar of Monkland, Herefordshire, during which time he rendered 'the Church great service by editing "Hymns Ancient and Modern," the most popular of modern hymn-books, to which he contributed a number of original hymns, metrical litanies, and translations. His most widely used hymn is his version of the twenty-third Psalm, the third verse of which formed his last utterance upon the bed of death:—

"THE LORD IS MY SHEPHERD."

PSALM xxiii. 1.

The King of love my Shepherd is,
   Whose goodness faileth never;
I nothing lack if I am His
   And He is mine for ever.

Where streams of living water flow
   My ransomed soul He leadeth,
And, where the verdant pastures grow,
   With food celestial feedeth.

Perverse and foolish oft I strayed,
   But yet in love He sought me,
And on His shoulder gently laid,
   And home, rejoicing, brought me.

In death's dark vale I fear no ill
   With Thee, dear Lord, beside me;
Thy rod and staff my comfort still,
   Thy Cross before to guide me.

Thou spread'st a table in my sight;
  Thy unction grace bestoweth,
And, oh, what transport of delight
  From Thy pure Chalice floweth!

And so through all the length of days
  Thy goodness faileth never;
Good Shepherd, may I sing Thy praise
  Within Thy house for ever.

FRANCES POWER COBBE, author of numerous original works, including "An Essay on Intuitive Morals," and editor of the works of Theodore Parker in twelve volumes, was the author of several poems, of which the hymn "God draws a cloud over each gleaming morn," given below, is the best known. Miss Cobbe was born at Dublin on the 4th of December, 1822. She died April 5th, 1904. The following verses were written in 1859.—

"REST IN THE LORD, AND WAIT PATIENTLY FOR HIM."

PSALM xxxvii. 7.

God draws a cloud over each gleaming morn,—
  Wouldst thou ask why?
It is because all noblest things are born
  In agony.

Only upon *some* cross of pain or woe
  God's Son may lie·
Each soul redeemed from self and sin must know
  Its Calvary.

Yet we must crave neither for joy nor grief;
  God chooses best:
He only knows our sick souls' best relief,
  And gives us rest

More than our feeble hearts can ever pine
  For holiness,
That Father in His tenderness divine,
  Yearneth to bless.

He never sends a joy not meant in love,
  Still less a pain:
Our gratitude the sunlight falls to prove,
  Our faith, the rain

In His hands we are safe. We falter on
  Through storm and mire.
Above, beside, around us, there is One
  Will never tire.

What though we *fall*,—and bruised and wounded lie,
  Our lips in dust!
God's arm shall lift us up to victory!
  In Him we trust

For neither life nor death, nor things below,
  Nor things above,
Can ever sever us, that we should go
  From His great love.

Among the most popular hymns of recent years, several of those written by the Rev. GODFREY THRING must be numbered. Mr. Thring was born at Alford, Somerset, on the 25th of March, 1823, and was educated at Shrewsbury School and Balliol College, Oxford. After holding several curacies, he became Rector of Alford in 1867, and Prebendary of East Harptree in Wells Cathedral 1876. He published "Hymns Congregational and Others" (1866), "Hymns and Verses" (1866), "Hymns and Sacred Lyrics" (1874), and "A Church of England Hymn-Book" (1880). Many of his hymns are in common use, some of them being great favourites for congregational purposes; they show an eye for the picturesque, a dramatic instinct, a sympathetic spirit, and a joyous disposition. The hymn commencing "Saviour, blessed Saviour," which in its complete form, as given in "Hymns and Sacred

Lyrics," comprises ten stanzas of eight lines each, is too long for selection. The same may be said of the fine hymn beginning "I heard a sound of voices." The following hymns are of general acceptance among the Churches:—

AFTERNOON HYMN.

The radiant morn hath passed away,
   And spent too soon her golden store;
The shadows of departing day
      Creep on once more.

Our life is but an autumn day,
   Its glorious noon how quickly past;—
Lead us, O Christ, Thou Living Way,
      Safe Home at last.

Oh! by Thy soul-inspiring grace
   Uplift our hearts to realms on High;
Help us to look to that Bright Place
      Beyond the sky,—

Where Light, and Life, and Joy, and Peace
   In undivided empire reign,
And thronging angels never cease
      Their deathless strain,—

Where saints are clothed in spotless white,
   And evening shadows never fall,
Where Thou, Eternal Light of Light,
      Art Lord of all.

II.
THE GREAT CALM

Fierce raged the tempest o'er the deep,
Watch did Thine anxious servants keep,
But Thou wast wrapt in guileless sleep,
      Calm and still.

"Save, Lord, we perish," was their cry:
"O save us in our agony!"
Thy word above the storm rose high,—
 "Peace, be still!"

The wild winds hushed; the angry deep
Sank, like a little child, to sleep,
The sullen billows ceased to leap,
 At Thy will.

So, when our life is clouded o'er,
And storm-winds drift us from the shore,
Say, lest we sink to rise no more,
 "Peace, be still!"

III.

(Martin Luther.)

A Fortress sure is God our King,
 A Shield that ne'er shall fail us,
His sword alone shall succour bring,
 When evil doth assail us;
  With craft and cruel hate
  Doth Satan lie in wait,
  And, armed with deadly power,
  Seeks whom he may devour,
 On earth where is his equal?

O who shall then our champion be,
 Lest we be lost for ever?
One sent by God,—from sin 'tis He
 The sinner shall deliver;
  And dost thou ask His Name?
  'Tis Jesus Christ,—the Same
 . Of Sabaoth the Lord,
  The Everlasting Word,—
 'Tis He must win the battle.

God's word remaineth ever sure,
  (To us no merit owing,)
The Spirit's gifts—of sin the cure—
  Each day He is bestowing;
    Though naught we love be left,
    Of all, e'en life, bereft;
    Yet what shall Satan gain?
    God's kingdom doth remain,
  And shall be ours for ever.

One of the most popular as well as one of the most beautiful of modern hymns is that of the Rev. HENRY TWELLS which follows. Mr. Twells was born in 1823, and educated at St. Peter's College, Cambridge. He was curate of Great Berkhampstead, 1849-51; Sub-Vicar of Stratford-on-Avon, 1851-54; Rector of Baldock, Herts, 1870, and of Waltham-on-the-Wolds, 1871; Select Preacher at Cambridge, 1873-74; and Canon of Peterborough, 1884. From 1854 to 1870 he was engaged in education. He has written several hymns, but his evening hymn is the one by which he is best known. In some collections the first line is altered and the fourth verse omitted. The word "when" is sometimes substituted for "ere" and the word "did" for "was" in the former. The following is the original form, though it was first published in "Hymns Ancient and Modern," Appendix, 1868, without the fourth verse.

At even, ere the sun was set,
The sick, O Lord, around Thee lay;
O in what divers pains they met!
O with what joy they went away!

Once more 'tis eventide, and we,
Oppressed with various ills, draw near
What if Thy form we cannot see?
We know and feel that Thou art here.

O Saviour Christ, our woes dispel,
For some are sick, and some are sad;
And some have never loved Thee well,
And some have lost the love they had;

And some are pressed with worldly care;
And some are tried with sinful doubt;
And some such grievous passions tear
That only Thou canst cast them out;

And some have found the world is vain,
Yet from the world they break not free;
And some have friends who give them pain,
Yet have not sought a friend in Thee.

And none, O Lord, have perfect rest,
For none are wholly free from sin;
And they, who fain would serve Thee best,
Are conscious most of wrong within.

O Saviour Christ, Thou too art Man;
Thou hast been troubled, tempted, tried;
Thy kind but searching glance can scan
The very wounds that shame would hide;

Thy touch has still its ancient power;
No word from Thee can fruitless fall:
Hear in this solemn evening hour,
And in Thy mercy heal us all.

ADELAIDE ANNE PROCTER (1825-1864) was born in Bedford Square, London, on the 30th of October, 1825. Her father, Bryan Waller Procter, better known to many by his *nom de plume* Barry Cornwall, himself a writer of classic verse, was for many years the centre of a choice literary circle, which included many of the leading writers of his time; his daughter's literary aspirations therefore may be said to have been set from the first in congenial surroundings. Her love for poetry early manifested itself first in fondness for that of others, and afterwards in the composition of original verse, though it was not until the year 1853 that she offered some of her poems for publication. These were sent under the assumed name Mary Berwick to Charles Dickens, who inserted them in *Household Words*. Dickens was a friend of Barry Cornwall's, and had known Adelaide Procter all her life; and it is a proof of the modest sincerity of her character that she did not take advantage of her personal knowledge of Charles Dickens, but sent her verses incognito to be judged on their merits by the Editor of *Household Words*. Adelaide Procter's general verse is represented in the volume of THE POETS AND THE POETRY OF THE CENTURY which is devoted to the Women Poets, and there examples of her lyrical and narrative poetry are given with a critical introduction from the pen of Mr. H. J. Gibbs. Here it is her devotional verse which calls for representation, and of this one example will suffice. Though all of Adelaide Procter's poems are characterised by an earnestness of purpose which gives them a religious tone, her actual output of definitely religious verse is very small. The poem "Thankfulness," quoted below, has, however, given voice to the religious feelings of so many that it certainly deserves a place in any collection of the religious poetry of the time. Much of Adelaide Procter's poetry was "made perfect through suffering," and in these lines she shows herself to have attained to a rare standard of Christian faith and culture. She died on the 2nd of February, 1864.

> My God, I thank Thee, Who hast made
>   The earth so bright,
> So full of splendour and of joy,
>   Beauty and light,
> So many glorious things are here,
>   Noble and right.

I thank Thee, too, that Thou hast made
    Joy to abound;
So many gentle thoughts and deeds
    Circling us round;
That in the darkest spot of earth
    Some love is found.

I thank Thee *more* that all our joy
    Is touched with pain;
That shadows fall on brightest hours,
    That thorns remain;
So that earth's bliss may be our guide,
    And not our chain.

For Thou Who knowest, Lord, how soon
    Our weak heart clings,
Hast given us joys, tender and true,
    Yet all with wings,
So that we see, gleaming on high,
    Diviner things.

I thank Thee, Lord, that Thou hast kept
    The best in store;
I have enough, yet not too much,
    To long for more;
A yearning for a deeper peace
    Not known before

I thank Thee, Lord, that here our souls,
    Though amply blest,
Can never find, although they seek,
    A perfect rest,—
Nor ever shall, until they lean
    On Jesus' breast!

Modern hymnody is rich in hymns for special purposes and occasions, among which the hymn of WILLIAM WHITING (1825-1878) "For Those at Sea" is a great favourite. Mr. Whiting was for some years master of Winchester College Choristers' School. He published "Rural Thoughts and other Poems" (1851), and contributed about a dozen hymns to various hymnals, the most popular of which is the one given here:—

> Eternal Father, strong to save,
> Whose arm hath bound the restless wave,
> Who bidd'st the mighty ocean deep
> Its own appointed limits keep;
> O hear us when we cry to Thee
> For those in peril on the sea.
>
> O Christ, whose voice the waters heard
> And hushed their raging at Thy word,
> Who walkedst on the foaming deep,
> And calm amid the storm didst sleep;
> O hear us when we cry to Thee
> For those in peril on the sea.
>
> Most Holy Spirit, who didst brood
> Upon the chaos dark and rude,
> And bid its angry tumult cease,
> And give, for wild confusion, peace;
> O hear us when we cry to Thee
> For those in peril on the sea.
>
> O Trinity of love and power,
> Our brethren shield in danger's hour;
> From rock and tempest, fire and foe,
> Protect them wheresoe'er they go;
> Thus evermore may rise to Thee
> Glad hymns of praise from land and sea.

LAURENCE TUTTIETT, son of John Tuttiett, surgeon R.N., was born at Cloyton in Devonshire in 1825, and was educated at Christ's Hospital and King's College, London. In 1854 he became perpetual Curate of Lea Marston, Warwickshire; in 1870 Incumbent of the Episcopal Church of St. Andrews, Scotland; and in 1880 Prebendary of St. Ninian's Cathedral, Perth. He published "Hymns for Churchmen" (1854), "Counsels of a

Godfather" (1861), "Hymns for the Children of the Church" (1862), "Germs of Thought on the Sunday Services" (1864), and "Through the Clouds, Thoughts in Plain Verse" (1866), all of which contain original verse. The most popular of his hymns are "Father, let me dedicate all this year to Thee," "Go forward, Christian soldiers," "O Jesu, ever present," and "O quickly come, dread Judge of all."

> O quickly come, dread Judge of all,
> For, awful though Thine advent be,
> All shadows from the truth will fall,
> And falsehood die, in sight of Thee:
> O quickly come; for doubt and fear
> Like clouds dissolve when Thou art near.
>
> O quickly come, great King of all;
> Reign all around us, and within;
> Let sin no more our souls enthral,
> Let pain and sorrow die with sin:
> O quickly come; for Thou alone
> Canst make Thy scattered people one.
>
> O quickly come, true Life of all;
> For death is mighty all around;
> On every home his shadows fall,
> On every heart his mark is found:
> O quickly come; for grief and pain
> Can never cloud Thy glorious reign.
>
> O quickly come, true Light of all;
> For gloomy night broods o'er our way;
> And weakly souls begin to fall
> With weary watching for the day:
> O quickly come; for round Thy throne
> No eye is blind, no night is known.

ELIZABETH CHARLES, daughter of John Rundle, M.P., was born at Tavistock, Devonshire, in 1827. She was the author of several widely popular works for the young, including "The Chronicles of the Schönberg-Cotta Family" and "The Diary of Kitty Trevlyan." She wrote and translated a number of hymns, and published, in addition to the works mentioned above, "The Voice of Christian Life in Song; or, Hymns and Hymn-Writers of Many Lands and Ages" (1858), "The Three Wakings and other Poems" (1859), "Poems" (New York, 1867), "The Women of the Gospels," etc. (1868), and "Songs Old and New" (1894). Among her most widely accepted hymns are "Age after age shall call thee blessed" and "Never further than Thy cross." She died at Hampstead on the 28th of March, 1896.

L.

Never further than Thy Cross
Never higher than Thy feet!
Here earth's precious things grow dross;
Here earth's bitter things grow sweet.

Gazing thus, our sin we see;
Learn Thy love while gazing thus!
Sin which laid the Cross on Thee,
Love which bore the Cross for us.

Here we learn to serve and give,
And, rejoicing, self deny;
Here we gather love to live,
Here we gather faith to die.

Symbols of our liberty
And our service here unite;
Captives, by Thy Cross set free,
Soldiers of Thy Cross, we fight.

Pressing onward as we can,
Still to this our hearts shall tend;
Where our earliest hopes began,
There our last aspirings end;

Till amid the hosts of light,
We, in Thee redeemed, complete,
Through Thy Cross made pure and white,
Cast our crowns before Thy feet.

II.

The strongest light casts deepest shades,
  The dearest love makes dreariest loss;
And she His birth so blest had made
  Stood by Him dying on the cross.

Yet since not grief but joy shall last,
  The day and not the night abide,
And all time's shadows earthward cast
  Are lights upon the "other side;"

Through what long bliss that shall not fail
  That darkest hour shall brighten on!
Better than any angel's "*Hail!*"
  The memory of "*Behold thy Son!*"

Blest in thy lowly heart to store
  The homage paid at Bethlehem;
But far more blessed evermore
  Thus to have shared the taunts and shame—

Thus with thy pierc'd heart to have stood
  'Mid mocking crowds, and owned Him thine,
True through a world's ingratitude,
  And owned in death by lips Divine.

III.

Around a Table, not a Tomb,
He willed our gathering-place to be ;
When going to prepare our home,
Our Saviour said—"Remember Me."

We kneel around no sculptured stone,
Marking the place where Jesus lay ;—
Empty the tomb, the angels gone,
The stone for ever rolled away.

Nay! sculptured stones are for the dead !
Thy three dark days of death are o'er ;
Thou art the Life, our living Head,
Our living Light for evermore !

Of no fond relics, sadly dear,
O Master! are Thine own possest ;
The crown of thorns, the cross, the spear,
The purple robe, the seamless vest.

Nay, relics are for those who mourn
The memory of an absent friend ;
Not absent Thou, nor we forlorn !
"With you each day until the end !"

Thus round Thy Table, not Thy Tomb,
We keep Thy sacred Feast with Thee ;
Until within the Father's Home
Our endless gathering-place shall be.

"Sacred Hymns from the German" (London, 1841; second edition, revised, and with additions, 1864), by FRANCES ELIZABETH COX, was another attempt to introduce hymns from German sources for English use. Originally these were printed with the German text and biographical notes of the authors. Two at least of these fifty-six translations have become widely popular—the translation from Schenck which commences "Who are these like stars appearing," and the following Easter hymn from the German of C. F. Gellert. The latter has been variously modified in successive editions and different collections. The text here given is from the edition of "Hymns from the German," published in 1890.

> Jesus lives! no longer now
>   Can thy terrors, Death, appal me:
> Jesus lives! by this we know
>   From the grave He will recall me.
> Brighter scenes at death commence;
> This shall be my confidence.
>
> Jesus lives! to Him the Throne
>   High o'er all the world is given:
> I may go where He is gone,
>   Live and reign with Him in Heaven.
> God, through Christ, forgives offence;
> This shall be my confidence.
>
> Jesus lives! who now despairs
>   Spurns the word which God hath spoken;
> Grace to all that word declares,
>   Grace whereby sin's yoke is broken:
> Christ rejects not penitence;
> This shall be my confidence.
>
> Jesus lives! for me He died;
>   Then will I, to Jesus living,
> Pure in heart and act abide,
>   Praise to Him and glory giving:
> Freely God doth aid dispense;
> This shall be my confidence.
>
> Jesus lives! my heart knows well
>   Naught shall me from Jesu sever
> Life, nor death, nor powers of hell,
>   Part me now from Him for ever;
> God will be my sure defence;
> This shall be my confidence.

Jesus lives! henceforth is death
  But the gate of life immortal;
This shall calm my trembling breath,
  When I pass its gloomy portal.
Faith shall cry, as fails each sense,
Lord, Thou art my Confidence.

The following popular hymn first appeared in "Hymns for Missions" (1854), and was written by the editor of that book, the Rev. HENRY COLLINS, M.A. Mr. Collins was educated at Oxford, and entered the ministry of the Church of England; but in 1857 he seceded to the Church of Rome, joining the Cistercian order in 1860. Another popular hymn from this source is that commencing "Jesu, meek and lowly, Saviour, pure and holy."

Jesu, my Lord, my God, my all!
Hear me, blest Saviour, when I call;
Hear me, and from Thy dwelling-place
Pour down the riches of Thy grace:
  Jesu, my Lord, I Thee adore,
  O make me love Thee more and more.

Jesu! alas! too coldly sought,
How can I love Thee as I ought?
And how extol Thy matchless fame,
The glorious beauty of Thy Name?
  Jesu, my Lord, I Thee adore,
  O make me love Thee more and more.

Jesu! what didst Thou find in me,
That Thou hast dealt so lovingly?
How great the joy that Thou hast brought!
So far exceeding hope or thought!
  Jesu, my Lord, I Thee adore,
  O make me love Thee more and more.

Jesu! of Thee shall be my song;
To Thee my heart and soul belong;
All that I am or have is Thine,
And Thou, my Saviour! Thou art mine.
  Jesu, my Lord, I Thee adore,
  O make me love Thee more and more.

The Moultries, father, son, and daughter, were all writers of verse which became more or less popular. The Rev. JOHN MOULTRIE (1799-1874) was for nearly fifty years Rector of Rugby, where his son, Gerard Moultrie, and his daughter, Mary Dunlop Moultrie, were born. While at Eton, where he was contemporary with Praed and the other brilliant boys who started the *Etonian*, he wrote a poem, " My Brother's Grave," in commemoration of a brother who had died at Eton, and was buried in the chapel —a noteworthy poem for one so young, and one which gave the title to a volume of poems published by him in 1837, " My Brother's Grave and other Poems." This volume contained two other poems, which have been many times reprinted, " The Three Sons," and a song " Here's to thee, my Scottish Lassie." He also published " Dream of Life, Lays of the English Church " (1843) ; " Memoir and Poetical Remains of W. S. Walker" (1852), etc., etc. He also wrote a number of hymns which were included in " Psalms and Hymns as Sung at the Parish Church, Rugby " (1851).

His son GERARD MOULTRIE (1829-1885) was educated at Rugby and Exeter College, Oxford. After taking Holy Orders, he became third master and chaplain in Shrewsbury School ; Curate of Brightwaltham, 1859; of Brinfield, Berks, 1860; Chaplain of the Donative of Barrow Gurney, Bristol, 1864; Vicar of Southleigh, 1869; and Warden of St. James's College, Southleigh, 1873. He published " The Primer set forth at large for the Use of the Faithful in Family and Private Prayer," edited from the post-Reformation editions (1864); " Hymns and Lyrics for the Seasons and Saints' Days of the Church" (1867); "The Espousals of St. Dorothea and other Verses" (1870); "Cantica Sanctorum; or, Hymns for the Black-Letter Saints' Days in the English and Scottish Calendars, to which are added a few Hymns for Special Occasions" (1880). Gerard Moultrie's hymns include translations from the Greek, Latin, and German. The following is a favourable example:—

MIDNIGHT HYMN OF THE EASTERN CHURCH

(FROM THE GREEK.)

Behold, the Bridegroom cometh in the middle of the night,
And blest is he whose loins are girt, whose lamp is burning bright;
But woe to that dull servant, whom his Master shall surprise
With lamp untrimmed, unburning, and with slumber in his eyes.

Do thou, my soul, beware, beware, lest thou in sleep sink down,
Lest thou be given o'er to death, and lose the golden crown;
But see that thou be sober, with a watchful eye, and thus
Cry—Holy, Holy, Holy God, have mercy upon us.

That Day, the Day of Fear, shall come; my soul, slack not thy toil,
But light thy lamp, and feed it well, and make it bright with oil;
Thou knowest not how soon may sound the cry at eventide,
"Behold, the Bridegroom comes. Arise! Go forth to meet the Bride."

Beware, my soul, beware, beware, lest thou in slumber lie,
And, like the five, remain without, and knock, and vainly cry;
But watch, and bear thy lamp undimmed, and Christ shall gird thee on
His own bright Wedding Robe of Light—the Glory of the Son.

MARY DUNLOP MOULTRIE (1837-1866) contributed a number of hymns to her brother's "Hymns and Lyrics" (1867), where they are distinguished by her initials.

By the publication of "Lyra Germanica" (first series, 1855; second series, 1858) and "The Chorale Book for England" (1863) CATHERINE WINKWORTH (1829-1878) enriched English hymnody from German sources, as Neale, Caswell, Chandler, Gerard Moultrie, and others enriched it from the hymns of the Eastern Church. Born at Alderley Edge, Cheshire, on the 13th of September, 1829, she lived successively in the neighbourhoods of Manchester and Bristol, and died at Monnetier, Savoy, in July 1878. In addition to her translations of German hymns, she translated, also from the German, "The Life of Pastor Fliedner" (1861) and "The Life of Amelia Sieveking" (1863), and published a biographical work, "The Christian Singers of Germany" (1869). Dr. Martineau says her translations "are invariably faithful, and for the most part both terse and delicate, and an admirable art is applied to the management of complex and difficult versification. They have not quite the fire of John Wesley's versions of Moravian hymns, or the wonderful fusion and reproduction of thought which may be found in

Coleridge. But if less flowing, they are more conscientious than either, and attain a result as poetical as severe exactitude admits, being only a little short of 'Native Music.'" One of the best known of her translations is the hymn commencing "Now thank we all our God." Others, which are very fine, are too long for quotation; the following must suffice, but all are worthy of attention:—

I.

THE ROSE OF SHARON.

I know a Flower so sweet and fair,
   There is no earthly blossom
With Sharon's Rose that may compare;
   Fain would I wear
   Its Fragrance in my bosom.

It is the True and Living Word,
   Whom God Himself hath given
To be our Guide, our Light, our Lord,
   In Whom is stored
   All hope for earth and Heaven.

Hark! how He saith—Come unto Me,
   Ye burdened and sad-hearted,
Granted your heart's desire shall be,
   And pardon free
   To mourning Souls imparted.

This is My Body that I give,
   For you in Mercy broken;
Whate'er is Mine with it receive,
   If ye believe
   And keep what I have spoken.

This is My Blood once shed for you,
   Ye hearts, now faint and sinking;
Drink of My Cup and find anew
   Fresh Strength to do
   My Bidding without shrinking.

Ah, Lord, by Thy most bitter Woes
  We pray Thee ne'er forsake us,
Since Thou couldst even die for those
    Who were Thy foes,
  Thy Children deign to make us.

And keep us ever close to Thee,
  Give courage to confess Thee
However dark the time may be,
    Till safe and free
  In Heaven at last we bless Thee.

II.

(ANGELUS, 1657.)

O Love, who formedst me to wear
  The image of Thy Godhead here;
Who soughtest me with tender care
  Through all my wanderings wild and drear;
O Love, I give myself to Thee,
Thine ever, only Thine to be.

O Love, who ere life's earliest dawn
  Thy choice on me hast gently laid;
O Love, who here as man wast born,
  And wholly like to us wast made;
O Love, I give myself to Thee,
Thine ever, only Thine to be.

O Love, who once in Time wast slain,
  Pierced through and through with bitter woe;
O Love, who wrestling thus didst gain
  That we eternal joy might know,
O Love, I give myself to Thee,
Thine ever, only Thine to be.

O Love, of whom is truth and light,
  The Word and Spirit, life and power,
Whose heart was bared to them that smite,
  To shield us in our trial hour;
O Love, I give myself to Thee,
Thine ever, only Thine to be.

O Love, who thus hast bound me fast,
  Beneath that gentle yoke of Thine;
Love, who hast conquered me at last,
  And rapt away this heart of mine;
O Love, I give myself to Thee,
Thine ever, only Thine to be.

O Love, who lovest me for aye,
  Who for my soul dost ever plead;
O Love, who didst my ransom pay,
  Whose power sufficeth in my stead,
O Love, I give myself to Thee,
Thine ever, only Thine to be.

O Love, who once shalt bid me rise
  From out this dying life of ours,
O Love, who once o'er yonder skies
  Shalt set me in the fadeless bowers;
O Love, I give myself to Thee,
Thine ever, only Thine to be.

III.

ON THE DEATH OF A LITTLE CHILD.
(W. Meinhold.)

Gentle Shepherd, Thou hast stilled
Now Thy little lamb's long weeping,
  Ah, how peaceful, pale, and mild,
In its narrow bed 'tis sleeping,
  And no sigh of anguish sore
  Heaves that little bosom more.

In this world of care and pain,
Lord, Thou would'st no longer leave it;
  To the sunny heavenly plain
Dost Thou now with joy receive it;
  Clothed in robes of spotless white
  Now it dwells with Thee in light.

Ah, Lord Jesus, grant that we
Where it lives may soon be living,
  And the lovely pastures see
That its heavenly food are giving;
  Then the gain of death we prove,
  Though Thou take what most we love.

PHILIP STANHOPE WORSLEY (1831-1866), whose early death closed a career of exceptional beauty and promise, though known best by his admirable translations of the "Odyssey" (1861) and the "Iliad" (1865), published also "The Temple of Janus," a Newdigate prize poem in 1857, and a volume of "Poems and Translations" in 1863, of which a second and enlarged edition was issued posthumously in 1875. His original poems differ widely in merit, but those on classical subjects reach a very high level indeed "Phaethon," the opening poem of the "Poems and Translations" volume, is a splendid work, and but for its length would have been included in the body of this work, though it may be added that its length is in itself hardly sufficient excuse for its omission. It displays fine imagination, and a capacity for the large handling of a great theme. Philip Stanhope Worsley had a rare personality and an impressive presence, and a beauty of character which shone out with the light of transfiguration in a face worn by acute and long-continued physical suffering. He was referred to in an obituary notice in the *Athenæum* as "the most perfect model of a Christian gentleman." Both of the following appear in Orby Shipley's "Lyra Eucharistica," and the latter is from "Poems and Translations." —

I.

OUT OF THE DEEPS.

Out of the deeps how often hath my cry
  Gone up to God on the wild wings of prayer!
  Even so often hath He deigned to hear,
So often hath He said—Thou shalt not die;
So often—Stand upon thy feet once more;
So often—Serve Me better than before

But I, the river of my pain being past,
 Slighted His Succour Who had borne me through,
 Daily deferring the sweet service due,
Till seem'd that Mercy's self might scarce refrain
 Her patient hands from vengeance at the last.
But Thee, still seeking Thy reluctant Sheep
'Mid thorny-tangled brakes that pierce Thee deep,
 Iron ingratitude repels in vain.

II.

THE TWO WILLS.

Oft as I act, or think, or speak,
 Comes battle of two Wills within,
This like an infant poor and weak,
 That like a Demon strong for sin.

This labours, flutteringly alive,
 As if a cold spark went and came
That other doth against it drive
 Red torrents of devouring flame.

Yet, mark th' exceeding Power of God,
 How like a rock His Promise stands—
That Demon to the dust is trod,
 Slain by the feeble Infant bands.

That fluttering life so faint and cold,
 That one pale spark of pure desire
Sun-like arises, and behold!
 God's Rainbow in the falls of fire.

O Mystery far beyond my thought!
 I trembled on the brink of Hell:
Into what Paradise am I caught!
 What Heavenly anthems round me swell!

RICHARD FREDERICK LITTLEDALE (1833-1890) was born at Dublin, and was educated at Bective House Seminary and Trinity College, Dublin, where he had a distinguished career. He was first class and gold medallist in Classics 1854, and won the Berkeley gold medal for Greek in 1856. He graduated B.A. 1855, M.A. 1858, LL.D. 1862, and was made D C.L. of Oxford in 1862 After holding curacies at St. Matthew's, Thorpe Hamlet, Norwich, and St. Mary the Virgin, Soho, London, he gave up parochial work in 1861 on account of his health, and devoted himself to literature. He has published works theological, historical, liturgical, and hymnological, too numerous to mention, including "The Priest's Prayer Book" (1864) and "The People's Hymnal" (1867). His translations comprise hymns from the Greek, Latin, Danish, Swedish, Syriac, German, and Italian, many of which are included in the "People's Hymnal." One of the best known of his poems is the one commencing "From hidden source arising," given below; another, the hymn for use during a vacancy of a see or parish, beginning,—

> Eternal Shepherd, God Most High,
> In mercy hearken as we cry,
> And send us, in our time of need,
> A pastor wise, Thy flock to lead.

Many of his hymns, like this one, which has been frequently reprinted, were written for special occasions, for which, as Julian says, there were at the time of their writing but few hymns provided. Dr. Littledale has used a great variety of measures with equal success. Many of his hymns are didactic in their aim, and therefore less poetical than others. Some are limited in their use by the doctrines they teach, but many are worthy of much wider use than they have yet attained.

I.

From hidden source arising,
  A mighty river ran,
Through Eden's pleasant garden,
  Where God created man.

Thence, parted into branches,
  In four great streams it rolled,
To water fields and vineyards,
  To wash down sands of gold.

And so, from highest heaven,
  The Lord, the Holy Dove,
In fourfold manner sends us
  The tale of Jesu's love.

The tale whose words are golden,
  The tale whose flood divine
Makes glad the Lord's own garden
  With plenteous corn and wine.

Four are the sacred voices,
  The story is but one;
In fourfold wise they praise Him,
  The Sole-Begotten Son.

A Man is Matthew's emblem,
  And Mark's the Lion's might,
The Ox is Luke's fit token,
  And John's the Eagle's flight.

True Man St. Matthew speaks Him,
  Mark gives the Victor laud,
Luke tells of His oblation,
  And John proclaims Him God.

To Him, the King and Victim,
  The God, whom Mary bore,
With Father and with Spirit
  Be praise for evermore.

II.

In Paradise reposing
  By Life's eternal well,
The tender lambs of Jesus
  In greenest pastures dwell

Their palms and tiny crownlets,
  Aglow with brightest gem,
Bedeck the baby Martyrs
  Who died in Bethlehem.

With them the rose-wreathed army
  Of children undefiled,
Who passed through mortal torments
  For love of Christ the Child.

With them in peace unending,
  With them in joyous mirth,
Are all the stainless infants
  Which since have gone from earth.

The Angels, once their guardians,
  Their fellows now in grace,
With them, in love adoring,
  See God the Father's Face.

The lullaby to hush them
  In that eternal rest,
Is sweet angelic singing,
  Their nurse God's Mother blest:

For she who rocked the cradle
  In Nazareth of old,
Now bendeth o'er the younglings
  Within that happy fold.

O Jesu, loving Shepherd,
  Who tenderly dost bear
The lambs in Thine own Bosom,
  Bring us to join them there.

SABINE BARING-GOULD, historian, antiquarian, novelist, and poet, was born at Exeter on the 28th of January, 1834. He was educated at Clare College, Cambridge, and, taking Holy Orders, became successively Curate of Horbury, near Wakefield; Incumbent of Dalton, Yorks; Rector of East Mersea, Essex; and Rector of Lew Trenchard, Devon (1881). His works are very numerous and varied, the most important being "Curious Myths of the Middle Ages" (2 series, 1866-68), "The Origin and Development of Religious Belief" (2 vols., 1869-70), and "Lives of the Saints" (15 vols, 1872-77). His hymns appeared in the *Church Times*, "Hymns Ancient and Modern," "The People's Hymnal," and other collections. Perhaps the most perfect of these is the Easter hymn "On the Resurrection morning." The most popular are "Onward, Christian soldiers" and "Now the day is over."

On the Resurrection morning
  Soul and body meet again;
No more sorrow, no more weeping,
        no more pain!

Here awhile they must be parted,
  And the flesh its Sabbath keep,
Waiting in a holy stillness,
        wrapt in sleep.

For a while the tirèd body
  Lies with feet toward the morn;
the last and brightest Easter
        day be born.

But the soul in contemplation
  Utters earnest prayer and strong,
Bursting at the Resurrection
        into song.

Soul and body reunited
 Thenceforth nothing shall divide,
Waking up in CHRIST's own likeness,
 satisfied.

Oh! the beauty, oh! the gladness
 Of that Resurrection day,
Which shall not through endless ages
 pass away!

On that happy Easter morning
 All the graves their dead restore;
Father, sister, child, and mother,
 meet once more.

To that brightest of all meetings
 Bring us, JESU CHRIST, at last;
To Thy Cross, through death and judgment,
 holding fast.

FOLLIOTT SANDFORD PIERPOINT, the author of the well-known hymn commencing "For the beauty of the earth," was born at Spa Villa, Bath, on the 7th of October, 1835. He was educated at Queens' College, Cambridge, where he graduated in 1871. He published "The Chalice of Nature and other Poems" at Bath, republishing it in 1878 as "Songs of Love, the Chalice of Nature, and Lyra Jesu," besides which he contributed hymns to the "Churchman's Companion" and to Orby Shipley's "Lyra Eucharistica. The hymn by which he is best known was contributed to the second edition of that work, from which it has been many times reprinted in various modified forms. The following is the original form:—

THE SACRIFICE OF PRAISE.

For the beauty of the earth,
  For the beauty of the skies,
For the Love which from our birth
  Over and around us lies;
Christ, our God, to Thee we raise
This, our Sacrifice of Praise.

For the beauty of each hour
  Of the day and of the night,
Hill and vale, and tree and flower,
  Sun and moon, and stars of light;
Christ, our God, to Thee we raise
This, our Sacrifice of Praise.

For the joy of ear and eye,
  For the heart and brain's delight,
For the mystic harmony
  Linking sense to sound and sight;
Christ, our God, to Thee we raise
This, our Sacrifice of Praise.

For the joy of human love,
  Brother, sister, parent, child,
Friends on earth, and friends above,
  For all gentle thoughts and mild;
Christ, our God, to Thee we raise
This, our Sacrifice of Praise.

For each perfect gift of Thine
  To our race so freely given,
Graces human and Divine,
  Flowers of earth, and buds of Heaven;
Christ, our God, to Thee we raise
This, our Sacrifice of Praise.

For Thy Bride that evermore
  Lifteth holy hands above,
Offering up on every shore
  Its Pure Sacrifice of Love;
Christ, our God, to Thee we raise
This, our Sacrifice of Praise.

For Thy Martyrs' crown of light,
　For Thy Prophets' eagle eye,
For Thy bold Confessors' might,
　For the lips of Infancy:
Christ, our God, to Thee we raise,
This, our Sacrifice of Praise.

For Thy Virgin's robes of snow,
　For Thy Maiden Mother mild,
For Thyself, with hearts aglow,
　Jesu, Victim undefiled,
Offer we, at Thine own Shrine,
Thyself, sweet Sacrament Divine.

MATILDA BARBARA BETHAM-EDWARDS, sister of Amelia B. Edwards, the Egyptologist, was born at Westerfield, near Ipswich, on the 4th of March, 1836. She published "Poems" (1885), besides several works of fiction. As a writer of hymns for children she was eminently successful. The following examples first appeared in *Good Words* for 1873:—

I.

God make my life a little light
　Within the world to glow;
A little flame that burneth bright,
　Wherover I may go.

God make my life a little flower,
　That giveth joy to all,
Content to bloom in native bower
　Although its place be small.

God make my life a little song
　That comforteth the sad;
That helpeth others to be strong,
　And makes the singer glad.

God make my life a little staff,
　Whereon the weak may rest,
That so what health and strength I have
　May serve my neighbours best.

God make my life a little hymn
　　Of tenderness and praise;
Of faith—that never waxeth dim,
　　In all His wondrous ways.

II.

The little birds now seek their nest;
The baby sleeps on mother's breast;
Thou givest all Thy children rest,
　　God of the weary.

The sailor prayeth on the sea;
The little ones at mother's knee;
Now comes the penitent to Thee,
　　God of the weary.

The orphan puts away his fears;
The troubled hopes for happier years;
Thou driest all the mourner's tears,
　　God of the weary.

Thou sendest rest to tirèd feet,
To little toilers slumber sweet,
To aching hearts repose complete,
　　God of the weary.

In grief, perplexity, or pain,
None ever come to Thee in vain;
Thou makest life a joy again,
　　God of the weary.

We sleep that we may wake renewed,
To serve Thee as Thy children should
With love, and zeal, and gratitude,
　　God of the weary.

A characteristic feature of the modern hymnal is the "Metrical Litany," examples of which have been contributed by Sir H. W. Baker, Rev. W. J. Irons,

Dr. Littledale, Dr. Monsell, and the Rev. Thomas Benson Pollock. Among the most successful of these are those by Mr. POLLOCK, published in his "Metrical Litanies for Special Services and General Use" (1870), his "Litany Appendix" (1871), etc., etc. Mr. Pollock was born in 1836, and graduated at Trinity College, Dublin, in 1859, where he gained the Vice-Chancellor's prize for English verse in 1855. Taking Holy Orders in 1861, he was successively Curate of St. Luke's, Leek, Staffordshire; St. Thomas's, Stamford Hill, London; and St. Alban's, Birmingham. Litanies are naturally too lengthy to quote entire. The following is the first part of Mr. Pollock's "Children's Litany":—

>Jesu, from Thy throne on high,
>Far above the bright blue sky,
>Look on us with loving eye,
>   Hear us, Holy Jesu.
>
>Little children need not fear
>When they know that Thou art near,
>Thou dost love us, Saviour dear,
>   Hear us, Holy Jesu.
>
>Little lambs may come to Thee;
>Thou wilt fold us tenderly,
>And our careful Shepherd be,
>   Hear us, Holy Jesu.
>
>Little lives may be divine,
>Little deeds of love may shine,
>Little ones be wholly Thine,
>   Hear us, Holy Jesu.
>
>Little hearts may love Thee well,
>Little lips Thy love may tell;
>Little hymns Thy praises swell,
>   Hear us, Holy Jesu.

Jesu, once an infant small,
Cradled in the oxen's stall,
Though the God and Lord of all,
    Hear us, Holy Jesu.

Once a child so good and fair,
Feeling want and toil and care,
All that we may have to bear,
    Hear us, Holy Jesu.

Jesu, Thou dost love us still,
And it is Thy holy will
That we should be safe from ill:
    Hear us, Holy Jesu.

Fold us to Thy loving breast,
There may we, in happy rest,
Feel that we indeed are blest:
    Hear us, Holy Jesu.

Among the most popular of modern hymns must be numbered the fine Epiphany hymn of WILLIAM CHATTERTON DIX which follows:—

I.

EPIPHANY HYMN.

As with gladness men of old
Did the guiding star behold,
As with joy they hail'd its light,
Leading onward, beaming bright;
So, most gracious LORD, may we
Evermore be led to Thee.

As with joyful steps they sped,
Saviour, to Thy lowly bed,
There to bend the knee before
Thee Whom Heav'n and earth adore;
So may we with willing feet
Ever seek Thy mercy-seat.

As they offer'd gifts most rare
At Thy cradle rude and bare;
So may we with holy joy,
Pure and free from sin's alloy,
All our costliest treasures bring,
CHRIST, to Thee our heavenly King.

Holy JESUS, every day
Keep us in the narrow way;
And, when earthly things are past,
Bring our ransom'd souls at last
Where they need no star to guide,
Where no clouds Thy glory hide.

In the Heav'nly country bright
Need they no created light;
Thou its Light, its Joy, its Crown,
Thou its Sun which goes not down;
There for ever may we sing
Alleluias to our King.

Mr. DIX was a son of Mr. John Dix, author of a "Life of Chatterton," "Local Legends," etc., and was born at Bristol on the 14th of June, 1837, and educated at the Bristol Grammar School. He published "Hymns of Love and Joy" (1861), "Altar Songs, Verses on the Holy Eucharist" (1867), "A Vision of All Saints and other Poems" (1871), and "Seekers of a City" (1878), and contributed hymns to "Hymns Ancient and Modern" and other collections of hymns for Church use and anthologies of sacred song. He has also cast in metrical form some of Dr. Littledale's translations of the Greek in his "Offices . . . of the Holy Eastern Church" (1863) and the Rev. J. M. Rodwell's translations of hymns of the Abyssinian Church, besides which he has written carols for Christmas and

Easter which have become widely popular. His other works are "Light" (1883), "The Risen Life" (1883), both devotional works, and "The Pattern Life" (1885), a book of instruction for children, which contains a number of original hymns. The following is from "A Vision of All Saints and other Poems":—

II.

PATIENCE.

"If Thou hadst come, our brother had not died."
  Thus one who loved, to One who came so late;
  Yet not too late, had she but known the fate
Which soon should fill the mourners' hearts with tide
Of holy joy. Now she would almost chide
  Her awful Guest, as though His brief delay
  Had quenched her love and driven faith away.
"If Thou hadst come," oh could we only hide
  Our heart's impatience and with meekness stay
To hear the Voice of Wisdom ere we speak.
  We mourn the past, the tomb, the buried dead,
  And think of many a bitter thing to say,
While all the time True Love stands by so meek,
  Waiting to lift anew the drooping head.

GEORGE MATHESON was born at Glasgow on the 27th of March, 1842, and, notwithstanding the loss of his eyesight in early life, pursued a brilliant university career at Edinburgh, graduating in 1862, and becoming successively parish minister at Innellan and St. Bernard's, Edinburgh. Besides several prose works, he published "Sacred Songs" (1890). The first of the following is his most widely accepted hymn. It was written at a time of great mental prostration :—

I.

O Love that wilt not let me go,
   I rest my weary soul on Thee;
I give Thee back the life I owe,
That in Thine ocean depths its flow
     May richer, fuller be.

O Light that followest all my way,
   I yield my flickering torch to Thee,
My heart restores its borrowed ray,
That in Thy sunshine's blaze its day
     May brighter, fairer be

O Joy that seekest me through pain,
   I cannot close my heart to Thee;
I trace the rainbow through the rain,
And feel the promise is not vain
     That morn shall tearless be.

O Cross that liftest up my head,
   I dare not ask to fly from Thee;
I lay in dust life's glory dead,
And from the ground there blossoms red
     Life that shall endless be.

II.

Gather us in, Thou Love that fillest all,
Gather our rival faiths within Thy fold,
Rend each man's temple's veil and bid it fall,
That we may know that Thou hast been of old,
     Gather us in.

Gather us in: we worship only Thee;
In varied names we stretch a common hand;
In diverse forms a common soul we see;
In many ships we seek one spirit-land;
     Gather us in.

Each sees one colour of Thy rainbow-light,
Each looks upon one tint and calls it heaven;
Thou art the fulness of our partial sight;
We are not perfect till we find the seven;
    Gather us in.

Thine is the mystic life great India craves,
Thine is the Parsee's sin-destroying beam,
Thine is the Buddhist's rest from tossing waves,
Thine is the empire of vast China's dream;
    Gather us in.

Thine is the Roman's strength without his pride,
Thine is the Greek's glad world without its graves,
Thine is Judæa's law with love beside,
The truth that censures and the grace that saves;
    Gather us in.

Some seek a Father in the heavens above,
Some ask a human image to adore,
Some crave a spirit vast as life and love:
Within Thy mansions we have all and more;
    Gather us in.

ADA CROSS, better known to many by her maiden name ADA CAMBRIDGE, was born at St. Germans, Norfolk, on the 21st of November, 1844. She married the Rev. G. F. Cross, who, after holding several curacies in England and Australia, became Incumbent of Coleraine, Ballarat, in 1877. Mrs. Cross published "Hymns on the Litany" (1865), "Hymns on the Holy Communion" (1866), "The Manor House and other Poems" (1875), besides which she contributed to "Lays of the Pious Minstrels" (1862) and "English Lyrics," and has written several works of fiction. Mrs. Cross's poems have all the grace and charm of her hymns, and display upon a larger scale her command of calm, smooth versification, and quiet, restful thought. "The Farewell" and "The Baptistry" are among the best of them. Several of her hymns are in constant use, the following, in a modified form, being perhaps the most widely accepted:—

THE FOURTH COMMANDMENT.

The dawn of God's dear Sabbath
  Breaks o'er the earth again
As some sweet summer morning
  After a night of pain.
It comes as cooling showers
  To some exhausted land,
As shade of clustered palm-trees
  'Mid weary wastes of sand;

As bursts of glorious sunshine
  Across a stormy sea,
Revealing to the sailors
  That Port where they would be,—
The calm and peaceful Haven,
  The dazzling, golden shore,
The home of saints and angels,
  Where sin is known no more.

O day when earthly sorrow
  Is merged in heavenly joy,
And trial changed to blessing
  That foes may not destroy,—
When want is turned to fulness,
  And weariness to rest;
And pain to wondrous rapture,
  Upon the Saviour's breast!

O we would bring or offering,
  Though marred with earthly soil,
A week of earnest labour,
  Of steady, faithful toil;

Fair fruits of self-denial,
  Of strong, deep love to Thee,
Fostered by Thine own Spirit
  In our humility.

And we would bring our burden
  Of sinful thought and deed,
At His dear Altar kneeling,
  From bondage to be freed;
Our heart's most bitter sorrow
  For all Thy work undone—
So many talents wasted!
  So few bright laurels won!

And with that sorrow mingling,
  A steadfast faith, and sure,
And love so deep and fervent,
  That tries to make it pure,—
In His dear Presence finding
  The pardon that we need;
And then the peace so lasting—
  Celestial peace indeed!

So be it, Lord, for ever:
  O may we evermore,
In Jesu's holy Presence,
  His blessèd Name adore!
Upon His peaceful Sabbath,
  Within His temple-walls,—
Type of the stainless worship
  In Zion's golden halls;

So that, in joy and gladness,
  We reach that Home at last
When life's short week of sorrow
  And sin and strife is past:
When Angel-hands have gathered
  The fair, ripe fruit for Thee,
O Father, Lord, Redeemer,
  Most Holy Trinity!

Most widely known as a writer of fiction—especially for girls—Miss SARAH DOUDNEY has composed much tender and sympathetic verse, which, buried in back numbers of magazines, escapes the attention it deserves. Her hymns are to be found in many collections, English and American, and one of her songs, "The Lesson of the Water Mill," which has for its refrain the lines

> The Mill cannot grind
> With the water that is past,

is said to have become nationalised in America. Miss Doudney has published "Psalms of Life," (1871), and later "Drifting Leaves" and "Thistledown," two dainty booklets of dainty verse. Space will not admit of adequate representation. The following poem has been frequently used as a funeral hymn :—

THE CHRISTIAN'S "GOOD-NIGHT."

The early Christians were accustomed to bid their dying friends "Good-night," so sure were they of their awaking at the Resurrection Morning.

> Sleep on, beloved, sleep on and take thy rest,
> Lay down thy head upon thy Saviour's breast;
> We love thee well, but Jesus loves thee best;—
>   Good-night!

> Calm is thy slumber as an infant's sleep;
> But thou shalt wake no more to toil and weep;
> Thine is a perfect rest, secure and deep;—
>   Good-night!

> Until the shadow from this earth is cast,
> Until He gathers in His sheaves at last,
> Until the Lenten gloom is overpast;—
>   Good-night!

Until the Easter glory lights the skies,
Until the dead in Jesus shall arise,
And He shall come—but not in lowly guise;—
      Good-night!

Until, made beautiful by love divine,
Thou, in the likeness of Thy Lord, shalt shine,
And He shall bring that golden crown of thine;—
      Good-night!

Only "Good-night," beloved, not "Farewell"!
A little while, and all His saints shall dwell
In hallowed union, indivisible;—
      Good-night!

Until we meet again before His throne,
Clothed in the spotless robe He gives His own;
Until we know, even as we are known;—
      Good-night!

It is, of course, impossible to include all the worthy hymns and sacred verses of the century in this selection; it must therefore be taken as merely an attempt to represent the more important writers who are not otherwise represented in this work.

      ALFRED H. MILES.

The Poets and the Poetry of the Nineteenth Century.

Edited by ALFRED H. MILES.

In TWELVE VOLUMES, Fcap. 8vo.

A Popular Encyclopædia of Modern Poetry, covering the area of Greater Britain and the limits of the Nineteenth Century.

The plan of this work is to give, as far as possible, a representative selection from the poetry of the century, together with a biographical and critical notice of each poet represented. In carrying out this plan the Editor has been assisted by the following well-known critics:—

Dr. F. J. Furnivall,	Havelock Ellis,
J. Addington Symonds,	Cosmo Monkhouse,
Dr. Garnett,	John H. Ingram,
Buxton Forman,	Samuel Waddington,
Austin Dobson,	Emily H. Hickey,
Joseph Knight,	Coulson Kernahan,
Robert Bridges,	J. Howlett Ross,
Lionel Johnson,	Walter Whyte,
Hon. Roden Noel,	Mackenzie Bell,
Arthur Bullen,	Herbert E. Clarke,
Hall Caine,	R. Le Gallienne,
W. J. Linton,	William Gisburn,
Arthur Symons,	Thomas Archer,
Ashcroft Noble,	Alex. H. Japp,
T. Herbert Warren,	W. G. Collingwood,
W. B. Yeats,	T. W. Littleton Hay,
Charles Sayle,	J. A. Blaikie,
Thomas Bayne,	Alexander Grosart,
J. Rogers Rees,	Garrett Horder,

AND OTHER WRITERS.

For Chronological Order, Contents of each Volume, and General Index of Authors, see the following pages.

CHRONOLOGICAL ORDER OF VOLUMES.

VOL. I.
GEORGE CRABBE TO S. T. COLERIDGE.

VOL. II.
ROBERT SOUTHEY TO P. B. SHELLEY.

VOL. III.
JOHN KEATS TO EDWARD LORD LYTTON.

VOL. IV.
FREDERICK TENNYSON TO A. H. CLOUGH.

VOL. V.
CHARLES KINGSLEY TO JAMES THOMSON.

VOL. VI.
WILLIAM MORRIS TO ROBERT BUCHANAN.

VOL. VII.
ROBT. BRIDGES AND CONTEMPORARY POETS.

VOL. VIII.—(WOMEN, I.)
JOANNA BAILLIE TO JEAN INGELOW.

VOL IX.—(WOMEN, II.)
CHRISTINA ROSSETTI TO CICELY FOX-SMITH.

VOL. X.—(HUMOROUS).
CRABBE TO CHRISTIAN.

VOL. XI.—(SACRED, I.).
MONTGOMERY TO WARING.

VOL. XII.—(SACRED, II.).
PLUMPTRE TO SELWYN IMAGE.

List of Authors in each Volume.

VOLUME I.

GEORGE CRABBE TO S. T. COLERIDGE

George Crabbe.
William Blake.
Samuel Rogers.
Robert Bloomfield.
James Hogg.
William Wordsworth.
Sir Walter Scott.
S. T. Coleridge.

VOLUME II.

ROBERT SOUTHEY TO P. B. SHELLEY.

Robert Southey.
Robert Tannahill.
W. S. Landor.
Charles Lamb.
Thomas Campbell.
Thomas Moore.
Ebenezer Elliott.
J. Sheridan Knowles.
William Tennant.
Leigh Hunt.
T. L. Peacock.
B. W. Procter.
Lord Byron.
Edwin Atherstone.
Sir Aubrey de Vere.
Percy Bysshe Shelley.

VOLUME III.

JOHN KEATS TO EDWARD, LORD LYTTON.

John Keats.
John Clare.
Sir T. N. Talfourd.
Thomas Carlyle.
Hartley Coleridge.
George Darley.
William Motherwell.
Thomas Hood.
William Thom.
Lord Macaulay.
Sir Henry Taylor.
Charles J. Wells.
William Barnes.
W. M. Praed.
J. Clarence Mangan.
R. H. Horne.
T. L. Beddoes.
Laman Blanchard.
Charles Whitehead.
R. S. Hawker.
Thomas Wade.
Edward, Lord Lytton.

VOLUME IV.

FREDERICK TENNYSON TO A. H. CLOUGH.

Frederick Tennyson.
C. Tennyson Turner.
Alfred, Lord Tennyson.
Arthur H. Hallam.
John Sterling.
R. C. Trench.
T. Gordon Hake.
Lord Houghton.
J. S. Blackie
Sir S. Ferguson.
Sir F. H. Doyle.
Alfred Domett.
Robert Browning.
W. Bell Scott.
W. J. Linton.
W. E. Aytoun.
Aubrey de Vere.
Thomas Westwood.
Charles Mackay.
Philip J. Bailey.
Charles Harpur.
W. M. W. Call
Ernest C. Jones.
J. Westland Marston.
John Ruskin.
Arthur Hugh Clough.

VOLUME V.

CHARLES KINGSLEY TO JAMES THOMSON.

Charles Kingsley.
Ebenezer Jones.
W. C. Bennett.
F. Locker-Lampson.
Sir J. Noel Paton.
Robert Leighton.
Matthew Arnold.
William Corry.
W. B. Rands.
Coventry Patmore.
W. C. Roscoe.
Sydney Dobell.
William Allingham.
George Macdonald.
F. T. Palgrave.
Thomas Woolner.
Mortimer Collins.
Robert Brough.
Gerald Massey.
George Meredith.
Walter Thornbury.
Dante G. Rossetti.
Alexander Smith.
Sebastian Evans.
T. E. Brown.
Robert, Lord Lytton.
Joseph Skipsey.
Sir Edwin Arnold.
R. Watson Dixon.
A. Lindsay Gordon.
John Nichol.
Lewis Morris
Sir Alfred Lyall.
James Thomson.

VOLUME VI.
WILLIAM MORRIS TO ROBERT BUCHANAN.

William Morris.
Hon. Roden Noel.
Alfred Austin.
Richard Garnett.
Lord de Tabley.
Thomas Ashe.
Theodore Watts-Dunton

A. C. Swinburne.
David Gray
Herman C. Merivale.
Austin Dobson.
W. S. Blunt.
Cosmo Monkhouse.
J. Addington Symonds.

and Robert Buchanan.

VOLUME VII.
ROBERT BRIDGES AND CONTEMPORARY POETS.

John Todhunter.
H. C. Kendall.
G. A. Simcox.
John Payne
F. W. H. Myers.
E. Dowden.
E. Myers.
Robert Bridges.
Gerard Hopkins
Arthur O'Shaughnessy.
Andrew Lang.
S. Waddington.
E. Lee-Hamilton.
William Canton.
George Barlow
Edmund Gosse.
W. E. Henley.
P. B. Marston
H. D. Rawnsley.
R. Louis Stevenson.

Eric Mackay
Herbert Clarke
F. Money Coutts
W. J. Dawson.
E. C. Lefroy.
Oliver M. Brown.
William Sharp.
Oscar Wilde
John Davidson
Alfred Hayes.
William Watson
Rennell Rodd.
H. Newman Howard
Norman Gale
J. H. Newbolt.
Stephen Phillips.
R. Le Gallienne
Rudyard Kipling
W. B. Yeats
Laurence Binyon.

AC ETIAM.

James Ashcroft Noble.
Walter H. Pollock
Henry B. Baildon

H. T. Mackenzie Bell.
Horace G. Groser
Arthur Symons.

AC ETIAM—*continued*.

Clement W. Scott.
A. Perceval Graves.
George R. Sims.
Frederick E. Weatherly.
Frederick Langbridge.
Arthur J. Munby.
Philip S. Worsley.
George F. Armstrong.
Edmund G. A. Holmes.
Theophilus J. H. Marzials.

Henry C. Beeching.
A. Eubile Evans.
John A. Goodchild.
F. Wyville Home.
Douglas B. W. Sladen.
Robert, Lord Houghton.
Charles G. D. Roberts.
James Dryden Hosken.
Henry J. Patmore.
Wilfred W. Gibson.

(Appendix Index, see p. xix., Vol. VII.)

VOLUME VIII.
WOMEN POETS, I.
JOANNA BAILLIE TO JEAN INGELOW.

Joanna Baillie.
Lady Nairn.
Caroline Bowles.
Felicia D. Hemans.
Mary Howitt.
L. E. Maclean.
Sara Coleridge.
Sarah F. Adams.
E. B. Browning.
Jane W. Carlyle.

Lady Dufferin.
Hon. Mrs. Norton.
Frances A. Kemble.
Eliza Cook.
Emily Bronte.
George Eliot.
M. B. Smedley.
Dora Greenwell.
Adelaide A. Procter.
D. M. Craik.

And Jean Ingelow.

VOLUME IX.
WOMEN POETS, II.
CHRISTINA ROSSETTI TO CICELY FOX-SMITH.

Christina Rossetti.
Ellen O'Leary.
Isa Craig Knox.
H. E. Hamilton-King.
Augusta Webster.
Isabella Harwood.
Emily Pfeiffer.
Sarah Williams.

Mary M. Singleton.
Emily Hickey.
L. S. Guggenberger.
C. C. F. Tytler-Liddell.
Mathilde Blind.
Michael Field.
Alice Meynell.
Annie Matheson.

Volume IX.—*continued.*

Ada B. Baker.	Mrs. Radford
Rosa Newmarch.	Graham R. Tomson.
M. F. Robinson-Darmesteter	Jane Barlow.
Constance Naden.	Katharine Tynan.
Edith Bland.	Cicely Fox-Smith.

And other Writers.

VOLUME X.
THE HUMOROUS POETS.
CRABBE TO CHRISTIAN.

George Crabbe.	W. M. Thackeray.
George Colman.	R. Browning.
John Hookham Frere.	Edmund Lear.
George Canning.	J. Sheridan Le Fanu.
Hon. W. R. Spencer.	R. H. Dalton Barham.
James Hogg.	C. Shirley Brooks.
S. T. Coleridge.	Theodore Martin.
Robert Southey.	A. H. Clough.
James Smith.	Whyte-Melville.
W. S. Landor.	F. Locker-Lampson.
Charles Lamb.	Charles Stuart Calverly.
Thomas Moore.	Lewis Carroll.
Horace Smith.	Henry S. Leigh.
Leigh Hunt.	J. Brunton Stevens.
Thomas L. Peacock.	H. C. Pennell.
Theodore Hook.	W. J. Prowse.
Lord Byron.	W. S. Gilbert.
R. H. Barham.	J. Ashby Sterry.
J. R. Planché.	Austin Dobson.
Samuel Lover.	Robert Buchanan.
T. Haynes Bayley.	W. J. Courthope.
Thomas Hood.	H. D. Traill.
W. M. Praed.	Sir F. Pollock.
E. Fitzgerald.	Coulson Kernahan.
C. R. Forrester.	May Kendall.
George Outram.	R. F. Murray.
Charles Lever.	Edmund Christian.

VOLUME XI.

THE SACRED POETS, I.

MONTGOMERY TO WARING.

James Montgomery.	Caroline Clive
Richard Mant.	Sarah F. Adams.
Sir R. Grant	R. C. Trench.
Reginald Heber.	Christopher Wordsworth
Bernard Barton.	Henry Alford
Kirke White.	H. Bonar.
Charlotte Elliott.	J. S. Blackie
Josiah Conder.	Henry Ellison.
Henry Hart Milman.	F. W. Faber.
John Keble.	Thomas Lynch.
Sir J. Bowring.	John Mason Neale.
H. F. Lyte.	T. H. Gill.
Robert Pollok.	C. Dent Bell
J. Henry Newman.	A. Lætitia Waring.

VOLUME XII.

THE SACRED POETS, II.

E. H. PLUMPTRE TO SELWYN IMAGE.

E. H. Plumptre.	E. H. Bickersteth.
J. D. Burns	H. S. Sutton.
C. F. Alexander.	John Ellerton.
W. Walsham How.	Richard Wilton.
William Alexander.	J. J. Murphy
W. J. Irons.	Christina Rossetti.
Aubrey de Vere.	Alexander Grosart.
Coventry Patmore.	John Owen.
F. T. Palgrave.	F. R. Havergal.
Walter C. Smith.	S. J. Stone.
George Macdonald.	F. W. Orde-Ward.

and Selwyn Image.

AC ETIAM.

- A. L. Barbauld.
- Thomas Kelly.
- Harriet Auber.
- J. Blanco White.
- Philip Pusey.
- Thomas Moore.
- Ann Taylor.
- Jane Taylor.
- W. J. Fox.
- Andrew Reed.
- Charlotte E. Tonna.
- James Edmeston.
- Samuel Rickard.
- Thomas Binney.
- Herbert Knowles.
- Matthew Bridges.
- Richard Massie.
- John R. Wreford.
- Harriet Martineau.
- Isaac Williams.
- John H. Gurney.
- Henry J. Buckoll.
- Samuel Greg.
- James Martineau.
- John F. Chandler.
- George Rawson.
- Edward A. Dayman.
- Joseph Anstice.
- John S. B. Monsell.
- Norman Macleod.
- Jane Borthwick.
- Edward Caswell.
- Arthur P. Stanley.
- Jane M. Campbell.
- Emily Brontë.
- Annie Brontë.
- Sir H. W. Baker.
- Francis Power Cobbe.
- Godfrey Thring.
- Henry Twells.
- Adelaide A. Procter.
- William Whiting.
- Laurence Tuttiett.
- Elizabeth Charles.
- Frances E. Cox.
- Henry Collins.
- John Moultrie.
- Gerard Moultrie.
- Mary D. Moultrie.
- Catherine Winkworth.
- Philip S. Worsley.
- Richard F. Littledale.
- S. Baring Gould.
- F. S. Pierpoint.
- M. B. Betham-Edwards.
- T. B. Pollock.
- W. C. Dix.
- George Matheson.
- Ada Cross.
- Sarah Doudney.

GENERAL INDEX OF AUTHORS.

	VOL.	PAGE
ADAMS, SARAH FLOWER	{ viii	141
	xi.	215
AINSWORTH, WILLIAM HARRISON	vii.	xi
AIRD, THOMAS	vii.	xvii
ALEXANDER, CECIL FRANCES	xii.	37
ALEXANDER, WILLIAM	xii.	59
ALFORD, HENRY	xi.	237
ALLINGHAM, WILLIAM	v.	241
ANDERSON, ALEXANDER	vii.	xviii
ANDERSON, ROBERT	vii	v
ANSTICE, JOSEPH	xii	333
ARMSTRONG, EDMUND JOHN	vii.	667
ARMSTRONG, GEORGE FRANCIS (SAVAGE)	vii.	666
ARNOLD, SIR EDWIN	v	573
ARNOLD, MATTHEW	v.	85
ASHE, THOMAS	vi.	219
ATHERSTONE, EDWIN	ii.	495
AUBER, HARRIET	xii.	292
AUSTIN, ALFRED	vi	147
AYTOUN—MARTIN	x	387
AYTOUN, WILLIAM EDMONDSTOUNE	iv.	447
BAILDON, HENRY BELLYSE	vii.	652
BAILEY, PHILIP JAMES	iv.	517
BAILLIE, JOANNA	viii.	1
BAKER, SIR HENRY WILLIAMS	xii.	355
BAKER, ADA BARTWICK	ix.	341
BALLANTINE, JAMES	vii	xviii
BANIM, JOHN	vii.	xvi
BANKS, GEORGE LINNÆUS	vii.	xiii
BANKS, MRS. LINNÆUS	vii.	xii
BARBAULD, ANNIE LÆTITIA	xii.	295
BARHAM, RICHARD HARRIS	x.	197
BARHAM, RICHARD HARRIS DALTON	x.	365

	VOL	PAGE
BARING-GOULD, SABINE	xii.	381
BARLOW, GEORGE	vii.	267
BARLOW, JANE	ix.	433
BARNES, WILLIAM	iii.	397
BARTON, BERNARD	xi.	69
BAYLY, THOMAS HAYNES	ix.	241
BEDDOES, THOMAS LOVELL	iii	521
BEECHING, HENRY CHARLES	vii.	668
BELL, CHARLES DENT	xi.	371
BELL, H T MACKENZIE	vii	655
BELL, HENRY GLASSFORD	vii.	xvii
BENNETT, WILLIAM COX	v.	37
BETHAM-EDWARDS, M. B.	xii.	395
BICKERSTETH, EDWARD HENRY	xii.	145
BINNEY, THOMAS	xii.	307
BINYON, LAURENCE	vii	621
BLACK, WILLIAM	vii.	xii
BLACKIE, JOHN STUART	{ iv.	269
	xi	257
BLACKMORE, R. D	vii.	xii
BLAKE, WILLIAM	i.	85
BLANCHARD, LAMAN	iii.	547
BLAND, EDITH (NESBIT)	ix	395
BLIND, MATHILDE	ix.	259
BLOOMFIELD, ROBERT	{ i.	151
	x.	19
BLUNT, WILFRID SCAWEN	vi.	425
BONAR, HORATIUS	xi.	247
BORTHWICK, JANE	xii.	340
BOWLES, WILLIAM L	vii	1
BOWRING, SIR JOHN	xi.	147
BRADDON, MISS	vii	xi
BRIDGES, MATTHEW	xii.	310
BRIDGES, ROBERT	vii.	113
BRODIE, E. H.	vii.	iii
BRONTÉ, ANNE	xii	352
BRONTÉ, EMILY	{ viii	283
	xii.	352
BROOKS, C. W. SHIRLEY	x.	375
BROUGH, ROBERT	v.	331
BROWN, OLIVER MADOX	vii.	445

	VOL.	PAGE
Brown, Thomas Edward	v.	521
Browning, Elizabeth Barrett	viii.	155
Browning, Robert	{ iv.	345
	x.	337
Brydges, Sir S. Egerton	vii.	iii
Buchanan, Robert	{ vi.	517
	x.	547
Buckoll, Henry James	xii.	321
Burbridge, Thomas	vii	x
Burns, James Drummond	xii.	23
Byron, Lord	{ ii.	363
	x.	189
Caine, Hall	vii.	xii
Call, Wathen Mark Wilks	iv.	575
Callanan, James Joseph	vii.	xv
Calverley, Charles Stuart	x.	433
Campbell, Jane Montgomery	xii.	351
Campbell, Thomas	ii.	149
Canning, George	x.	49
Canton, William	vii.	257
Capern, Edward	vii.	xiv
Carlyle, Jane Welsh	viii.	229
Carlyle, Thomas	iii.	117
Carrington, Noel Thomas	vii.	ix
Carroll, Lewis	x.	443
Caswell, Edward	xii.	342
Chandler, John F.	xii.	327
Chapman, Elizabeth Rachel	ix	475
Charles, Elizabeth	xii.	365
Cherry, Andrew	vii.	xv
Christian, Edmund B. V.	x.	633
Clare, John	iii.	79
Clarke, Herbert Edwin	vii.	389
Clive, Caroline	xi.	201
Clough, Arthur Hugh	{ iv.	645
	x.	409
Cobbe, Frances Power	xii.	356
Coleridge, Hartley	iii.	131
Coleridge, Samuel Taylor	{ i.	435
	x	89

	VOL.	PAGE
COLERIDGE, SARAH	viii.	127
COLLIER, JOHN PAYNE	vii.	XI
COLLINS, HENRY	xii.	370
COLLINS, MORTIMER	v.	315
COLMAN, GEORGE	x.	9
CONDER, JOSIAH	xi.	95
COOK, ELIZA	viii.	269
COOPER, THOMAS	vii.	XIV
CORY, WILLIAM	v.	141
COURTHOPE, WILLIAM JOHN	x.	559
COX, FRANCES ELIZABETH	xii.	368
CRABBE, GEORGE	{ i. x.	1 1
CRAIK, DINAH MARIA	viii	377
CROLY, GEORGE	vii	IX
CROSS, ADA (née Cambridge)	xii.	392
CUNNINGHAM, ALLAN	vii.	XVII
DARLEY, GEORGE	iii	149
DAVIDSON, JOHN	vii.	477
DAVIS, THOMAS OSBORN	vii.	XV
DAWSON, WILLIAM JAMES	vii	429
DAWSON, C AMY	ix	475
DAYMAN, EDWARD ARTHUR	xii	332
DIX, WILLIAM CHATTERTON	xii.	388
DIXON, RICHARD WATSON	v.	599
DOBELL, SIDNEY	v	211
DOBSON, AUSTIN	{ vi. ix	391 533
DOMETT, ALFRED	iv.	315
DOUBLEDAY, THOMAS	vii.	III
DOUDNEY, SARAH	xii.	395
DOWDEN, EDWARD	vii	81
DOYLE, SIR FRANCIS HASTINGS	iv	299
DUFFERIN, LADY	viii	235
EARLE, JOHN CHARLES	vii.	III
EDMESTON, JAMES	xii.	304
EGERTON, LADY	ix.	475
ELIOT, GEORGE (Mary Ann Cross)	viii	293
ELLERTON, JOHN	xii	173

	VOL.	PAGE
ELLIOT, LADY CHARLOTTE	ix.	475
ELLIOTT, CHARLOTTE	xi.	87
ELLIOTT, EBENEZER	ii.	231
ELLISON, HENRY	xi.	261
EUBULE-EVANS, ALBERT	vii.	669
EVANS, SEBASTIAN	v.	497
FABER, FREDERICK WILLIAM	xi.	299
FANE, HON. JULIAN	vii.	iii
FANU, LE, JOSEPH SHERIDAN	x.	357
FERGUSON, SIR SAMUEL	iv.	281
FIELD, MICHAEL	ix.	291
FITZGERALD, EDWARD	x.	285
FLEMMING, MRS	ix.	476
FORRESTER, CHARLES ROBERT	x.	293
FOX, WILLIAM JOHNSON	xii.	298
FRANCILLON, R E	vii	XII
FRERE, JOHN HOOKHAM	x.	23
FRISWELL, JAMES HAIN	vii.	XIII
FURLONG, ALICE	ix.	476
GALE, NORMAN	vii.	549
GALLIENNE, LE, RICHARD	vii.	583
GARNETT, RICHARD	vi.	165
GIBSON, ELIZABETH	ix.	475
GIBSON, WILFRED WILSON	vii.	680
GILBERT, WILLIAM S.	x.	501
GILL, THOMAS HORNBLOWER	xi.	361
GOODCHILD, JOHN ARTHUR	vii.	669
GORDON, ADAM LINDSAY	v.	613
GOSSE, EDMUND	vii.	281
GRANT, SIR ROBERT	xi.	41
GRAVES, ALFRED PERCEVAL	viii.	690
GRAY, DAVID	vi.	335
GREENWELL, DORA	viii.	341
GREG, SAMUEL	xii.	323
GRIFFIN, GERALD	vii.	XIV
GROSART, ALEXANDER B.	xii.	215
GROSER, HORACE G.	vii.	656
GUGGENBERGER, LOUISA S.	ix.	227
GURNEY, JOHN HAMPDEN	xii.	320

INDEX OF AUTHORS.

	VOL.	PAGE
HAKE, THOMAS GORDON	iv.	207
HALLAM, ARTHUR HENRY	iv.	157
HALL, WILLIAM	xii.	245
HAMILTON, SIR WILLIAM ROWAN	vii.	iii
HAMILTON-KING, HARRIET ELEANOR	ix.	81
HANMER, LORD	vii.	iii
HARPUR, CHARLES	iv.	551
HARWOOD, ISABELLA (Ross Neil)	ix.	147
HAVERGAL, FRANCES RIDLEY	xii.	251
HAWKER, ROBERT STEPHEN	iii.	573
HAYES, ALFRED	vii.	491
HEBER, REGINALD	xi.	49
HEMANS, FELICIA DOROTHEA	viii.	53
HENLEY, WILLIAM ERNEST	vii.	309
HERAUD, JOHN ABRAHAM	vii.	XII
HERVEY, THOMAS KIBBLE	vii.	XVII
HICKEY, EMILY HENRIETTA	ix.	215
HINKSON, KATHARINE TYNAN	ix.	443
HOGG, JAMES	i.	173
	x.	77
HOLMES, EDMUND G. A.	vii.	667
HOME, F. WYVILLE	vii.	670
HOOD, THOMAS	iii.	215
	x.	249
HOOK, THEODORE	x.	175
HOPKINS, GERARD	vii.	179
HORNE, RICHARD HENRY	iii.	487
HOSKEN, JAMES DRYDEN	vii.	681
	vii.	XIV
HOUGHTON, LORD	iv.	241
HOUGHTON, ROBERT, LORD	vii.	675
HOWARD, HENRY NEWMAN	vii.	529
HOW, WILLIAM WALSHAM	xii.	49
HOWITT, MARY	viii.	81
HUNT, LEIGH	ii.	301
	x.	157
IMAGE, SELWYN	xii.	279
INGELOW, JEAN	viii.	385
INGRAM, JOHN KELLS	vii.	XVI
INGRAM, SARSON C. J.	ix.	475
IRONS, JOSEPH	xii.	69

	VOL.	PAGE
Irons, William Josiah	xii.	69
James, G. P. R.	vii.	xi
Jones, Ebenezer	v.	19
Jones, Ernest Charles	iv.	599
Keats, John	iii	1
Keble, John	xi.	119
Kelly, Thomas	xii.	290
Kemble, Frances Anne	viii.	253
Kendall, Henry Clarence	vii	11
Kendall, May	x.	613
Kent, William C. Mark	vii.	XIII
Kernahan, Coulson	x.	595
Kingsley, Charles	v.	1
Kipling, Rudyard	vii	593
Kipling, Mrs.	ix.	476
Knowles, Herbert	xii.	309
Knowles, James Sheridan	ii.	261
Knox, Isa (Craig)	ix.	65
Lamb, Charles	ii / x.	131 / 123
Landor, Walter Savage	ii / x.	87 / 115
Lang, Andrew	vii.	211
Langbridge, Frederick	vii.	662
Langhorn, Charles Hartley	vii.	XVI
Lear, Edward	x.	343
Lee-Hamilton, Eugene	vii.	241
Lefroy, Edward Cracroft	vii.	439
Leigh, Henry S.	x.	455
Leighton, Robert	v.	73
Lever, Charles	x.	309
Levy, Amy	ix.	476
Lewis, Matthew Gregory	vii.	VII
Linton, William James	iv.	429
Littledale, Richard Frederick	xii.	378
Lloyd, Charles	vii.	x
Locker-Lampson, Frederick	v. / x.	49 / 423
Lockhart, John Gibson	vii.	XVII
Lorne, Marquis of	vii.	XVIII

	VOL.	PAGE
LOVER, SAMUEL	x.	229
LYALL, SIR ALFRED	v.	665
LYNCH, THOMAS TOKE	xi.	313
LYSAGHT, EDWARD	vii.	xv
LYTE, HENRY FRANCIS	xi.	157
LYTTON, EDWARD, LORD	iii.	621
LYTTON, ROBERT, EARL OF	v.	535
MACAULAY, LORD	iii.	277
MCCARTHY, DENIS FLORENCE	vii.	XVI
MACDONALD, GEORGE	v.	255
	xii.	129
MACKAY, CHARLES	iv.	505
MACKAY, ERIC	vii.	369
MACLEAN, LÆTITIA ELIZABETH	viii.	103
MACLEOD, NORMAN	xii.	338
MAGINN, WILLIAM	vii.	xv
MAHONY, FRANCIS	vii.	xv
MANGAN, JAMES CLARENCE	iii.	453
MANT, RICHARD	xi.	29
MARSTON, JOHN WESTLAND	iv.	611
MARSTON, PHILIP BOURKE	vii.	317
MARTINEAU, HARRIET	xii.	355
MARTINEAU, JAMES	xii.	325
MARZIALS, THEOPHILUS JULIUS HENRY	vii.	667
MASSEY, GERALD	v.	347
MASSIE, RICHARD	xii.	312
MATHESON, ANNIE	ix.	331
MATHESON, GEORGE	xii.	390
MEREDITH, GEORGE	v.	387
MERIVALE, HERMAN CHARLES	vi.	371
MEYNELL, ALICE	ix.	315
MILLER, THOMAS	vii.	XIV
MILMAN, HENRY HART	xi.	109
MITFORD, MARY RUSSELL	vii.	XI
MOIR, DAVID MACBETH	vii.	XVII
MONEY-COUTTS, F. B. T.	vii.	407
MONKHOUSE, COSMO	vi.	453
MONSELL, JOHN S. B.	xii.	335
MONTGOMERY, JAMES	xi.	1

	VOL.	PAGE
MOORE, THOMAS	ii.	187
	x.	133
	xii.	295
MORRIS, LEWIS	v.	635
MORRIS, WILLIAM	vi.	1
MOTHERWELL, WILLIAM	iii.	185
MOULTRIE, GERARD	xii.	371
MOULTRIE, JOHN	xii.	371
MOULTRIE, MARY DUNLOP	xii.	373
MUNBY, ARTHUR JOSEPH	vii.	663
MURPHY, JOSEPH JOHN	xii.	195
MURRAY, R. F.	x.	627
MYERS, ERNEST	vii.	99
MYERS, FREDERIC W. H.	vii.	61
NADEN, CONSTANCE C. W.	ix.	387
NAIRNE, LADY CAROLINA	viii.	17
NEALE, JOHN MASON	xi.	337
NEWBOLT, JOHN HENRY	vii.	561
NEWMAN, JOHN HENRY	xi.	185
NEWMARCH, ROSA	ix.	351
NICHOL, JOHN	v.	629
NICHOLL, ROBERT	vii.	xviii
NICHOLSON, WILLIAM	vii.	xviii
NOBLE, JAMES ASHCROFT	vii.	646
NOEL, HON. RODEN	vi.	81
NORTON, HON. MRS.	viii.	241
O'DONNELL, JOHN FRANCIS	vii.	xvi
O'LEARY, ELLEN	ix.	55
OPIE, AMELIA	vii.	vi
O'SHAUGHNESSY, ARTHUR	vii.	189
OUTRAM, GEORGE	x.	299
OWEN, JOHN	xii.	229
PALGRAVE, FRANCIS TURNER	v.	275
	xii.	93
PATMORE, COVENTRY	v.	163
	xii.	89
PATMORE, HENRY JOHN	vii.	682
PATON, SIR JOSEPH NOEL	v.	65
PAYNE, JOHN	vii.	37

INDEX OF AUTHORS.

	VOL.	PAGE
Peacock, Thomas Love	ii.	331
	..	169
Pennell, H. Cholmondeley	x.	479
Pfeiffer, Emily	ix.	161
Phillips, Stephen	vii.	571
Pierpoint, Folliott Sandford	xii.	393
Planché, James Robinson	x.	217
Plumptre, Edward Hayes	xii.	1
Pollock, Sir Frederick	x.	585
Pollock, Thomas Benson	xii.	397
Pollock, Walter Herries	vii.	650
Pollok, Robert	xi.	167
Praed, Winthrop Mackworth	iii.	425
	x.	271
Prince, John Critchley	vii.	xiii
Probyn, May	ix.	475
Procter, Adelaide Anne	viii.	359
	xii.	361
Procter, Bryan Waller	ii.	351
Prowse, William Jeffery	x.	491
Pusey, Philip	xii.	294
Radcliffe, Mrs.	vii.	xi
Radford, Mrs. Ernest	ix.	409
Raffalovich, Mark André	vii.	iii
Ragg, Thomas	vii.	xiv
Rands, William Brighty	v	147
Rawnsley, Hardwick Drummond	vii.	341
Rawson, George	xii.	330
Redding, Cyrus	vii.	xi
Reed, Andrew	xii.	301
Reynolds, John Hamilton	vii.	x
Rickards, Samuel	xii.	305
Roberts, Charles George Douglas	vii.	676
Robinson-Darmesteter, A. Mary F.	ix.	359
Rodd, Rennell	vii.	519
Rogers, Samuel	i.	123
Roscoe, William Caldwell	v.	193
Rossetti, Christina Georgina	ix.	1
	xii.	213

	VOL.	PAGE
ROSSETTI, DANTE GABRIEL	v.	439
ROSSETTI, WILLIAM MICHAEL	vii.	iii
ROXBY, ROBERT	vii.	vi
RUSKIN, JOHN	iv.	629
SACKVILLE, LADY MARGARET	ix.	475
SAWYER, WILLIAM KINGSTON	vii.	xiii
SCOTT, CLEMENT WILLIAM	vii.	660
SCOTT, SIR WALTER	i.	347
SCOTT, WILLIAM BELL	iv.	403
SHAIRP, JOHN CAMPBELL	vii.	xviii
SHARP, WILLIAM	vii.	455
SHEEHAN, JOHN	vii.	xvi
SHELLEY, PERCY BYSSHE	ii.	515
SIMCOX, GEORGE AUGUSTUS	vii.	29
SIMS, GEORGE ROBERT	vii.	661
SINGLETON, MARY M. (Violet Fane)	ix.	201
SKIPSEY, JOSEPH	v.	559
SLADEN, DOUGLAS BROOK W.	vii.	674
SMEDLEY, MENELLA BUTE	viii.	327
SMITH, ALEXANDER	v.	465
SMITH, CICELY FOX-	ix.	463
SMITH, HORACE	x.	139
SMITH, JAMES	x.	101
SMITH, JAMES	vii.	xviii
SMITH, WALTER CHALMERS	xii.	109
SOTHEBY, WILLIAM	vii.	viii
SOUTHESK, EARL OF	vii.	xviii
SOUTHEY, CAROLINE (Bowles)	viii.	39
SOUTHEY, ROBERT	ii.	1
	x.	93
SPENCER, HON. WILLIAM ROBERT	x.	71
STANLEY, ARTHUR PENRHYN	xii.	347
STEPHEN, JAMES KENNETH	x.	599
STEPHENS, JAMES BRUNTON	x.	469
STERLING, JOHN	iv.	179
STERRY, ASHBY	x.	521
STEVENSON, ROBERT LOUIS	vii.	351
STONE, SAMUEL JOHN	xii.	257
SULLIVAN, TIMOTHY DANIEL	vii.	xvi
SUTTON, HENRY SEPTIMUS	xii.	151

INDEX OF AUTHORS.

	VOL.	PAGE
SWAIN, CHARLES	vii.	XII
SWINBURNE, ALGERNON CHARLES	vi.	381
SYMONDS, JOHN ADDINGTON	vi.	477
SYMONS, ARTHUR	vii.	657
TABLEY, LORD DE	vi.	183
TALFOURD, SIR THOMAS NOON	iii.	107
TANNAHILL, ROBERT	ii.	73
TAYLOR, ANN (Gilbert)	xii.	296
TAYLOR, JANE	xii.	296
TAYLOR, SIR HENRY	iii.	311
TENNANT, WILLIAM	ii.	285
TENNYSON, ALFRED, LORD	iv.	67
TENNYSON, FREDERICK	iv.	1
THACKERAY, WILLIAM MAKEPEACE	x.	315
THOM, WILLIAM	iii.	249
THOMSON, JAMES	v.	671
THORNBURY, WALTER	v.	413
THRING, GODFREY	xii.	357
THURLOW, LORD	vii.	111
TODHUNTER, JOHN	vii.	1
TOMSON, GRAHAM R.	ix.	421
TONNA, CHARLOTTE ELIZABETH (née Browne)	xii.	302
TOWNSEND, CHAUNCY HARE	vii.	XII
TRAILL, HENRY DUFF	x.	575
TRENCH, RICHARD CHENEVIX	iv.	191
	xi.	225
TUPPER, MARTIN FARQUHAR	vii.	XIII
TURNER, CHARLES TENNYSON	iv.	45
TUTTIETT, LAURENCE	xii.	364
TWELLS, HENRY	xii.	360
TYNAN, KATHARINE (Hinkson)	ix.	443
TYTLER-LIDDELL, C. C. FRASER (Mrs. Edward Liddell)	ix.	245
VERE, DE, SIR AUBREY	ii.	507
VERE, DE, AUBREY	iv.	467
	xii.	83
WADDINGTON, SAMUEL	vii.	229
WADE, THOMAS	iii.	597

	VOL.	PAGE
Walker, William Sidney	vii.	xii
Waller, John Francis	vii.	xv
Ward, F. William Orde	xii.	269
Waring, Anna Lætitia	xi.	397
Warren, T. Herbert	vii.	421
Watson, William	vii.	501
Watts, Alaric A.	vii.	vii
Watts-Dunton, Theodore	vi.	255
Waugh, Edwin	vii.	vi
Weatherly, Frederic Edward	vii.	661
Webster, Augusta	ix.	105
Wells, Charles Jeremiah	iii.	359
Westwood, Thomas	iv.	487
White, Henry Kirk	xi.	81
White, Joseph Blanco	xii.	293
Whitehead, Charles	iii.	559
Whiting, William	xii.	363
Whyte-Melville, George John	x.	415
Wiffen, Benjamin Barron	vii.	vi
Wiffen, Jeremiah Holmes	vii.	vi
Wiffen, Priscilla Maden	vii.	vii
Wilde, Oscar	vii.	465
Williams, Isaac	xii.	305
Williams, Sarah ("Sadie")	ix.	179
Wilson, John	vii.	xvii
Wilton, Richard	xii.	181
Winkworth, Catherine	xii.	361
Wolfe, Charles	vii.	iv
Woods, James Chapman	vii.	iii
Woolner, Thomas	v.	295
Wordsworth, Christopher	xi.	229
Wordsworth, William	i.	211
Worsley, Philip Stanhope	{ vii. xii.	665 377
Wreford, John Reynell	xii.	313
Wynne, Frances	ix.	475
Yeats, William Butler	vii.	683

Lightning Source UK Ltd.
Milton Keynes UK
UKOW07f0856291215

265473UK00005B/84/P